JUST BEYOND THE

LIGHT

Also by D. Randall Blythe

Dark Days: A Memoir

JUST BEYOND THE LIGHT

MAKING PEACE WITH THE WARS INSIDE OUR HEAD

D. RANDALL BLYTHE

GRAND
CENTRAL

New York Boston

Grand Central Publishing
Hachette Book Group
1290 Avenue of the Americas, New York, NY 10104
grandcentralpublishing.com
@grandcentralpub

First Edition: February 2025

Grand Central Publishing is a division of Hachette Book Group, Inc. The Grand Central Publishing name and logo are registered trademarks of Hachette Book Group, Inc.

The publisher is not responsible for websites (or their content) that are not owned by the publisher.

The Hachette Speakers Bureau provides a wide range of authors for speaking events. To find out more, go to hachettespeakersbureau.com or email HachetteSpeakers@hbgusa.com.

Grand Central Publishing books may be purchased in bulk for business, educational, or promotional use. For information, please contact your local bookseller or email the Hachette Book Group Special Markets Department at Special.Markets@hbgusa.com.

Print book interior design by Bart Dawson

Library of Congress Cataloging-in-Publication Data

Name: Blythe, D. Randall, 1971– author.
Title: Just beyond the light: living with the war inside our head / D. Randall Blythe.
Description: New York: Grand Central Publishing, 2025.
Identifiers: LCCN 2024035662 | ISBN 9780306828188 (hardcover) |
    ISBN 9780306828195 (trade paperback) | ISBN 9780306828201 (ebook)
Subjects: LCSH: Blythe, D. Randall, 1971– author. | Rock musicians—United States—
    Biography. | Conduct of life.
Classification: LCC ML420.B6525 A3 2025 | DDC 782.42166092 [B]—dc23/eng/20240913
LC record available at https://lccn.loc.gov/2024035662

ISBNs: 9780306828188 (hardcover); 9780306837753 (B&N signed edition);
9780306837760 (signed edition); 9780306828201 (ebook)

Printed in the United States of America

LSC-C

Printing 1, 2024

For my grandmother, Mary Blythe,
and my friends
Wayne Ford and Dave Brockie.
Thank you for being my teachers while you were here—
I will see you again on the other side.

You tell me nothing matters
You're just fucking scared...

You tell me that I make no difference
At least I'm fucking trying...

What the fuck have you done?

—MINOR THREAT, "IN MY EYES"

CONTENTS

CONTENTS

Introduction

KNOWLEDGE

There was a time in my life when I could not see reality. For over twenty years, I viewed my entire existence through the blurry lens of active alcoholism. Each and every one of my actions—where I went, who I hung out with, what I spent my money on, when I ate, when I slept, when I woke up—was controlled by alcohol, everything determined by my drinking. In the final days of my drinking, I had to choke down a beer before I could eat anything each day. My thoughts, clouded and dull, struggled to solidify in the haze of booze. My emotions were out of control: a bladed pendulum swinging wildly between hubris and self-loathing, drunkenly hacking my spirit into smaller and smaller pieces. Physically, mentally, and emotionally, I was exceedingly unhealthy. My family, friends, and coworkers watched my alcoholism progress and get worse and worse each year. Many expressed their concern about my drinking to me, but I was not having it. *I would be fine if all these clueless squares would just get off my goddamn back and leave me the fuck alone.*

It's been over a decade since my last drink, and looking back on that period of my life through sober eyes is like watching a horror movie starring my mentally ill doppelgänger as the main character. He stumbles drunkenly through a nonsensical plot, doing all sorts of bizarre and distasteful things as he wreaks havoc on everything and everyone around him. Obviously, I know that person was me, but at times I struggle to understand my old self. It seems utterly ludicrous that I allowed the consumption of a cheap fermented liquid packaged in twelve-ounce aluminum cans and readily available at any corner convenience store to define my existence, but that was indeed the case. How could I not see what I was doing to myself? Why on earth would I keep staggering down such a horrible path for so long?

Because my perspective was all fucked up.

That's how. That's why.

I allowed my drinking to warp my perspective to the point that I no longer had an accurate view of reality, much less any idea how to exist within it. When I could no longer run away from the painful truth of my alcoholism, I put down the bottle, and my life began to resemble that of a relatively sane human being. However, having viewed existence through the bottom of a beer glass for so long, my newfound sobriety didn't instantly transform me into a well-adjusted person. To start seeing the world through rational eyes, I had to learn new ways of thinking, of managing my emotions. Before I could do that, I had to understand which of my habits and beliefs were harmful and needed to be discarded. I had to get honest with myself about myself, and that meant looking in the mirror and asking some uncomfortable questions.

As a teenager growing up in the 1980s punk rock scene, I'd learned the importance of questioning *everything*—society, the system, and especially all manner of authority figures—and I maintain that skeptical attitude to this day. My angry refusal to blindly conform to the suffocating social mores and materialistic "values" so widely celebrated during that hideous Era of Excess was legitimate; that way of living wasn't for me then, and it isn't for me now. *But...* even though I was a pretty smart kid, I was still just a kid. As such, I tended to conveniently ignore (and foolishly still do at times) the obvious fact that contained within the *everything* that I constantly questioned were *myself* and *my own beliefs*—and unexamined, self-righteous, reactionary beliefs are inherently shallow, no matter how cool they look in a spiked leather jacket (or, today, paraded around in the insipid costume of an internet meme). I never once stopped to ask my snotty little self deeper questions about why I was so pissed off at the way the world was misbehaving. If something is worth believing in—a political position, a religion, a scientific theory—surely it should withstand a little rigorous examining from a rational, educated observer employing critical thought, yes? If not, that belief should be discarded. In theory, no one is more educated about your individual beliefs and why you hold them than yourself, but if you are resolutely unwilling to question your own beliefs, if you just accept your habitual thought patterns, prejudices, and beliefs at face value without rigorous analysis simply because it is uncomfortable to do so...then you are driven by *fear*.

Fear kept me drunk for two decades and destroyed my ability to maintain a proper perspective. Every time I woke up feeling like shit and thought, "Maybe this drinking thing ain't working out for you, dude," fear would come screeching forth demanding to know, "But what will you do without alcohol?" As insane as it seems to me now, the astoundingly obvious answer ("Um...*anything I want*") never popped into my head. *Not once.* I was so afraid I would die without drinking that I was drinking myself to death.

My fucked-up, fear-driven perspective was, quite literally, killing me.

People ask me all the time, "How did you get sober? I can't seem to do it!" The answer is annoyingly simple: on tour with my band in Australia, while sitting on a hotel-room balcony one dreadfully hungover morning, I realized that I would die if I kept on drinking. I was so exhausted from years of drinking that a great part of me did not care whether I checked out right then and there. But just for kicks, I decided to try something different on the off chance it might make me feel a little better. I sat there for a moment, then simply made a conscious decision to not go get a beer from the refrigerator.

The second I made that choice, I felt a great sense of peace. It was as if I had been walking through life blindfolded, constantly injuring myself as I crashed into everything in my path, but with that simple decision, I ripped off the blindfold and opened my eyes for the first time in decades.

However, alcoholism is a tricky motherfucker, so approximately forty-five seconds after that blissful wave of relief washed over me, a little voice in the back of my head spoke up. "Wait, wait, wait—hold up now, dude. Let's not rush this. Don't you think we're being a little rash here? Today is probably just a bad day, don't you think? Let's not jump to any hasty conclusions…"

Incredibly, after twenty-two years of hard drinking and drugging accompanied by all sorts of unpleasant consequences, even in the face of my own impending doom, I was still watching my newfound perspective on life rapidly slipping away. Yet by some inexplicable miracle, I recognized that my own head was lying to me, that I could no longer trust myself or my own reasoning. Five or six guys on that tour were sober, so I decided to try to not drink until I saw them at the venue that evening. Maybe they would have some advice for me? Somehow I toughed it out until I got to the gig, found those dudes, and said to them: "Please. Help me."

I did not ask for help from my parents or a spiritual guru or even a world-famous doctor specializing in addiction treatment for creative types. No, I asked a bunch of sweaty, tattooed, alcoholic musicians and guitar techs. Why? Because I knew they used to drink like me, they didn't anymore, and they all seemed pretty damn happy about it. Deep within my beer-battered skull, I somehow still possessed enough logic to deduce that these men possessed a rational, *experience-based perspective* on their own alcoholism and had figured out how to deal with it without drinking. I could plainly see that they were successfully accomplishing something I had thus far spectacularly failed at, so I stopped trying to do everything *my way*. Obviously, my way *sucked*, so I looked for a better example to follow. I asked these men for advice, then I shut my big mouth and did what they told me.

I'm still following their example today, and I'm a reasonably happy dude.

I learned enough from quitting drinking to know that my perspective on life is not always a healthy, clear one, with or without alcohol. Today, when I am confused or upset about something, I know I need to shift my perspective. When I seek the counsel of others, *reliable and experienced* people I know and trust, my perspective shifts in a healthy way. Conversely, when I rely solely on myself to sort through distressing situations, most of the time my perspective turns dark and nihilistic. I become overwhelmed and resentful at the world. I get stuck wandering around inside my head, which (sadly for me) happens to be a really bad neighborhood to get lost in. The anger and anxiety increase to an unbearable fever pitch until finally the light bulb goes off in my thick skull: *You idiot! Why don't you ask someone for help or search for a better example to follow?*

Maybe you're reading this and thinking, "What a total loser this guy is—why did I buy this book?" You've got it all figured out, and you feel your life is perfectly under control. Everything is exactly the way you want it to be, and you're never, ever scared or confused. You never make poor decisions, so you don't need outside perspectives to help you figure things out. Congratulations! You must be very pleased with yourself! Regrettably, this also almost certainly means that you're an insufferable and highly delusional asshole who will eventually die alone and unloved, so I hope isolation is your cup of tea. As for me, the older I get, the more I realize that I'm totally clueless about the vast majority of things. This continually comes as a big relief because it's utterly exhausting trying to have all the answers and be "right" all the time. So I'm going to keep asking others for advice and searching anywhere I can for better examples to follow, hoping for the best.

Modern-day life is complex, to put it mildly: we walk through the world under constant assault by a never-ending digital stream of dogmatic opinions, envy-inducing advertisements, and doomsday news items. This incessant barrage of for-profit information, often delivered straight into our hands by addictively designed mobile devices, is enough to induce anger, fear, and confusion in anyone. But with the exception of our very real ability to render the planet incapable of sustaining human life in relatively short order, history shows that all the problems we face today are exactly the same ones ancient civilizations confronted—they've just been given a facelift and electronically amplified in our consciousness to a ridiculous level. This noise in our heads can become overwhelming, but when we consciously pause, step back, and broaden our perspective by looking at the experiences of those who have gone before us, we see that life has *always* been complex, yet somehow it continues on unabated.

Since we first banded together for protection in tribes, humanity has faced the inherent difficulties of existing in complex social groups (i.e., two or more people). Although we cannot eliminate these difficulties—once again, life is complex and always has been—we can lessen our confusion about our problems by consciously searching for a wider, experience-based perspective. With the proper perspective, we can determine what actually matters in life and what is inconsequential, thereby saving a ton of mental, physical, and emotional energy. When we are not so exhausted by endless worry over a ton of trivial bullshit, we can instead clearly and calmly face issues of true gravity without losing our minds. We do not have to buy into the many, many lightweight for-profit lies society is selling that keep us anxious and prisoner to the status quo—we can *choose* to decide for ourselves what our lives should look like, what our standard of happiness or "success" is.

Life is hard, but it used to be a lot harder. When we get honest with ourselves about ourselves and our present-day reality, we are forced to stop lying and complaining about how tough our cushy modern lives are. Countless people everywhere have endured much, much worse and under far more difficult circumstances. We must remember that and learn from these people and their examples. If we do not, then we deserve all the misery we heap on ourselves like the spoiled children that we are.

To strive for a rational, healthy perspective on life without blissfully ignoring reality or being consumed by anger and nihilism—this is the struggle, the war inside my head. I may not know much, but I know enough to look outside myself for better examples to follow while I attempt to fight the good fight. This book is about some of the people and experiences that have provided me those examples.

JUST

BEYOND

THE

LIGHT

Chapter One

THE DUKE

L et me tell you your future: if you read one more sentence of this book, you are going to die.

Of course, it doesn't matter whether or not you read another sentence, you are still going to die. Even if you hated this book's introduction so much that you never even read this far—you cursed aloud over the money you just wasted, doused this thing in lighter fluid, grabbed a book of matches, and now these unread words are currently drifting into the heavens on a cloud of ash and smoke—you're still going to die. It's way too late to do anything about it now; in fact, it's *always* been too late. You were doomed from the second you emerged bloody and screeching from your mother's womb. You—yes, I'm talking to *you*—are going to cease to exist. No more hopes and dreams and walks on the beach and whatever your favorite dessert is. No more you. Bye-bye life. *Finis.*

Don't feel bad—it's going to happen to everyone, including me. In fact, I might already be dead by the time you read this. Although I know with absolute certainty that I am going to die, I have zero clue when it is going to happen—my guess is probably within fifty years, but that is mere speculation. Theoretically, I could last at least as long as my grandmother, who made it to one hundred years old, or I could have a heart attack and die five minutes from now. The timing of the whole thing is a rather convenient mystery, so I'm not going to stress over it. I only know that it's coming, and there's nothing I can do to stop it. (By the way, if I *am* dead when you read this, just know that I got a big kick thinking about the creepy feeling some of y'all are experiencing as I speak to you *right now* from beyond the grave—spooky! Ain't reading and writing cool?)

Death is the great leveler, coming for us all regardless of how much power, money, or fame we achieve in our lifetimes. As the great Stoic philosopher-king Marcus Aurelius put it: "Alexander the Great and his mule driver both died and the same thing happened to both. They were absorbed alike into the life force of the world or dissolved alike into atoms." Death is the one immutable fact of all our lives—the good news about death is that we will all be *perfectly* dead. In fact, being dead is the *only* thing each and every single one of us is guaranteed to get exactly right. One day, each of us will stop breathing, and no one not-breathes better than anyone else. If you're harboring delusions of superiority, this is probably going to come as a real bummer and rude shock to your swollen ego, because no matter how hard you've worked to get ahead of everyone else, in death you're going to be just the same as everyone else. The nerds, geeks, and losers you picked on in high school. All those mindless schmucks at work who just didn't have what it takes to get where you are. That filthy bum you pass on the street corner every afternoon as you drive your Mercedes home from the gym. Even the neighbor's dog that bit you decades ago when you wouldn't stop pulling its tail—you're going to wind up exactly like them. Everyone is perfectly equal in death, and in the end, you're no better than a piece of roadkill rotting beside the highway. So come down off your high horse there, buster, and stop being such an atrocious jerk to your waitress.

Conversely, if you've spent your entire life thus far feeling lesser-than, like a terminal screwup, like you'll never ever ever get anything right, this should come as *great* news. The president of the United States, the pope, the richest bazillionaire on earth, the person you had a crush on in ninth grade who publicly humiliated you when you finally got up the nerve to ask them out—none of those people will be dead any better than you. For your grand finale, you will succeed effortlessly and brilliantly at attaining the exact same level of deadness as the most respected and revered humans in all history. It's literally *impossible* to screw up being dead. Death is life's participation trophy. Congratulations, we're all winners in the end!

If we know with absolute certainty that we are going to die, then why have humans always worried about it so much? It's not like we can do anything about it. I think it's the surrounding uncertainty accompanying death that bothers most people, the peripheral aspects that remain forever, maddeningly, obtuse. *When will it happen? Will it hurt? What will happen after?* Furthermore, if you're like me and have spent your life reading a bunch of hero-filled classical mythology and modern literature in which the main character always dies steely-eyed, with grim resolve, while doing the right thing in the face of insurmountable odds, you have to add: *Will I embarrass myself? Please, God, don't let me go out looking like a little bitch.* (Yes, I worry about that.)

Death is the great boogeyman, the unknowable absolute, the ultimate unstoppable uncertainty. In the face of this uncertainty, many people (myself included) find comfort in the belief that when they die they will continue on in some form, traveling eternally through some sort of afterlife. Some people (particularly those of the fundamentalist-religion persuasion) present a belief in their particular brand of afterlife as an ironclad certainty—but they are fooling themselves, because let's face it, *no one* knows what happens when we die. An old story from Zen Buddhism illustrates this perfectly: A monk asks a Zen master, "What happens when you die?" The Zen master replies, "I have no idea." The irate monk says, "What do you mean you have no idea? Aren't you supposed to be a Zen master?" The Zen master replies, "Yes, but I've never been a dead Zen master." Even those with "near-death experiences" (being clinically dead for a short time, then revived) have no definitive answer about what happens— some report floating outside of themselves, many report being drawn to some sort of light, some recall blackness, and others do not recall anything at all. Plus, all the people telling these stories are alive when they tell them, so what do they actually know about being dead?

I hope I carry on in some way, and I believe that I will, but I just can't say for certain. If there is no afterlife and every aspect of this thing I call "me" simply vanishes, then I don't suppose my nonexistent self will be too bummed about being wrong.

To be perfectly clear, those who emphatically insist that there is nothing after we die annoy me just as equally as those who insist that they know exactly what the afterlife is. "When you die, that's it. There is no scientific evidence of an afterlife, you superstitious buffoons," says the oh-so-self-satisfied supposedly rational modern person. Although it is irrefutable that there is no scientific evidence for the existence of an afterlife, there's no scientific evidence *against* it either—there is simply no evidence, *period*. Nobody knows, no matter which dogmatic tool they reach for to hammer home their belief. It's like stating with great conviction: "I will not sneeze on the second Tuesday of March, two years from now," and then attempting to back up that statement with either religion or science—both are equally useless in this case. First, you have no idea whether you will make it to Tuesday next week, much less a Tuesday in March two years from now. And supposing that you do live that long, even if in the interim you constantly pray to whatever deity you wish or study the science of sneezing under the most famous otorhinolaryngologist in the world...immediately after 11:59 p.m. on that fateful Monday night, all bets are off. You may or may not be holding a box of tissues and struggling mightily to hold back a sneeze (don't do that, by the way—you can rip your larynx).

My friend Carlos loves to say, "Life is full of uncertainty!" He usually says this whenever something goes abysmally wrong during one of our surfing trip adventures in South America. This drives me crazy, because many times it would be far more accurate to say, "Carlos's wildly careening lack of proper planning is full of uncertainty!" but at the root, he's absolutely correct. And in an era when all the knowledge in the world is available at the click of a button, humans seem to be growing less and less capable of dealing with uncertainty. This is a big problem because no matter how much knowledge we accrue, life is, well, it's full of uncertainty. People always want answers (and today they are used to getting them immediately), but sometimes there is no answer. The only answer we have about death is that it's coming for us all, and you can bet every penny in your bank account on that—not that you could collect on that bet when you win.

As I get older, I think about my mortality more and more. I always used to joke that everyone was going to die except my own cockroach self, but as I head into my fifties and the aches and pains get worse every year, it's becoming very apparent that this much-abused body of mine ain't gonna last forever. And that's okay—after the insane way I lived my life for so long, I realize that the game is now in overtime. Honestly, the drugs and alcohol should have killed me decades ago, so I try to view every day aboveground as a bonus. When I think about dying (which I am absolutely in no hurry to do), there are many, many unpleasant ways of meeting my end that I definitely do not wish to experience. And I do get panicky from time to time when I begin to dwell on the fact that I may not get to accomplish certain things I want to do during my time on earth or visit places I've dreamed of going or say all the things I want to say through music, writing, and photography—my ego wants to leave behind a well-rounded body of work for posterity, preferably one that is filed away in some immaculately maintained Ivy League university's climate-controlled archive. But the idea of being dead itself doesn't scare me. Why should it? It's inevitable, so I might as well accept it. In the interim, I want to make the most of what time I have left so that when my time comes, hopefully I will die peacefully, with dignity and grateful acceptance. That sort of death seems good enough for me today.

But that's easy enough for me to say right now, with the unknowable future stretching forth and no idea of when I will expire. My future is a blank slate, one that I intellectually recognize as having a finite end, but right now I'm still (theoretically) a good way away from that end. Therefore, I can't even begin to truly comprehend it with any sort of clarity at all. My death is not immediate enough to seem real to me (although I know that can change any second), so I can't really be bothered to worry much about the timing of its arrival. For now, I've accepted the fact that worrying about dying doesn't change a thing (in fact, it only makes it worse and might actually make it happen sooner), so I might as well enjoy my life in this moment and handle death when it gets a bit closer.

Some people attempt to deal with mortality by pretending that death won't happen to them, by denying the truth until the bitter end and their last panicked, wasted breaths. I've heard deathbed stories about these kinds of people directly from my doctor and nurse friends who watched their demise. It's an ugly, pathetic way to die, and I don't want to go out like that—so I refuse to ignore the fact that the Reaper is already sharpening his scythe to collect my head. But either way, whether we meditate on death daily like a samurai preparing for battle or push the idea as far from our minds as possible, statistically it's not something most of us will deal with until we are much older.

But what if something happened that forced you to face your own death a lot sooner than you thought you would have to? What if you were made aware with 100 percent certainty that you were going to die, and die soon? That your time on earth was swiftly coming to an end, and that there was absolutely nothing you could do about it? How would you handle it? I like to think I would come to a place of acceptance, enjoy what time I had left, tie up some loose ends, and die with serenity in my heart, but honestly, I do not know. I haven't been in that situation yet, so I can't say if I would meet that romantic ideal.

But I do know for a fact that it is possible to handle impending death with courage. I knew someone who was thrust into that terrifying situation. Although I had the pleasure of his friendship for only a brief time, I learned a lot about strength and dignity from watching this man. This is how he handled it.

His name was Wayne Ford, and he was The Duke.

On October 30, 2012, I was in Phoenix, Arizona. My band, lamb of god, was starting a tour and that night was the first gig of the run. The first night of any tour is always a mess, prone to all sorts of equipment malfunctions, guest list disasters, and the generally neurotic on-edge vibe that comes with not having played in front of an audience for a few months. In addition, I had been released on bail from a Czech prison just three months earlier, and my future as a free man was extremely uncertain. (If you want to know that whole story, I tell it in detail in my previous book, *Dark Days*.) With a possible five- to ten-year prison sentence in a foreign country hanging over my head, getting onstage to entertain a few thousand people was the very last thing I felt like doing—inside, I was a mess, to put it lightly. But all the lawyers and transcontinental airfares involved in securing my release had been very, very expensive, so it was time for me to get up and sing for my multiple attorneys' suppers.

Concertgoers do not fork over their hard-earned money to watch someone teetering on the edge of a nervous breakdown; they buy tickets to lose themselves in the music and forget their troubles for an hour or two. If you're a true professional (and I am), your own problems are entirely irrelevant for as long as you are onstage, especially as a frontman. It's your job to ensure that everyone is having a good time, and even if your own life is completely falling to pieces—the audience can never know that. My life was in an extremely scary place at that time, but I knew I had to push that out of my mind every single night of the tour and show the fans a good time. That evening before our set, I was standing around backstage, wheels spinning in my head. I was wondering how in the hell I was going to hold it together long enough to get through a seven-week tour when a young man came up to me and introduced himself as Adam.

"Hey, man, I hate to bother you, but my friend Wayne Ford is a huge fan—he's in the audience tonight. He got diagnosed with leukemia not too long ago, and he wanted you to have this." Adam handed me a T-shirt with the words FUCK CANCER printed on it. "Will you give him a shout-out, man? He's got a hard fight ahead of him, and he could use the encouragement."

"Of course," I said, then asked Adam for his friend's name again. As preoccupied as I was, I'd need a reminder—so, in permanent marker I wrote WAYNE FORD in big block letters on my hand, going over each character several times to make sure his name wouldn't sweat off during our set. Adam thanked me and left.

Onstage later that night, I dedicated the song "Ruin" to Wayne, saying, "This one goes out to Mister Wayne Ford—fuck cancer, motherfucker! You're gonna beat this thing!" Not the most delicate way to encourage someone fighting for their life, but lamb of god fans are generally not fragile, delicate people. Wayne would certainly prove that in the years to come.

Despite all the worries crashing around in my head, lamb of god had a great show that evening—it felt good to be onstage again, doing what we had done so many times before. It also felt great to shout Wayne out, to hear the crowd of thousands roar after I said his name, to know that together we had concentrated our mighty, indomitable human spirit en masse and were directing that energy toward him for the coming fight. Whenever I am lucky enough to help orchestrate moments like this as a frontman, I do not take them for granted. It is a very special part of my life as a musician, and it's very humbling. Even though this sort of thing takes so little effort on my part, I know that it means something to people. I feel a great swell of love for everyone who joins their voice with mine because these moments of grand unity can make a real difference in someone's life. Trying to help someone else who is going through a difficult time, even if it's just dedicating a song to a person I've never met, also gets me out of my own head.

After the show was over and the gear was being loaded out, I walked to our tour bus. The vast concrete oven that is

Phoenix had released most of the brutal heat it had soaked up that day, and the temperature had dipped to a very pleasant seventy-something degrees. As usual, a group of fans by the tour buses waited for autographs. I was signing concert tickets and posing for photos when a handsome shaved-headed young man with piercing dark brown eyes behind horn-rimmed glasses introduced himself as Wayne Ford. I asked Wayne to hang out a few minutes until I was done so that we could chat. After the last ticket was signed and the last blurry cell phone photo taken, I stepped away from the line of fans, bringing Wayne and his wife, Courtney, with me.

"Thanks so much for the shout-out," Wayne said. "I had zero idea that was going to happen—that was awesome."

"No problem, dude," I said. And standing on the sidewalk, we began to talk about the cancer he had been diagnosed with in March 2010. Leukemia had already hit close to home for my band—our sweetheart of a merch girl, Evie Carrano, had died in 2008 a mere week after being diagnosed with the disease. As well, our friend Adam "Nergal" Darski, singer of the Polish metal band Behemoth, had just undergone a bone marrow transplant to treat the disease—thankfully, he had made a full recovery, but it was touch and go for a while there.

I told Wayne and Courtney that after Evie died, I had learned a bit about leukemia, its treatment, and in the process had signed up for Be The Match, an American bone marrow transplant registry (the National Marrow Donor Program, also known as NMDP). Bone marrow types are much more specific than blood types, and a patient's likelihood of finding a matching bone marrow donor ranges from 29 percent to 79 percent, depending on ethnic background. The number of folks registered as bone marrow donors is woefully insufficient, and leukemia patients die every year for lack of matching donors who can provide healthy blood-forming cells. We talked about the need for more donors, took a photo together, then I wished Wayne good luck before climbing on the tour bus and heading to Los Angeles for the next gig.

"What a nice dude," I thought as we pulled away. "I hope he beats it."

Almost three years later, in January 2015, lamb of god was writing and recording our album *VII: Sturm und Drang*. One afternoon I read an email our publicist had forwarded me from a dude named Sammy. "Hey dude, I don't know if you even remember, but a few years ago in Phoenix you got a T-shirt from my friend Wayne Ford who has leukemia. He fought it hard for five years, but the treatments aren't working anymore—Wayne's not gonna make it, man. He's decided to go home and spend his last days with family instead of in some hospital bed. I know it's a lot to ask, but do you think you could get the whole band together and maybe say hello on the phone or something?"

I clearly remembered my conversation with Wayne and replied to Sammy immediately. Regrettably, it was impossible to get the entire band together for a call—I was in Virginia finalizing lyrics and they were in California recording the instrumental tracks for our new album. However, I was certainly willing to talk to Wayne if Sammy could put us in touch. Sammy sent me Wayne's info, and I emailed him and suggested we set up a video chat—I thought that would be more personable than a phone call. We made plans to talk via Skype in a few days, and I went back to working on lyrics.

But very shortly after making these plans, I became exceedingly nervous. The weight of what I had agreed to do settled in swiftly, and self-doubt reared its ugly head. This was a very serious situation, and I felt like an impulsive moron for even reaching out to Wayne. A fan of my band was facing his own imminent demise. What could I possibly say that would be of any use to this dying man? I was just a singer in a stupid heavy metal band, not a psychiatrist or a grief counselor. Was I supposed to do my little frontman song and dance, maybe tell him a few funny war stories from tour and hope for a laugh? Wayne was dying, not having a birthday party at a comedy club. I became full of fear: fear that I would offend Wayne, fear that I would say something that would make him feel even worse about his situation, maybe even upset him to the point where it would deteriorate his already poor health. For a day or two, this fear overwhelmed me until I realized that (just as with virtually all cases of fear I experience) I was really just thinking about myself. I was obsessing over my own emotions, my feelings of discomfort, my desire to not look bad or stupid or ineffective.

Me, me, me—that's what I was really thinking about, not a dying man.

So I put those self-centered thoughts on pause for a moment, pondered deeply how to not screw this up, and finally did what I should have done in the first place: I called my dad for advice. Unlike me, my father has extensive experience with grief counseling, and he confirmed what I already intuitively knew: it was not my job, in this instance, to try to "fix" the situation or be an entertainer or even make Wayne feel better. I just needed to be a human being and talk to this man. Although I had questions I wanted to ask Wayne, things I hoped we would talk about, I knew the right thing to do was to talk about whatever Wayne wanted to discuss, whether it was cancer, my band, politics, or what we were having for dinner that evening. I would let Wayne steer the ship. I would not ignore the fact that he was dying or foolishly pretend that everything was okay and that he would somehow get better. I would not make some ham-fisted effort to cheer him up— that would be selfish, a lame attempt to make *me* feel better in an uncomfortable situation. Most importantly, I decided I would shut my big mouth and just *listen* to the man. If I were the one dying, that is what I would want, just someone to hear what I was saying, whatever that may be.

After I talked to my dad, I called my rabbi to get a second opinion. No, I am not Jewish, but my buddy Michael "Stick" Shefrin is, and as a rabbi, he too had experience with grief counseling. Plus, as we say down south: "Every good redneck needs a rabbi." (Okay, okay, so we don't say that down south, but it's true.) Rabbi Stick gave me the same advice: just listen. Even at the end of our lives, the search for connection, for understanding, continues. Connection and understanding occur only when people listen to each other. Wayne had listened to me screaming for years. Now it was my turn to be the audience and open my ears.

I was still very nervous when I hit the video call button on my laptop, but the second Wayne's face popped up on my computer screen I relaxed. A huge smile spread across his face as soon as he saw me. Wayne's head was still as bald as when I had met him years ago, but now that the poisonous chemo was no longer coursing through his veins, a bushy red beard framed his jaw. Seeing him grinning at me looking like some bespectacled Viking who had somehow gotten sidetracked in Arizona immediately put me at ease, and I felt my own smile automatically stretching across my own bespectacled face. Science tells us that smiling is literally contagious—it also triggers automatic chemical reactions in our brain that produce serotonin and dopamine, leading to an elevated mood. For all my nervousness, we were off to a good start.

And just how does one start a conversation with a dying man?

"What's up, duuuude?" I said.

"Hey, man, what's up," Wayne replied.

Just like that. Like any other normal conversation I would have with a friend I ran into on a street corner. And that was the tenor of all our communications going forward from there—startlingly normal. Most modern-day conversations start with some version of the following question: "How are you doing today?" (In my case, "What's up, duuuude?") This is just an automatic pleasantry, a colloquialism used to open conversation, not an actual inquiry into someone's current emotional/physical/mental/financial state. (But I know better than to use that greeting with some people as they will immediately proceed to actually tell me in great misery-filled detail about the latest banal tragedy that has consumed their perpetually angst-ridden existence.) And although I did not want to beat Wayne over the head with the obvious fact that he was dying, I did want to give him the opportunity to speak about the elephant in the room if he wished. So the next question I asked was, "How are you feeling, man?"

"How are you feeling?" is a very different question from "What's happening, bro?" especially in the context of a conversation with someone who will be leaving the earth soon. I had many questions I wanted to ask Wayne—"Are you scared?" "What are your spiritual beliefs?" "What do you think will happen after you die?" just to name a few. But I had thought deeply about how to broach the inescapable subject of his death, and asking him how he was feeling seemed the most respectful way to let him open that door if he wanted to. I am a pragmatic (if rather clumsy) man, so if someone in my life is having a problem, my instinct is to immediately try to help them figure out how to fix that problem. Being present, just sitting and listening to someone discuss a hardship they are going through, is *much harder* for me than trying to help them find a solution to their difficulty. My racing monkey mind screams, "Figure it out! Figure it out!" because I am uncomfortable in sad and painful situations, and I want to change the circumstances so that the problems will go away (this, by the way, has led to many of what can only be characterized as *unfortunate* conversations with various women I have dated over the years—sometimes you just need to shut up and listen, dummy). But Wayne had a problem I was powerless to help solve, no matter how much I thought about it. Making myself feel better wasn't the object here—I was there to be present for a fan of my band during one of his last days, to discuss whatever he wanted to discuss, to hear whatever he wanted to say. Although I could not pretend to truly grasp what Wayne was going through, my job was to display as much empathy as possible. Empathy requires attentive listening, so I shut my mouth and listened.

"I'm feeling okay today, man," Wayne replied calmly. Then, in that same even, measured tone he began to tell me about what he was going through.

We discussed his cancer openly and how hard he had fought it for the past five years. For a long time, Wayne had been living in the brutal war zone that is a human body undergoing chemotherapy, and he was tired of it. He told me he was tired of not being at home for the holidays, having spent the previous three Christmases in the hospital—in fact, less than a month earlier, just two days before Christmas, doctors in the hospital had told him he was dying. He told me he was tired of not being able to eat what he wanted for years now because of the cancer treatment's dietary restrictions. He told me he was tired of the way the treatments had disrupted virtually every aspect of his life, of the physical, mental, and emotional roller-coaster ride that is chemotherapy. And he told me of a possible clinical trial that maybe, *maybe* could have prolonged his life a bit but that he wasn't interested in participating—Wayne was tired of hospitals and treatments. He was just *tired*, and I could not blame him.

But in that all-pervasive weariness of his body and soul, Wayne had made a decision. He had taken back control of his destiny, wrestling it from the same cruel hands of fate that had delivered the cancer into his bloodstream. With the same fierce self-determination that he had used to fight the cancer, Wayne had decided how he would spend the end of his days. He would live out the rest of his life as *he* wished, not at the mercy of doctors and hospitals, not even at the terrible whims of leukemia. And so he told me he planned to simply enjoy whatever time he had left. He told me what a relief it was to have a decent meal of his choice whenever he wanted. He told me how nice it was to be at home, not stuck in some hospital with chemicals running through his veins. He told me how he was taking natural cannabis oil for his pain instead of pharmaceutical opiates. He told me that what he most wanted to do was spend what time he had left with his wife, his family, and his friends—and that was exactly what he was doing.

Wayne knew the cancer would end his life, but he would be damned if it would decide how he would live it anymore.

Not once during our conversation did Wayne complain of the unfairness of his situation, nor did he bemoan his fate or burst into tears—he didn't seem to be that sort of guy (and I knew this to be true after further conversations with him, his wife, and his family). Instead, he appeared quite stoic about the whole thing, and I mean that both in the commonly understood modern usage of that word as a calm, uncomplaining manner in the face of adversity and in the deeper philosophical manner from which the term is derived. Historically, members of the Stoic school of philosophy have made it one of their foremost goals to clearly perceive and understand what is within their control and what is not. Then, in accordance with that understanding, they strive to act on only what is within their realm of influence and not let the rest bother them much. To use the ancient Greek terminology, Wayne possessed *katalêpsis*, a clear perception of what was not in his control (the fact that he was going to die soon) and what was (the way he lived and handled that impending death). He then employed *prohairesis* (reasoned choice and free will) to live and die on his own terms, as he saw fit, in his own home and surrounded by his loved ones.

It only seems natural that at the end of a long life, most elderly people seem to settle into a place of acceptance of their mortality. They understand that they will die soon, and many prepare to meet their end calmly and with a full heart, grateful for the long life and many experiences they have had. I have witnessed this manner of transition with my own two eyes, and it is something, indeed, to behold. But Wayne was still a young man, and I found his stoic demeanor utterly remarkable. We tend to picture philosophers as wise, old bearded men, puttering about in some simple seaside dwelling and occasionally uttering profound bits of wisdom. Ironically, because of his impending mortality, at age thirty-three Wayne had become the finest living, breathing embodiment of ancient philosophy I had ever seen, or have since, some seven years after his death. Surely, he had to have moments when he shed tears walking the black dog of depression, feeling helpless and terrified in the face of what was coming—he would not have been a human being otherwise. But I never saw those moments. This was a deeply dignified man, a real warrior who showed me what true strength looked like. In the short time I knew him, Wayne's manner during his final days had a profound impact on me, one that lasts to this day.

During our talk, I asked Wayne whether he had any questions for me, and I believe we briefly discussed what my band had been up to lately. But mostly I remember asking him a few questions and then listening to his answers—unlike my own loudmouthed self, Wayne was what I would call a reserved man, but he did not hesitate to share openly when asked.

I cannot explain what it feels like to have a dying stranger give you a few of their remaining moments on earth. To this day, when I think about what our conversation truly meant in practical terms, I become overwhelmed and tear up. My band's music meant something to Wayne, and so I understood it must have been neat for him to talk to me; after all I am first and foremost a music *fan*, one who has been lucky enough to have the pleasure of conversation with members of my favorite bands, and I treasure those talks. But our time here on earth is our only true possession, and it comes in a very finite supply. Wayne's supply was swiftly running dry, and his willingness to share some of it with me displayed an astounding generosity of spirit. I honestly don't think Wayne understood what sharing his time meant to me—I know I didn't at first. But I do now. It was a gift of the highest magnitude. When someone's life is coming to an end and they spend time with you, don't take a single second of it for granted.

They are giving you a piece of the only thing they have left.

As I recall, we talked for about an hour, then at the end of our conversation we exchanged telephone numbers. "Holler at me anytime, man," I said, and we promised to keep in touch. Over the next few weeks, we did just that, mostly via text message. Every now and then I would text Wayne to ask how he was doing, and he did the same. During this time, my band finished recording the music for our new album, and I flew to California to track vocals. Wayne's friends and family were throwing a goodbye party for him, and I remember joking with him about jumping out of the airplane as I passed over Arizona, crashing the party via parachute. And I would have loved to have gone to that party, but I had a recording schedule to meet. Tracking vocals for a lamb of god album is one of my least favorite parts of being in our band—I hate singing along to music in headphones instead of music blasting from amps onstage; there is none of the live-show energy that I get onstage from my bandmates and our audience, the already constant ringing in my ears gets even louder, and I develop a perpetual headache from screaming all day that lasts until I'm done recording the album. The worst comes at night when I lie down to sleep—in my head, I hear my own voice, endlessly repeating fragments of lyrics I recorded that day, sometimes just a single word. It's like having a doppelgänger who also happens to be the world's most annoying roommate, one who never, ever shuts up while you're trying to crash after a long day at work, one you can't kick out or run away from because he is *you.*

As the recording sessions went on and I slid deeper and deeper into the neurotic, irritable, self-loathing mind frame that is my natural state of being while making an album, one morning Wayne texted me to see how I was doing.

"This fucking record is making me crazy," I wrote. "I think I would rather chew glass than go back into that goddamned studio today."

"Wow," he replied. "Must be tough to be you. You need a tissue?"

Holy CRAP, I thought as I burst into hysterical laughter. *This bald-ass ginger motherfucker is talking shit!* Immediately, my opinion of Wayne rocketed up several notches, and from that point on, we engaged in a bit of mutual ballbusting here and there. If I am friends with a person, I feel compelled to pick on them every now and then, just to remind them that I care. If I don't like you, I just won't address you at all. Why would I? It's an utter waste of time, like arguing politics with people online or trying to explain to a teenager why 90 percent of the stuff they worry about doesn't matter. And by this point, Wayne and I had become friends, so we talked a little shit. Busting balls is a fine art, one I love practicing with my family and friends, and Wayne gave as good as he got. I was impressed that someone in his situation still had such a sharp wit—I mean, what are you gonna say when a dude who's about to check out lights you up and tells you to stop being such a pussy? It's hard to think of a witty comeback to that one.

Well done, bro, *well done.*

One afternoon as Wayne and I were texting in between takes, I asked him if he wanted me to video-conference him into the studio so he could check out some vocal sessions. Aside from guest vocalists and the occasional photographer, *no one* comes to the studio while I am tracking—not my bandmates, not our management, not anyone. Usually, the singer goes last when making a record, and I've learned through hard experience that it's a process most successfully undertaken with minimal distractions. I have never understood musicians who bring an entourage into the studio; I am there to work, not party. Would an accountant invite ten of his non-accountant buddies to sit around the cubicle all day smoking weed, drinking beer, and giving their opinions on how he should calculate deductions for the taxes of his firm's biggest client? No, he would not, and for the same reason I like to be left the fuck alone when I am recording. But for obvious reasons, Wayne was an exception—plus, he was just a super mellow guy. So we talked a little about the record, then Wayne watched me track for a while. He got to hear how some of the new lamb of god tunes would sound with vocals before anyone else, including my bandmates. It felt nice to share that creative process with him, just a small experience I could give him that none of our other fans will ever have.

After I turned off our video chat, Josh, my producer, looked over at me and said, "Whoa. That was heavy—you guys just seemed so *normal.*" Once again, that was how our conversations were: normal. I didn't constantly bring up the fact that he was dying, but I didn't ignore it and pretend that he was going to live forever, either. Wayne didn't need either of those things, so I tried to adjust my perspective to what had become his "normal" reality—if he seemed to be accepting it with grace, then I damn sure could try to do the same.

One of the last messages Wayne sent me spoke of how he was heading into a diner with his wife and was about to "destroy some food"—it made me so damn happy to read that. Wayne was going to enjoy something that he had been denied for years, something so important to our happiness as humans but that most of us take for granted: a good meal of our own choice. I remember grinning like a crazy man, pumping my fist into the air as I read those words—*YEAH, BRO! FUCK SHIT UP, MAN! GO! GO! GO!* I screamed in my mind. Wayne messaged me one more time after that asking what I was up to, but I was busy recording and got distracted. *I'll hit him up later,* I thought, then promptly forgot to do so. The only regret I have (and it is a real one) when I think about our brief friendship is not replying to that text message immediately because I never heard from him again.

Shortly after his last message, I received an email letting me know that on February 3, 2015, Wayne had died. Wayne left this world peacefully, at home with his beloved wife by his side. He was just thirty-three years old. I was sad to know he was gone, but happy he was finally out of pain. He had fought as hard as he could for five long years—the man deserved some peace.

Earlier, when I was in the studio, I had an idea of something I could do for Wayne, a small gift I could give him. On our video chat, I asked him if there was anything he wanted to say to the world, any particular words he wanted to be remembered by. My idea was to record him saying those words over the phone, and then I would layer them into a tune on the album or work his words into a lyric. That way, a part of him would be immortalized in song, and "immortalized" quite literally—I am a firm believer in science, and as such I believe in the law of conservation of energy, also known as the first law of thermodynamics. Albert Einstein famously summarized this principle by stating, "Energy cannot be created or destroyed; it can only be changed from one form to another." Music is composed of sound waves, which move through solids, liquids, and gases, thereby causing objects and substances to vibrate. (This is how we hear—sound waves vibrate our eardrums, and the brain processes the vibrations via the auditory nerve.) Those sound waves are called *kinetic mechanical energy*. In short, music is an externally and purposefully organized collection of kinetic energy (the energy of motion), and because energy can neither be created nor destroyed, music is, in a very real way, *eternal*. From the moment of their creation (or rather *organization*, I should say), songs travel endlessly outward through the universe, ever moving and changing form as they pass through the cosmos. I do not know what will happen after my bandmates and I are dead, but I do know that our music will exist as some form of energy forever. I thought maybe Wayne would like to be a part of that eternal creative expression.

"That's really cool. Let me think about it, man," he'd said, but he never got back to me. I don't know whether he ran out of time before he decided what he wanted to say or just didn't feel like it. I'm sure he had weightier matters on his mind than being on a heavy metal record. Regardless, after he died I still wanted to honor him in some way. I felt that this level-headed, collected man who had become my friend, all the while staring down his own death, should be remembered through the music of the band that he loved. Seeing how calm Wayne remained at the end of his life was (for lack of a better term) inspirational—he provided me with a living example of how to leave this world with courage, dignity, and grace. I owed him something for that, so I decided to write a song for him.

By that time, most of the songs on the album already had lyrics written for them, but there was one that was completely blank: "The Duke." As I sat down to work on it, I decided to write the lyrics in a first-person narrative style, speaking in

Wayne's voice. It was impossible for me to step into his shoes, to truly know what he had gone through, but I did my best to use my feeble understanding of Wayne's perspective as I wrote. I was honoring him in my way by letting what I knew of his character speak through my pen. Shortly after Wayne's death, I had a conversation with Courtney, his recently widowed wife. Courtney was very generous with me as we talked about her husband, recalling his bravery and composure at the end of his days. She shared some very personal things about his very final moments and things he had said to her leading up to them. I won't betray her trust by going into details about that private conversation, but I will say some of the lyrics for "The Duke" arose from things Courtney told me during that phone call. Other words came from things Wayne had said to me, and some came from my own head. I was quite emotional as I recorded the vocals, and I worked hard with Josh to get it right. The song felt important to me. It still does.

Before I get around to putting lyrics and vocals to our music, the guys in my band come up with the most hilarious and ridiculous working titles for the songs they are working on ("Elephant Sex," "Chicken Chicano Dinner," "Mark Bunster's Bunker Buster," "The Corbin Bernsen," and "The Fudgsicle Dental Dam," to name a few of my favorites from over the years). At one point, the song I was writing for Wayne was called "The Hazardous Duke Nukem," but somewhere along the way the guys had shortened it to "The Duke." After the vocals were done, I settled on "Immortalis" as a real title, but after a conversation with Wayne's father, Frank, I decided to stick with the abbreviated working title the guys had landed on months before I had reconnected with Wayne. I talked to Frank about the song, and when I mentioned the working title, he laughed out loud. He was a big John Wayne fan; in fact, he had named his son after the actor. Wayne's namesake also just happened to be referred to famously as . . . The Duke. Synchronicity at work.

After I was finished recording, the band began the process of sequencing the album, and for various reasons we decided not to release "The Duke" as an album track. I was perfectly fine with that. I thought the song, and the story behind it, would get more attention if it was released on its own. And I absolutely wanted the song to get a lot of attention, for more than one reason. As I sat with the tune, I began to feel that the song had the potential to do better than just being a shout-out to a departed fan. Perhaps we could raise some money to help out cancer patients or to fund researchers looking for a cure for leukemia. I reached out to Wayne's widow and his family to get their opinion on this—it was important that they be aware of and approve anything we did with this song. The Fords are as fine a group of people as you will meet and were happy we were trying to do some good in Wayne's honor. His mother, Londi, named a few different organizations she liked, one being the Leukemia and Lymphoma Society. With that in mind, I asked 5B, lamb of god's management company, to help us figure out the best way to raise money with the song.

In lieu of attempting the almost impossible task of explaining the bewildering, constantly changing, and insanely Byzantine reality that is the modern-day music industry, I will simply say this: except for a *very small* percentage of actual superstars, making money from the sale of music these days is pretty much impossible. We would have to sell millions of copies of *The Duke* EP before we ever recouped the recording budget our label had advanced, much less saw a penny of profit to donate to charity. Another way I like to explain my career is this: although my job title on tax forms is "professional musician," I am actually a glorified traveling black T-shirt salesman. In other words, kids: merchandise is where the money is. Knowing that, 5B proposed that we do a charity auction campaign with Propeller, an organization that works with artists to help raise funds for nonprofits and charitable causes. For The Duke campaign, we made limited-edition T-shirts. As well, my bandmates donated signed guitars and drum equipment. I donated signed copies of my book *Dark Days*, handwritten lyrics to "The Duke," and my gold record plaque for our album *Ashes of the Wake*. At the time, it was our first (and only) gold record, but I felt like it would do a lot better in a charity auction than in its current location in a cardboard box at the bottom of my cluttered closet. Plus, it would go to a fan, and I wouldn't have had a gold record in the first place without fans like Wayne. It felt very full circle to pack up that record and ship it off to be raffled.

On November 18, 2016, lamb of god released "The Duke" as part of a five-song EP of the same name. At the end of the Propeller auction campaign around the EP's release, we sent a check for $13,364 to the Leukemia and Lymphoma Society in honor of Wayne Ford and the memory of our merch girl Evie Carrano. Although that might not seem like much compared to the millions of dollars a massively famous musician, like, let's say, Bruce Springsteen, has raised for charitable causes...this is lamb of god, not Led Zeppelin. Plus, it's $13k more than they had before, and I was proud of my band—everyone, no matter what their supposed level of status or "success," has the ability to help others. The opportunities are endless. All you have to do is care and be willing to try.

There was one other thing I wanted to accomplish with "The Duke": a way to help leukemia patients that wouldn't cost people a single penny. As I did press around the release of the EP and the Propeller campaign, I always made sure to mention the bone marrow registry, Be The Match. Wayne and I had discussed Be The Match when we first met in Phoenix. He was gone now, but that didn't mean his story couldn't help save someone else's life. So I spoke a lot about Be The Match, the urgent need for more registered potential bone marrow donors, and how easy, painless, and free it was to register. All you have to do is go to www.bethematch.org, sign up, and they will send you everything you need, absolutely free.

So, what are you waiting for? Seriously, put this book down *right now* and do it—you might just save someone's life.

Conversations with Wayne (and further talks with his wife and family after his death) established that he was a pretty private dude, a quiet and humble man. He wasn't a big attention seeker, but in his final days he opened up and talked more about his disease. He knew that his death could help bring awareness to leukemia, the need for both bone marrow donors and research funding to find a cure for this terrible disease. If Wayne were still alive, I have no doubt that he would be annoyed by all the attention I tried to draw to him with *The Duke* EP release—he definitely would have busted my chops good for harshing his mellow. But right before the release, his wife reassured me that he would have understood why I was doing it, to try to help people, and that "he would be so honored to have not died in vain."

And Wayne didn't die in vain—we *did* raise money to help fight leukemia, and we *did* raise awareness in his name. That has already happened, and perhaps sharing his story again here might give someone else a few more years on earth, years that Wayne himself was denied—who knows? I can only use the tools at my disposal to try to help others to the best of my ability, then hope for the best. My music is one of those tools, and I need the guys in my band to help me make that tool. This book is another tool, one I have to fabricate myself. But Wayne gifted me the most important tool for this particular job, merely by speaking with me—he gave me his story. Stories have power if we use them well.

We are all going to die. Wayne showed me how to die well and to make the most of the time I have left. When my end comes, I will be grateful if I go out with half the dignity of that young man. Wayne wasn't some character in a best-selling thriller or Hollywood action movie; he was a regular dude, a thirty-three-year-old fan of my band from Phoenix, Arizona. But I learned a lot from him in the short time I got to be his friend. He showed me a perspective I hadn't seen before, and I will never forget him.

All hail The Duke.

Chapter Two
DOOMSDAY

If I had the power to remove one word from the English language until everyone swore a blood oath to use it properly, that word would be *unprecedented*. (Although *literally* comes in a very close second.)

For the last few years, *unprecedented* has been a nauseating constant, endlessly slipping from the anemic lips of every talking head bobbing on the vast, omnipresent array of glowing screens surrounding us. These professional harpies, screeching their particular brand of biased doom and gloom, simply love *unprecedented*. It is the chic term du jour used to describe any of a myriad of current unpleasantries— deadly pandemics, economic downturns, environmental disasters, sociopathic heads of state, violently insane toilet paper hoarders. Because all these things have, in fact, occurred multiple times within the last one hundred years (yes, even the toilet paper hoarding), and because the definition of *unprecedented* is "never known or done before," *not* "something-that's-already-happened-a-zillion-times-before-but-we-haven't-bothered-to-stop-watching-football-and-reality-TV-long-enough-to-think-about-it-until-now-that-it's-actually-affecting-us," its current overuse is not only blatantly incorrect but also *dangerous*.

Besides driving me insane, *unprecedented* subtly works to instill panic in the populace, a sense of facing some gruesome, nebulous foe that may or may not be possible to conquer. Whereas its incessant usage to torque up the constant anxiety spasm that passes for news these days is good for ratings and advertiser satisfaction, currently *unprecedented* is a fallacy, a lie, an ethical and linguistic abomination. If I had my way, I would replace *unprecedented* with *mayonnaise*—I mean, why not? If we're going to throw words around because they sound good regardless of their actual meaning, then "in these mayonnaise times" makes about as much sense. Plus, for a man of my highly refined palate, it's a far more accurate modifier to employ if you want to impart a "this sucks, it's scary, and it makes me feel kind of nauseous to contemplate being near it" emotional vibe when describing something unpleasant.

Unprecedented simply means *new*, and despite what the media doomsayers, politicians, and peddlers of designer handbags would have us believe, there is nothing new under the sun. Regrettably, people are very attracted to *new*, even if it's *bad new*. The feeling of excitement imparted by watching the latest bright, shiny thing unveiled—even if it's a bright, shiny disaster—is irresistible. And although history shows us again and again that politicians lie, people go broke, strange diseases from foreign lands wipe out large numbers of people, and the earth acts in unpredictable ways, the giant media conglomerations know that people would eventually unglue their weary selves from their screens if the corporate mouthpieces were to get honest and say, "Okay, admittedly, some of us ain't gonna make it, but this is the same old crap we've survived repeatedly in the past—it's just wrapped in plastic now instead of papyrus. Hang in there, y'all—we've seen all this before." So newscasters keep cashing paychecks and toeing the company line, acting as if this is an utterly new terrifying reality instead of an entirely predictable continuation of historical patterns. Regrettably, it seems most folks can't be bothered to further strain their LCD-battered eyes, rendered feeble and myopic by the luxury that is modern life, to peer into the brutal truth of the past.

But we as a global society ignore history at our own peril—the endless rise of petty dictators riding into power on the back of populist fears (not to mention the resurgence of Day-Glo 1980s-style fashion apparel) proves this irrefutably. And on a personal level, if we don't bother learning from the past, we can easily begin feeling as if the mundane, historically repetitive difficulties woven into the fabric of our day-to-day lives are actually extraordinary and, um, *unprecedented*. This corrosive belief can manifest in various poisonous ways—uncontrollable anger, bitter envy, and worst of all, *paralyzing fear.*

Fear is a real motherfucker, a top-shelf, Grade A son of a bitch that will ruin your whole week if you let it run the show. It also has a purpose, rooted in evolution, so FDR wasn't quite right when he said "The only thing we have to fear is fear itself"—there's some shit you should *definitely* be afraid of. If you are sunbathing on the banks of the River Nile and your first thought when a crocodile beelines toward your beach towel is "What a beautiful lizard! I wonder what he had for lunch?" instead of *"Jesus Christ, I gotta get the hell outta here right now!"* then your lack of fear is a very, very unhealthy perspective (but the crocodile will certainly appreciate it). But aside from those rare life-or-death situations, Roosevelt was right for the most part—unchecked fear is a pernicious, caustic presence in our lives, and it needs to be fought to a standstill at every single opportunity. If we don't halt fear in its tracks, it can become overwhelming, paralyzing us mentally and emotionally, even physically.

There has been only one time in my life that I can recall being physically paralyzed by fear. To my knowledge, I am not afflicted with any of the common, everyday phobias; I actually like creepy-crawly things like spiders and snakes, even the poisonous ones, because they look pretty to me and I know they serve a valuable purpose in the natural order. I'm not scared of needles or enclosed spaces, so giving blood in a broom closet wouldn't bother me much. I've spent way too much time on airplanes crammed full of coughing people who probably don't wash their hands after using the bathroom to be afraid of flying in a long metal tube full of germs. And I've been climbing trees since before I read my first Tarzan book as a boy, so heights haven't ever freaked me out—except once.

For years before my band got big enough to actually pay the bills, all of us worked straight jobs to make rent. Although traveling up and down the East Coast in a series of constantly breaking-down vans while drinking cheap beer and playing music for fifteen people in some kid's basement is undeniably fun, it doesn't keep a roof over your head. So I've had a job since high school, mostly sweating over an oven or dish sink in various restaurant kitchens, but for several years I was a roofer (as was our guitarist, Mark Morton—he was much better at it than I). The roofing company I worked for was run by our friend Noal Clark, another local musician I had previously worked with at a crazy all-night diner. Noal is a big, strapping, physically powerful dude who taught me a lot about roofing and metalwork—I always trusted him to keep me safe on the job, and he never asked me to do anything I was truly uncomfortable with. Under Noal's watchful eye, I walked the steeply pitched slate roofs of old-money mansions on Richmond's Monument Avenue, ran up and down a forty-foot extension ladder loaded down with heavy tools, even perched myself high above my state's capitol grounds while we roofed an addition on the exquisite Virginia Governor's Mansion (my coworker Dave smoked a joint up there, à la Willie Nelson at Jimmy Carter's White House). Although

I had been on some pretty hair-raising roofs, I was always careful, and I always felt confident that I would return safely to the ground to have a few cold beers with the boys at the day's end. Heights didn't bother me then, and they don't now.

One summer afternoon, Noal and I were on a small job in Windsor Farms, a well-to-do neighborhood modeled after an English village in Richmond's West End. My task that day was to solder the seams on a new flat-lock copper roof, really not much more than an ornamental ledge sticking out of the house beneath some windows. We set up the extension ladder and up I went, climbing about two stories with my canister of propane gas and soldering iron. At the top of the ladder, I set my tools down on the roof, then hopped up there and set up my soldering rig. The roof was pretty small, I'd say about eight feet by four feet total, but it was virtually flat, with almost no slope, so I sat comfortably on the foam guts of an old couch cushion with what felt like plenty of room. Noal went to another part of the house to handle a different project, and I began to work, applying flux paste with a small brush to the copper seams to clean them before soldering them shut with my iron.

It was a typical summer day in Richmond, hot and muggy. After about an hour's work, I was almost halfway done, making slow but steady progress on the seams. I sat there sweating and fluxing and soldering away, wondering whether I would catch a glimpse of Patricia Cornwell, the famous crime novelist who lived in the neighborhood at the time. I put my iron down and reached to take a drink of water when something happened—I froze.

I don't know how to describe it any other way. One second I was fine, concentrating on my work. The next second I looked up, saw the roof I was sitting on, saw the ground two stories below me, saw the ladder I had climbed up just an arm's length away...and I was instantly and completely paralyzed, gripped by a full-body experience of fear. I remember thinking it was so hot up there, and the sweat was dripping from my body in the afternoon sun, but I physically felt a chill run through me to my core. I just knew that if I moved, even an inch, I was going to fall off that roof. I remember looking at the copper panels, seeing the little bit of excess flux on the edges of the seam I had just soldered, and thinking how slick that flux had made the copper, how easily I could just slide across it and off the roof. I remember thinking, "I need to get off this roof, *NOW*," but being totally unable to move. In an instant, for no discernible reason, I was utterly terrified on a molecular level, the entirety of my existence completely overwhelmed by fear.

Never before had I felt anything like it, and I never have since—I was stricken completely immobile. I get goosebumps just thinking about it.

I don't know how long I sat there, frozen with fear like a cat stuck in a tree. Eventually, I called for help in a quavering voice: "Noal...NOAL!" I didn't have to say anything else. Noal heard the terror in my voice and was running up the ladder in an instant. It took him the better part of half an hour to get me off that roof, coaxing me along in a calm voice as I slowly moved inch by inch from the roof onto the ladder and then down to the ground, my whole body shaking the entire time. I had never been more happy to feel grass beneath my feet in my life. (Thanks, Noal—love ya, buddy!)

To this day, I have zero idea *why* I froze on the roof that afternoon. It confuses me when I think about it, as I had certainly worked on much steeper and higher roofs before (and would do so again repeatedly without the slightest problem). Unlike most roofing jobs I'd been on, there was even grass below that particular roof—it would have sucked to fall that far, but people have survived falling onto concrete from much higher heights. I suppose what happened could be called a panic attack, but it was so very specific in nature, rooted entirely in a sudden and inexplicable transient fear of heights. Not only was I unafraid of heights, but they also were a routine part of my daily life, so I still have no clue what triggered it. It makes no sense to me. I have been locked up in a European prison, walked through the middle of a massive riot in Southeast Asia, had bullets whiz past my head on an American city street, even voluntarily jumped out of an airplane thousands of feet above the Nevada desert—all things I consider much more dangerous and far scarier than just another day at my roofing gig—and I have never, ever frozen. I've certainly been afraid before, but never terrified to the point of immobility.

For the most part, immobility in dangerous situations is how you die, like a deer frozen in the headlights of a Mack truck. From an evolutionary standpoint, freezing from fear is the next option after the fight-or-flight response is exhausted, when your brain determines that you can neither battle off danger or run away from it. You are stricken immobile, perhaps in a last-ditch psychic defense of disassociating yourself from whatever traumatic experience you are undergoing. But roofing was not a traumatic experience for me, and I could have simply climbed down the ladder, as I had hundreds of times before while on the job. Failing that, with very little difficulty I could have smashed out the large window behind me using my roofing hammer and crawled through it to safety. I had easy options to get off that roof, so my freezing up that day served no purpose, other than perhaps to teach me a lesson: paralyzing fear *sucks*. It can get you hurt badly, or even killed, so learn to recognize it when it's happening and fight to not let it consume you. Fear thoroughly kicked my ass that day, and I didn't even attempt to put up my dukes to ward it off—this will not do.

Unbridled fear can also paralyze you mentally and emotionally, keeping you stuck in a swirling pool of crap: crappy relationships, crappy jobs, and crappy habitual responses to any of life's crappy situations. (In my case, habitual responses like ignoring the situation while drinking a case of Heineken in the hopes it would eventually go away, just like an alcoholic ostrich on spring break sticking his head into the beer-soaked sand of a South Florida beach. By the way, ostriches—alcoholic or not—don't really do that, but I think it's funny to think about.) Most of the time, we already know what we should do to make our lives better, but the thought of actually committing to change and taking action to effect it can produce so much anxiety that we often stay stuck in the same old familiar highly uncomfortable comfortable bullshit (the devil you know...). To my knowledge, telling your power-tripping boss at your sketchy minimum-wage telemarketing job to go fuck herself as you ride off into the sunset in search of a better job hasn't gotten anyone executed lately, so why on earth do people stay working gigs that make them miserable? (I mean, has there ever been a *happy* telemarketer?) And why in the hell haven't you dumped your loser hobosexual boyfriend yet? You know, the unshaven mess that's been sitting on your couch smoking pot and playing video games all day for the last three months while you go to work? He ain't *that good* in the sack—yet there he sits, cursing into his headset to his "squadron" as some eleven-year-old sniper in South Korea blasts his virtual ass to smithereens. Why don't you just tell him to kick rocks?

The answer, as always, lies in history. For thousands of years, our ancestors lived as prey to larger, stronger, faster predators—enormous saber-toothed cats, huge hyenas, massive snakes, cave bears, and maybe even giant eagles and carnivorous kangaroos. Although it's true that various species of animals still snack on humans from time to time, for the most part it's extremely unlikely you're going to get eaten while running an errand to the post office. But burned into our genetic code is the memory of that most primal of fears: winding up as lunch for something much bigger than you. Back in the day, that primal fear was invaluable, as it kept your ancestors alive—at least long enough to mate and raise offspring, which eventually produced you: the end product of a few million years of screwing and running away from enormous hungry animals (don't you feel special now?). But these days, this fear of monsters with sharp teeth doesn't have anything to attach itself to. Instead, it manifests as anxiety over any of a million different nonlethal things your brain perceives as threats to your well-being. That primal fight-or-flight survival response was designed to deal with immediate, short-term, life-threatening situations, like a pack of wolves circling you in the forest. It was not designed to deal with giving a PowerPoint presentation outlining the abysmal first-quarter profit margins to the CEO of your corporation, but the mechanism is not sophisticated enough to tell the difference—that's why your hands get so sweaty when you have to give the boss bad news. This sort of fear is an evolutionary hangover, a once-useful ancient response cloaked in the modern and counterproductive costume known as anxiety. So, even though we cannot eradicate fear and anxiety from our lives, it helps to know their source, to understand why we feel these emotions, and to recognize them for what they are—echoes from a time when the stakes were much, much higher. That way we can train ourselves to calmly deal with things that scare us or make us nervous.

Remaining calm when we get scared or encounter a stressful situation is *good*. Freaking out, no matter what is happening, is *bad*. It solves absolutely nothing. I mean, when was the last time you went to a friend for advice concerning a difficult situation you were facing and they said, "Wow. That *is* a tough one. Lemme think about it.... Okay, if I were you, I would just go ahead and *panic*"? Unless you have really crappy friends, "totally freak out" is advice we never, ever hear, yet we do it all the time. There is so much anxiety in the world today, and while admittedly there are certainly some nerve-wracking things happening across the globe, the vast majority of stuff people get worked up over is ultimately insignificant *bullshit*. Let's face it, kiddos, most modern humans are not constantly engaged in a life-or-death struggle for survival; they are too busy getting upset over minor inconveniences or obsessing over what some idiot said online.

Can you imagine a caveman going postal because his flight was delayed or bursting into tears when someone is mean to him on social media? Get the fuck outta here. Primitive man would look at what we modern-day humans consider "stressful situations" and say, "Hey, assholes, chill out and enjoy your magically convenient existences—nothing is debating whether or not to have you for lunch, ya dig?" Besides, even when something actually *is* considering eating you, trust me, it's *much better* to remain calm.

I am a surfer. I love, love, *love* to surf, and I go every chance I get. I wind up discussing surfing fairly often with fans, the music press, and friends. By far, the number one question I get from nonsurfers is: "Have you ever seen any sharks while you were surfing?" *Of course I have.* I am around sharks quite often because sharks are always there in the ocean. We just don't see them most of the time because they are busy swimming around below us looking for food. I've seen a fin or two over the years, but it's a pretty rare occurrence. However, I know they are always nearby. I accept it, and furthermore, I am fully aware that one day I could be severely injured or even die after being bitten by a shark while doing what I love. Although it would undoubtedly be an extremely unpleasant experience in the moment of occurrence, that possibility is just a part of what I do, and if it happens to me, then so be it—I am 100 percent at peace with that. As we've previously discussed, everyone is going to die one day. If I die surfing, I will have died on my own terms. I can't ask for much more than that.

I am also 100 percent fully aware of the facts that sharks don't actually want to eat humans (we are far too bony), that most of the time a shark bites you merely out of curiosity to see if you taste yummy (then spits out your not-so-tasty flesh and promptly swims away in disgust), and that movies such as *Jaws* have unfairly portrayed sharks as bloodthirsty man-eating monsters (I must admit, though, it's *really fun* to hum the *Jaws* theme song on a crowded beach during peak tourist season). For decades, shortsighted idiots have been hunting sharks to the edge of extinction just to make a crappy-tasting soup from their fins—this both enrages and disgusts me. I hold these beautiful apex predators of the sea in very high esteem because eradicating them would be disastrous for the health of our oceans, and thereby the entire planet (which includes, of course, the apparently moronic human race). Furthermore, I know that I am a thousand times more likely to die in my rental car on the way to the studio to record an album than to ever suffer even the tiniest nibble from a shark; so, unlike every single terrifying time I have to drive in Los Angeles, I don't worry too much about dying when I paddle out into the ocean. (In 2021, 3,246 people died in car crashes in the state of California alone. Conversely, 11 people died from shark attacks in 2021 throughout the *entire world*—I'm not here on a physics scholarship, but the math seems simple enough to me.) So, although I know shark attacks are incredibly rare, and I also know the vast majority of attacks are nonfatal...they *do* happen. (And yes, I know, I know—some scientists and shark experts are pushing to abolish the term *attack*, preferring to call them "incidents" or "negative encounters." I understand their reasoning, but I would use "negative encounter" to describe a run-in with a rude barista at the coffee shop, not getting my leg ripped off in the ocean. Sharks didn't develop all those lovely teeth to better argue semantics.)

I know all these things, but I can assure you, no matter how well-versed in shark behavior and dietary preferences you are, when a big one suddenly appears beside you in the water...you *will* feel that most ancient and primal fear.

One beautiful September morning in 2016, I was surfing at Oak Island, North Carolina, with my buddy David and his son Ernie. We were at The Point, as the western end of the island is known, surfing very near a river mouth. We were the only ones in the water, and the fall swell was providing exceptionally good waves that day; endless waist- to chest-high beautifully glassy peelers that gave us really smooth, long rides. We had been in the water for about half an hour, catching wave after perfect wave, and the stoke was very high. We were out past the breakers, relaxing in between sets and laughing about how awesome the surf was, when from my left I heard Ernie say:

"Dad. *DadDadDAD!!!!!*"

I looked over to where David was lying on his board, about four feet away from me. All the way at the tail end of his nine-foot longboard, I saw a tiny little fin surfacing. I remember thinking, "Oh, what a cute little baby shark!" Then I looked toward the nose of David's board and saw the dorsal fin.

Emerging from the water near David's head, sitting perfectly still about a foot or two away from him, the dorsal was *huge*. It seemed to rise forever, a mottled gray wedge that kept getting taller and taller. With both fins sticking out of the water directly beside David's board, I could see very clearly that the distance from tail to dorsal was longer than David was tall, at least six feet. That meant that the shark was an eight- to nine-footer, *minimum*.

The Landlord had arrived.

Surfers around the world have different nicknames for sharks—The Man in the Gray Suit, Noah, Mack (as in

"Mack the Knife")—but my personal favorite is *The Land-lord*. The ocean is the shark's house. He owns it, he knows it, and make no mistake, every time you enter the ocean, there's a chance he may come cruising by to check out what you're doing fooling around in his crib. Most of the time he just does a slow drive-by to remind you whose house it is, then splits. But every now and then, on rare occasions, The Landlord decides to collect rent.

Rent can be very, very high.

It's *intense* to be in the ocean when a big shark appears right beside you. They do not splash, they do not blast the *Jaws* theme from fin-mounted stereo speakers as they approach, they do not jump playfully out of the water like a not-so-cute Flipper with fangs—they just silently *materialize*, like dark primordial oceanic magic. One second you are sitting there on your surfboard chilling with the homies on a perfect day, and the next second all you see is a giant fin that makes you instantly reevaluate your place in the universe. You realize for the first time in your life that something, in this case, the massive oceanic apex predator floating just a few feet away, might *eat you*. It's *fucking scary*, and I am not ashamed to admit that just like that day on the roof, I immediately felt a chill run through my entire body when I saw that terrible fin.

But the way I processed that fear was very different. Unlike the day on the roof, I did not freeze or yell for help. Instead, I saw the shark, calmly turned my board around, and paddled very smoothly toward shore. I did not splash, I did not scream, I did not flail and panic and dig my arms in like a human speedboat engine to jet-propel me to shore. The Landlord can get irritated by that sort of behavior or mistake you for injured sea life and decide you are a low-effort snack. Every inch of my body was drawn up on that board, as far away from the surface of the water as possible (I think it's the only time I've ever paddled using just my fingertips), but my breathing was steady and my mind was level and clear. In fact, after the initial shock of seeing the fin, I wasn't even scared anymore, just extremely focused on getting to shore. So I paddled a few feet, caught a nice wave, and rode it in to the beach, David and Ernie following closely on waves right behind me. We stepped off our boards into knee-high water, took off our leashes, and walked calmly onto the dry sand. I felt strangely serene as I turned and looked out on the water, scanning for the fin. *Damn, I handled that perfectly*, I thought, and gave myself a smug little pat on the back.

Then the adrenaline hit.

"*OH FUCK, OH FUCK, OH FUCK, OH FUCK!*" I heard myself blabbering. I looked down and my knees were shaking.

"*JESUS CHRIST, HOLY SHIT, DID YOU SEE THAT THING? IT WAS FUCKING HUGE!*" Ernie hollered as he hopped back and forth from one foot to the other. We were *shook*.

David scowled at us and put his finger to his lips. "Shh-hhhhhhh! Be quiet, you idiots—you're gonna scare the kid," he said, pointing at the only other people on the beach, a couple sitting in beach chairs a few feet away. A three-year-old boy was playing in the sand near the water's edge in front of them. David walked over to them, leaned down, and whispered into the father's ear. The father sprang from his beach chair, grabbed his son, and brought him farther inland. We gathered our stuff, walked off the beach, and drove a few miles down the road to surf elsewhere. The waves weren't as good at the next spot, but The Landlord had let us know in no uncertain terms that the party was over at his hunting grounds by the river mouth.

Good hunting to you, Mister Landlord—we see you, we respect you, and we thank you for not tasting us that day.

Later that evening over dinner, we were telling the story to some friends, and Ernie said to me, "We saw *God* today, bro." Ernie was raised in Hawaii, and there are many shark gods within the native Hawaiian mythological pantheon, so maybe he was thinking of legends he had heard as a child. I'm a *haole* who hasn't set foot on those islands yet, but I still agreed with him 100 percent. Like some terrible deity, that shark could have obliterated our existence had he so chosen. But he didn't, so we were extra grateful to be sitting in one piece that evening, breaking bread together. (Ironically, relief at not being eaten makes food taste especially delicious.)

And like that time on the roof, to this day if I think deeply enough about the experience, I can still get creeped out and feel a strong echo of that fear. But I do not permit the memory of that experience to stop me from surfing (I certainly don't reminisce about it in the water), and I've even tried to learn something from the way David handled it on the beach that day.

I had handled things very well in the water, but once on dry land and away from danger, I pretty much lost my shit. The shark had undoubtedly scared David just as much, if not more, than me—after all, it was basically touching his surfboard. But unlike me, he took mastery over even his delayed response to that fear. David controlled the adrenaline rushing through his body, stayed composed, and didn't let it make him alarm a small child. Even though he had just undergone a bad scare, he wasn't thinking only of himself in the aftermath but was mindful of how his behavior might affect others and their future. I have adult friends who are terrified of the ocean because of a negative experience they had at the beach as children. David didn't want to create that sort of situation for that kid. His restraint showed me that I still had a lot of work to do on how I handle things that scare me, because uncontrolled responses to fear only beget more fear in others, and the last thing this world needs is more fear. I do not wish to be a part of that ever-growing problem, so merely handling fear in the moment, for myself, is no longer good enough for me. I have to learn to control my fear completely, to ride it into the ground until it is nothing but dust beneath my feet. Science has long proven that fear is contagious, and if I truly want the world to be a better place, I must not spread even an echo of fear with careless words and actions lest it infect others.

Regardless of the work I still have to do on controlling fear, I've historically been a pretty calm guy in real-life oh-shit-this-is-actually-terrifying type situations (with the exception of that strange time on the roof). That's nice and makes me feel good about myself and all, but because I'm not a caveman clawing my way through a brutal existence while hoping to survive to the ripe old age of thirty-five, those situations are quite rare and aren't really my problem—the situations I create inside my head are. On a daily basis, even though I know better, *goddammit*, if I don't watch it, I can become completely riddled with fear and anxiety over the dumbest things. There is a constant conflict inside me to reconcile what I know to be reality (*I'm doing waaaaay better than okay*) with how I feel when I have to do irritating things like call customer service at the bank (*oh my God, they are going to figure out that I am a no-talent hack, tell me I don't deserve any money, then throw me in prison on charges of impersonating an artist as I publicly disgrace my family's name*). Repeatedly, I abandon hard-earned lessons on perspective and instead catastrophize my entire existence as soon as some trivial annoyance raises its ugly head. I forget how grateful I was to stand on the shore unbitten, I forget the example of how calm David was telling that father about the very real death lurking in the water, I forget how lucky I am to be alive and healthy after drinking enough booze to give the entire state of Texas cirrhosis of the liver. My life is really quite easy, but I still go berserk as soon as I hear the robot voice on the phone say, "For English, press one. *Para Espanol, oprima el numero dos.*" I let the dumbest shit get into my head, irritate me, then the doom monkeys start running amok, and soon enough I am controlled by fear and anxiety and eventually express that fear and anxiety through the rot-gut cheap whiskey of emotions: anger. Even when I do attempt to get a handle on this ridiculous fear, anxiety, and anger, I usually go about it in one of a couple of highly ineffective ways.

I need to unlearn this shit.

Chapter Three

MY WAR

There is a war inside my head, an incessant conflict ignited daily by my constantly shifting perception of reality. This internal Ragnarok kicked off when I was around eight years old, the age I first became aware that adults were not infallible beings, that I could not trust all grown-ups to act in an upright manner, that some of them were not even worthy of my childish respect. Before then, I moved blissfully through life, walking happily along in the feather-light footsteps of innocence. Because I was lucky enough to be raised by moral and loving parents, I believed that everyone thought the same way that I had been taught to—we were all equal, no one better than anyone else for any reason. My parents told me that we were all children of a loving and caring God, and as such we should love one another equally in kind.

This seemed a sensible way to live, and the people within my tiny immediate orbit gave me no reason to think otherwise. I was never abused in any manner by any adult, but at a certain point I became aware that not everyone or everything was what it first seemed to be.

Most people generally wore a mask of decency in public, but in private or under duress, sometimes cracks would appear in the facade of decorum. Adults would say they believed one thing and then do another as angry and unguarded glimpses of true feelings peeped through the splintered face of their civility. Oddly to my young mind, this seemed to happen more freely around children such as me, as if these adults considered us so dim-witted as to be beneath notice. But children are nothing if not great noticers, and as I cataloged incidents of the hypocrisy and sheer stupidity some adults displayed, my childish illusions of their flawless benevolence were ripped away. Despite this rude awakening, a great part of me still saw so much beauty in the world, still felt so much love for and from many different good people that I couldn't automatically sink into a prepubescent riot of nihilism and apathy. Life could be extremely painful, yes, but it was also full of incredible joy. At that point, the long fight with myself began, a battle between hope and despair for the character of my soul.

One man inside me is almost unbearably sunny, a yam-mering, hippieish sort of dude who not only wants everyone to get along but also firmly believes that's possible. Indeed, at times Mister Relentless Optimism feels like we are on the brink of a planetwide social *satori*, a mass realization that we are nothing other than one great interconnected web of light. He believes that progress is not only possible but also actually occurring—just look at the advances in science, technology, and medicine! Comparing our modern medical knowledge to the ludicrous superstitions of the past ("When people acted weird back in the day, they used to *drill holes in their heads* to let the demons out! Imagine being that primitive—thank God we live now!"), he sees irrefutable progress. If he ever becomes discouraged about ongoing social inequities, he quickly reminds himself to consider life just over a hundred years ago, when women didn't have the right to vote and Jim Crow laws ruled the land. This cheerful dude believes that even the worst, most incorrigible criminal-minded sociopathic assholes can be rehabilitated if they are just given a chance, shown some compassion, and gently prodded in a constructive direction. Mister Relentless Optimism's heart often hurts, but only because it's ripping apart at the seams with a wild and savage love for every atom in the universe.

Mister Relentless Optimism wakes up at dawn, hums a verse or two of "Kumbaya," then throws open his antique French windows to take in all that glorious sunshine. He smiles at the beauty unfolding before him and says to the world: "Hang in there, everyone—we're all going to be okay!" Then he spins old-school seventies dub reggae albums and bounces around his well-lit apartment having encouraging conversations with his houseplants.

Then there's the other guy.

The Dark One looks around and sees a world full of conflict and strife. He knows that it has always been this way and always shall be, because history has proven that the urge to war with others is an intrinsic and inescapable component of human nature. For each publicly celebrated altruistic action and advance in our society, he scans the news and quickly finds what he's looking for: a multitude of vile reactions and regressions in the name of self-interest and greed. The Dark One knows that despite all our advances in technology, we are swiftly sinking to the bottom of an awful abyss of moronic, narcissistic self-destruction. As his keen and cynical eye notes, this downward moral and intellectual trajectory is aided—nay, *propelled*—by the for-profit misuse of that same technology. On devices and in forums made possible solely by the rigorous labor of scientifically minded individuals, the demonization of science and the rejection of reason, knowledge, and objective reality itself are not only accepted but also celebrated and weaponized. The irony would be so judgmentally delicious if it wasn't so goddamned pathetic. The Dark One sees a willful, gleeful embrace of ignorance; a roiling human sea of hubris, stupidity, and hatred rising faster each day, much like the levels of our actual oceans. He knows that even if we come to some sort of peace with each other and manage not to destroy Earth, it doesn't really matter because in approximately five billion years the sun will burn out and our planet will die. The Dark One sits writhing not so much in an existential crisis (which implies the possibility of a solution) but in the continual dawn of an existential Armageddon.

The Dark One wakes up at three in the afternoon with a splitting headache, groans, then stumbles off the couch to make sure the deadbolts on his reinforced steel door are still locked. Through the peephole, he sees a slushy wintry mix falling on the dirty sidewalk outside and mutters to himself: "It's too late. Drop the bomb now—*NOW!*—and wipe 'em all out. Maybe something that deserves to live will evolve next." Then, beneath the flickering light of a single naked bulb hanging by frayed wires from his nicotine-stained ceiling, he flips the early-nineties Norwegian black metal album to hear the other side and sharpens his knife.

In fact, both of these guys are undeniably right about some things. Equally as important, both of them are dead wrong about even more things. Much like our asinine two-party political system here in America, both of them are blind to the actual reality unfolding right in front of them.

Mister Relentless Optimism is a schmuck. His cheerfully myopic vision fails to see the magnitude of the problems the world faces. He mostly just sits around blissfully hoping for the best. "Hoping for the best" without action to back it up is worse than useless. What if Martin Luther King Jr. had never gotten past the "dream" part of his famous "I Have a Dream" speech? What if he had just sat around *dreaming* about the day little black boys and black girls would be able to join hands with little white boys and white girls as sisters and brothers instead of getting his ass handed to him by redneck cops across the South? I highly doubt I would have sat down at my favorite Mexican restaurant the other day for dinner and conversation with my friend Puma, a black man I refer to as "brother" without a second thought. And yes, MLK paid for his dream with his life—but sometimes that's the cost of progress.

The Dark One is no fun at parties. And no matter how much I let other people twist my head into misanthropic knots, I am still a human being and as such a social animal. Like it or not, I need human connection to carry on with some degree of mental stability. James B. Stockdale was a US Navy fighter pilot and student of Stoic philosophy who was captured and kept prisoner in the infamous Hanoi Hilton during the Vietnam War. During his seven years as a POW, Stockdale was both repeatedly tortured and kept in isolation for lengthy periods. Years after his brutal ordeal, he concluded that long-term erosion of human purpose was more effectively achieved through isolation than torture. Although I am no scholar of seventeenth-century poetry, John Donne's famous "no man is an island" line rings irritatingly true to my ear—experience has shown me that if I isolate myself too much, things get *weird*. And yes, it's true, many, many people suck—but I can't maintain a healthy existence without them.

These two drastically different characters, whipping the ship of my emotional state back and forth through the stormy seas of existence, resemble very closely the highs and lows of my active alcoholism. While drinking and drugging, at times I reveled in states of ecstatic bliss, periods when all was right in the universe (at least in my muddled perceptions), and I felt on top of the world. Matching that grand and delusional mountain peak were rapid descents into a foul-smelling valley of self-pity and sadness, a wretched place where all I saw was darkness. Every little inconvenience was merely more evidence that life was an entirely pointless exercise. This up-and-down emotional roller-coaster ride was exhausting, but people with experience told me that if I got and stayed sober things would start to level out and eventually I would find some balance and be content to walk a middle path.

"Walking a middle path" sounded so dreadfully boring to me, so . . . *average*. I have never really been interested in "average" *anything*. But after decades of the highest highs and lowest lows, I was just too damn tired to climb aboard the roller-coaster anymore, so I threw in the towel and quit drinking. At first, the highs and lows were still there (minus the hefty bar tab and attendant hangovers), but slowly I began to find my emotions more on the beam. Now I am just content to be sober, no longer annoyingly overjoyed at the fact I no longer drink nor morosely romanticizing the not-so-good old days. My sobriety is overwhelmingly pedestrian, and unless I am discussing it with someone else, I don't really think about it much throughout the day—it just *is*. Being sober is my normal state these days, and that's good enough for me.

Being a middle-of-the-road sober dude has helped my mentality in general, but I am definitely still a work in progress, as the war in my head constantly reminds me. My drinking was, in part, a way to deal with that war. Alcohol muffled the constantly screaming voices...until it didn't. In fact, eventually it amplified those voices to a ridiculous level, but they are much quieter now that the booze is gone. Regrettably, they are still present, and I still listen to them with embarrassing regularity—and it still exhausts me.

But if I quiet myself, I can remember a time before the axe of experience fell on my head, splitting me into warring factions ever shifting between the polarities of extreme joy and sorrow (e.g., falling in love for the first time to watching far too many friends die far too young to eating fresh ramen in a Tokyo subway station to doing federal income taxes). Before life got so goddamned complex, I was just one person, a well-balanced, good-natured child who saw things in the world as either right or wrong and didn't get too caught up in a million insignificant conflicting details. That tiny human didn't have the experience or skills to navigate the complex and problematic realities that plagued adults, but in his small way he tried his best to do the right thing, even if he made a mess of it at times.

For instance, when I was just a boy of six years old, I bankrupted my family by giving away every penny we had.

Or at least I tried to, according to my mother. I barely remember this attempted financial catastrophe, just vague flickering images on an old TV set in the den of the tiny one-story brick house where I lived with my parents and two younger brothers. My pretty mother was in the kitchen, ensconced among the pine cabinetry and Formica countertops and macramé plant holders (presumably preparing some sort of *casserole*—isn't that what everyone ate for basically every meal in the 1970s?), when I told her "the lady on the phone" wanted to speak to her. I handed her the avocado-green handset with its curlicue cord. In speaking to the woman on the other end, Mom discovered to her surprise that I had just pledged *all* the money in the family bank account to a foreign aid organization.

On one of the three channels our TV set received, I had been watching a special about starving children in Africa (or it could have been Southeast Asia or South America or maybe even Appalachia or Los Angeles—as now, there were hungry children in all those places, but Africa seemed the de facto choice for adolescent malnutrition fundraising purposes back then). On the small screen, I saw swollen bellies, thin limbs, and sad faces. I had become extremely upset at the state of these children, so I decided to help them. By American standards, my background could never be described as wealthy, but as a child, I never had to wonder where my next meal was coming from. At six years old, my grasp of the family's fiscal reality (it was tight) was nonexistent—my understanding of money itself was extremely minimal. But I understood enough about cash to know that sometimes you had to spend it to get food, and because we always had breakfast, lunch, and dinner, I knew we had to have some loot in that building my parents called "the bank."

"Well, we have enough food," I thought, "and these kids have none. So we just need to send them some money so they can eat. And why on earth are they starving? Hasn't anyone else helped them? Doesn't anyone care? Where are their adults? Mister Ray next door gives us vegetables from his garden all the time—don't these kids have neighbors? Maybe Mister Ray can send them some okra or corn if I let him know, but they look hungry *now*—I better give them our money."

And so I quietly called the toll-free number and told the lady that we had plenty of food, so would she please take all our money and buy some lunch for these kids. It made perfect sense to me then.

Cut away all the bullshit excuses society has shoveled in greedy, complicated heaps into our heads, and it still does.

My mom talked to the bemused woman and then explained to me that we each give according to our means. My means was a piggy bank, so I dumped out all my coins and gave them to Mom to send off to those hungry kids, which she did (along with a little supplemental parental contribution).

I had seen a problem and I simply took action.

At six years old, I did not know about the brutal, demoralizing history of slavery and colonialism on the African continent, much less where on the map Khartoum was. I did not know about genocidal dictators and droughts in Ethiopia because I had no conception of politics and it always seemed to rain plenty in my little corner of southeastern North Carolina. I was not aware of the corruption running through some fundraising organizations and *all* governments that diverts funds meant for humanitarian relief into the pockets of administrators and bureaucrats. I knew nothing about the cost of monetary wire transfers or the complexity of food supply chains or the arcane discipline of logistics. If I had known any of that stuff, I probably would have just thrown up my grubby little hands and said, "What's the use? This is all way too complicated for me—maybe someone else will figure out how to help those kids," then stomped outside to play beneath the canopy of pines behind the house. But I was just an "ignorant" child, and I only knew that those kids were starving to death while my family always had leftovers.

I need to help them was all I thought, and so I tried. No one told me I needed to do this. I just knew.

As children, all of us knew—and we still know today. Our sense of morality is instilled in us not only by our parents and society; evolution has written it into our genetic code. Once again, human beings are social animals, and our very survival as a comparatively weak species (no claws, no fangs) has depended on assisting one another. Alongside the instinct for self-preservation, the urge to do the right thing lives on within each of us, even if its shine is dimmed by the daily abrasive cynicism, self-interest, and ennui that coats life in the modern era. We can try to ignore this inner moral imperative by adopting a cool and dispassionate attitude, sprucing up our hip shiftlessness with a few choice Nietzsche quotes in a lame attempt to intellectualize life as meaningless. Or we can maintain appearances, pretending we are actually doing something by pushing a few buttons on a glowing screen, joining the billion-voice social media choir of outrage that screeches out the latest highly offended Top 40 hit. But apathy is the refuge of the intellectual coward, and outrage without action is self-righteous masturbation. No matter how we try to justify our inertia in the face of injustice, be it hipster nihilism or the angry circle jerk of social media, each of us knows right from wrong. And if we don't roll up our sleeves and get to work actually giving a crap about the world around us by taking actions to make it a better place, who will? Are we gonna wait for the adults to figure it out?

Since the days of Carl Jung, psychologists have spoken of "getting in touch with your inner child" and rediscovering a sense of wonder in simple things like playing on a swing set in the summertime or healing the trauma inflicted by that wicked witch of a second-grade teacher. All that is well and good, but I think we can take it a step further. Perhaps instead of constantly trying to fix the little motherfucker or retaste his first lick of ice cream, perhaps we ought to pause and ask him some questions, break down some large, complex, "adult" problems into simple terms his wee brain can understand, and see if he's got any answers. Let's say, something like, plastic pollution in the ocean.

"Hey, kid, I got a question for ya. There's this giant floating patch of plastic garbage in the ocean, made out of a bunch of stuff we used once and then threw away. It looks like doo-doo and it's bad for all the fish and sea turtles. All this plastic trash is breaking down into tiny pieces, getting into everything, even humans now. It seems to keep on growing. What do we do?"

"Hmm... don't use so much plastic. Find something else."

Duh.

And a great groan arises from the world-weary adult masses: "Nice try, sunshine, but that whole 'see-the-world-through-the-eyes-of-a-child' crap doesn't cut it in real life. We can't just look at complex issues, make a few decisions, and then run around 'fixing stuff.' These are giant, global, systemic problems with a million moving pieces to sort out. You're vastly oversimplifying things."

Am I? Am I really?

Or has society methodically broken the smartest, best part of us?

And so we carry on walking the aisles of the grocery store and throwing cases of plastic bottled water into the shopping cart instead of drinking the perfectly good tap water at home from a glass, and the amount of plastic in the sea keeps on growing and killing everything because we've grown "too complex" (aka stupid and lazy) on an *individual level* to simply do the right thing.

Sometimes a child's perspective is the most logical. Insane, nonsensical things like racial prejudice and subscribing to an economic caste system don't exist in children... until adults shove those things down their innocent little throats. Little kids notice if someone is a different color than them, but they are more likely to be fascinated by that difference than afraid of it. A small child might see that someone has on a different style of sneakers than them, but they won't care which pair costs more because no one has told them they need to assign a value to shoes yet. So, what exactly is the point in a grown-ass adult believing someone is inferior to them because of the shade of their skin? By what bizarre metric do we assign social status to fucking *footwear*? It makes precisely zero sense, yet society conditions these things into us, beats them into us…but to a child they are insignificant. Why shouldn't I look to my unpolluted six-year-old self for simple answers to big problems? Once again, the kid knows.

Of course, my six-year-old self would rather eat a five-pound bag of candy instead of a single piece of broccoli. He wants to sit around reading *The Hobbit* instead of doing his math homework. So if I want to look to him for a healthy perspective, I have to keep my questions simple. Matter-of-fact issues of right and wrong. Once I have my answers, the adults can work out all the confusing details and start fixing the mess we have landed in.

Because, by the way, that's *our fucking job*—what are we waiting for?

Maybe we ought to shut up and let the kid speak.

Chapter Four

HEAVEN KNOWS I'M MISERABLE NOW

I n the notes section of my phone, there is a long jumble of half-accomplished to-do lists, song and story ideas ("What would happen if I suddenly started growing again at age fifty-one?"), books and movies people have recommended, quotes from folks a lot smarter than me, fragments of overheard conversations ("So everybody was happy, and then..."—what a great opening sentence for a novel!), English words I've stashed away for future lyrics (*apotheosis, truculent, liminal*), and several of the wonderful and insanely *specific* terms the Germans specialize in, such as *drachenfutter* (noun, very rare, meaning "dragon food; a gift given to placate someone, especially a spouse, who is angry at the giver") and *Rindfleischetikettierungssüberwaacgungsaufgrabenübertragungsgesetz* (noun, now defunct, meaning a law for the delegation monitoring beef labeling). Among this digital farrago sits a note dated May 21, 2012. It reads:

"I am offended by humanity."

There is no explanation for the note, no supporting example given from the endless list of annoying things people constantly do in public that make me ask myself, *Why? Why do people have to act that way?* Yakking away on a cell phone in the bookstore/library/quiet car on Amtrak (shut up, you *savage*—no one needs to hear the details of your hair salon appointment or end-of-quarter business meeting). Abandoning shopping carts in the middle of the grocery store parking lot (the cart corral is ten feet away, you lazy fuck). Being rude to waitstaff in a restaurant (may you burn in hell forever, and also a shout-out to all the servers and bartenders out there). Screaming things like, "I AM A DIAMOND-CLASS ELITE MEMBER, YOU STUPID FUCKING BITCH!" at the poor lady behind the departure gate counter when your flight to Los Angeles gets delayed until eight o'clock the next morning (dude, you should know that your face looks very, very punchable). Let's not even get into big-picture, high-consequence stuff that affects society as a whole: corporate malfeasance, institutionalized racism, morally bankrupt government officials, et cetera, et cetera. No, that note is not specific at all, just one brief and highly misanthropic sentence that I can very easily justify with countless examples, because, well, let's face it—*people suck.* There's just one problem.

No matter how much I may feel like a space alien (and I often do), like it or not...I am a people.

And yes, I most definitely *suck* at times. We all do.

But no one likes to feel sucky, so we play little games to convince ourselves that we are not just like all those other crappy human beings. In fact, mentally separating myself from the rest of humanity used to be one of my favorite pastimes, one I regrettably still indulge in during my weaker moments. It makes me feel so much better about myself, smug and elevated above the parade of clueless, self-obsessed clowns bumbling loudly across my path. All I have to do is look around to see countless examples of shitty behavior that I would *never* engage in, and my opinion of myself instantly rises a few notches.

Except I *have* been that clueless, self-obsessed clown many, many times. Although I've managed to stuff Bozo back into his crowded little car for the most part (I hope), I know the inner clown is still there, pounding shitty beer and yanking away with greasepaint-smeared gloves on the childproof door lock. And without doubt, if I let him out to go on one last wild bender, I will quickly cut myself off from the rest of the population behind a wall of booze and hatred again, and before you know it, I'll be making ridiculous, self-pitying excuses for my own clownish behavior. This would be a fine return to alcoholic form—I often employed that imaginary separation from my fellow man to justify my drinking itself as well as the attendant highly offensive behavior. Because I am an artist and a storyteller, it was always an oh-so-cinematic interior exercise. One of my favorite fantasies when I was feeling like shit the morning after a good drunk looked like this:

I am sitting alone in a dim and dusty room at a small, rickety three-legged table, out-of-tune old-timey piano music tinkling softly in the background. On the table is a half-full bottle of whiskey (no label) and a dirty glass. Every now and then, I pour myself a stout shot, toss it back with a grimace, then rub my weather-beaten and dust-covered hands into my throbbing temples, a grim and stoic look embossed on my face as I debate pulling out my six-shooter and just ending it all right there. (In real life, it was more like eighteen shitty beers and five shots of Jägermeister mixed with an energy drink in some crowded basement heavy metal pub in Amsterdam, but since I'm obviously a goddamned cowboy in some lawless 1800s Texas border town in this version of myself, and since they didn't have cans of cheap Euro-lager and Jäger bombs in Old West gun-slingin' saloons, generic whiskey it is—just hand over the bottle, partner.)

Eventually, the batwing doors of the saloon swing open, and a beautiful woman with enormous tits squeezed into one of those elaborate hoop dresses swishes through, taking my hand as she kneels at my side. She tells me that a famous European doctor has just arrived in town and begs me with teary eyes to go see him because she just *can't bear* to watch me suffer anymore.

I cough out a weak protest: "No, darlin', no…it's… hopeless."

But she convinces me to see the doctor. (After all, the town needs me—hell, *she* needs me to protect the farm from the marauding bandits who oh-so-conveniently killed her husband just last week.)

I stumble out of the saloon and into the blazing sun, leaning heavily on her wonderful-smelling shoulder as I shuffle across the dusty street, almost collapsing under the weight of some immense and generic pain. We walk into a small and cluttered doctor's office (he just got into town twenty minutes ago—how in the hell did he get set up so soon? Where did that skeleton and all those weird vials come from?), where the doc (who just happens to be the world's top neurologist specializing in extremely rare brain disorders) gives me a brief physical exam, muttering to himself as he gently pokes and prods my extremities with archaic wooden-handled medical instruments. After five minutes or so, he sets down the instruments, looks at me through his monocle, and says in a thick German accent that sounds remarkably like Werner Herzog's (okay, okay—so the doctor *is* Werner Herzog):

"Herr Blythe, I regret to inform you that you are one of zee very few people in zee entire vorld who hast ever been diagnosed mit Strappenheimer's syndrome. *Mein freund*, I know it is excruciating to live like zis, but don't vorry—vee are going to get you some help, *ja?* Frankly, I don't know how you've survived zis long—most never make it to zheir twenty-first birthday, yet here you are. *Gott im Himmel*, such strength you possess! It's a miracle you are alive at all. No vonder you drink so much! *Natürlich!*"

Then my family, friends, bandmates, and (of course) all my exes gather around me and apologize profusely for the atrocious way they badgered me about my drinking. I just grit my teeth and say, "No, no...it's okay. You couldn't have known." Then I painfully climb aboard a fancy stagecoach and ride off into the sunset, bound for the coast where the doctor and I will catch an ocean liner to Europe and make our way to his exclusive clinic high in the Austrian Alps, where my ridiculously expensive treatment will begin. *Fade to black.*

What a horrendous load of self-pitying horseshit. But it was a lot more pleasant to imagine that than to face up to reality: dude, last night you peed in the corner at the party, then told everyone you loved them, then horribly insulted the host's girlfriend for no good reason. *What in the flying fuck is wrong with you?* I asked myself with increasing regularity as the drinking years swished boozily by.

I was a drunk—that's what was wrong with me, *duh*. I didn't mean to become one, and my alcoholism doesn't in any way excuse any of my shitty behavior, but it explains it (well, at least a very large portion of it). I didn't like the way the world behaved, so to blot it from my consciousness, I drank so much that I had no control over the only thing any individual has control over: myself.

Once I got some help and got sober, I started to regain control over myself, my thoughts and emotions. And during that process, I was told to worry about just one person—*myself*. I needed to fix my own bullshit and let the rest of the world take care of itself. And as the years went by, I was taught to view people who were acting in idiotic, unsavory ways with some sympathy if possible—I didn't know what that person was going through that day that might have made them act like such a douchebag (maybe they just got fired because their boss didn't like their political opinions or perhaps their wife just left them that morning for the dude with the mullet at the gym). I just had to keep my side of the street clean, control myself, and try not to be so goddamned judgmental. After all, hadn't I publicly made an ass of myself on many occasions? So, I try to do this when I can, I really do.

But it's getting harder and harder these days, because let's face it—if the last few years have proven anything, it's that standards of public behavior, consideration for others, and plain old common decency have sunk pretty low. An aggressive cult of toxic narcissistic individualism has grown way out of control, made increasingly obvious by the large numbers of people willing to openly and vociferously express their opinions on subjects they have zero real knowledge or experience of. It's fucking incredible the numbers of *really angry* instant scientists, doctors, foreign policy experts, and economists that have suddenly appeared over the last few years. Just scroll through a few random social media comment sections and you will be subjected to a blaze of invective and ignorance that baffles the rational mind. Who *are* these people, and who told them they were qualified to comment with such authority on things they clearly know nothing about? And why are they so goddamned angry?

The medical experts burn me up the most. Let's imagine what would happen if I were to walk into a hospital operating room during an open-heart surgery, wearing no scrubs or mask, stroll over to the team of doctors and nurses, then begin arguing with them about the specifics of a double bypass while poking away at the patient's bleeding ticker with my grubby paws: "No, no, no, dipshit. You're fucking with the wrong arteries. Plus, you don't even have to graft new veins in, just flush the old ones out with WD-40."

"Who in the flying fuck are you? How did you get in here? Are you a doctor? And where did you hear that crazy idea?"

"I just walked in. Y'all left the door wide open. I sing for a heavy metal band that's sold millions of records, so that should tell you something, Doc—*lots* of people listen to me. I mean, how many records have *you* sold? Yeah, that's what I thought. And I heard about the WD-40 on a podcast last week—the supermodel chick who hosts it gets a million downloads per episode. Um, how hot are you, Doc, and how many downloads do *you* get a week? Yeah, once again, that's what I thought. Now why don't ya put that scalpel down for a second while I run to the Home Depot real quick and grab a can of lube to blast those veins out?"

Sounds completely crazy, right? But it's really no crazier than some of the online arguments actual doctor and scientist friends of mine have had with laypeople over everything from the cause of breast cancer to the polio vaccine—endless buffoons emailing them or charging into a comment section, stomping around in their gigantic virtual clown shoes and shouting idiotic nonsense. Some people will shrug and say, "Well, that's the internet for ya!" but this bizarrely hubristic online behavior has spilled over into the real world, bringing real-world ramifications and consequences with it. For instance, as I write this, the polio virus has been detected in the wastewater of New York City. *Polio?* My grandfather (who died before I was born) had polio. He spent most of his childhood in a body cast and lived the rest of his life walking with a limp and a hump in his back because of it. I've never met anyone with polio, because applied science almost completely eradicated it here in America, but apparently some people think that their children are better off without a proven vaccine that has kept the rest of us safe for over a half century now. To those parents whose unlucky and unvaccinated children will be paralyzed by *fucking polio* because *"no one* is going to tell *me* what's right for *my* child"— congratulations! You've ensured that your kid will grow up to hate you.

How in the world has this repulsive and embarrassing I-know-more-about-science-and-stuff-than-highly-educated-

and-trained-medical-professionals-even-though-I'm-a-real-estate-agent mentality become commonplace enough to bring back something as horrifying as polio? Is it because utterly bonkers conspiracy theories (aka the security blankets of the witless) spread much faster now via the internet than they did the old-school way (that is, by disheveled crazy-looking people shouting on street corners while parading around wearing sandwich board signs with messages like "Fluoride in our water is a communist plot to destroy America!")? Are people simply flat-out *dumber* now than they used to be? Are a sizable group of folks just constantly having a bad day and blowing off a little steam by insulting a highly specialized expert or two? I know I'm not supposed to judge since I can't know a person's motivations for acting like a jackass, but I simply can't reconcile the idea of someone who wakes up with a bad case of the squirts believing their opinion on polio vaccines is just as valid as those of an immunology PhD.

Personally, I blame two things: (1) decades of shitty parents incessantly telling their children they are the most special thing in the world and hanging on their every word as if the little brats are constantly on the edge of delivering a Churchillian triumph of oration. These kids grow up to be adults, in this case, adults crammed full of unrealistic ideas about their abilities, adults who get their panties in a twist the second it is suggested they might want to shut up and listen to someone smarter than them when they don't know what in the hell they are talking about. And (2) the increasing inability of human beings of all ages to accept uncertainty in their lives, an intolerance increased in no small part by the ubiquitous tiny computers that can seemingly answer any question instantly with just a few swift taps on the screen (aka the cell phone, or as I like to call it, "the pocket Jesus"). No one likes feeling intellectually inferior to someone else, and no one likes to feel clueless in the face of an onrushing future full of a never-ending stream of potentially catastrophic eventualities, but guess what? That's life. Maybe Mom has been telling you that you're some sort of mental prodigy since the afternoon you finally figured out how to tie your own shoelaces, but remember, there's *always* someone much, much smarter than you. And yes, the internet is great, but no matter how many times you google "When will the next earthquake hit Los Angeles?" *no one*, not even the best seismologist in all human history, can predict exactly when The Strip will start vibrating like a sex toy from the Hustler store on Sunset Boulevard. Deal with it.

But it doesn't really matter who or what I blame for this weird modern state of affairs, because pointing fingers doesn't change anything other than my blood pressure. I need to remember that, even in the face of the roiling mass of screeching imbeciles who insist that their uneducated opinions on everything from pandemics to foreign policy matter more than empirical facts put forth by world-renowned experts who have devoted their entire lives to studying such things. I am in full possession of the knowledge that I am a man of average intelligence; in fact, a lot of the time I feel like a complete moron because I *make it a point* to hang out with people a lot smarter than me whenever I can on the off chance that some of their smarts will rub off on me (and it works sometimes, maybe a little, *I hope?*). I'm definitely smart enough to know I'm not that smart, but that's about it. Somehow I missed the boat full of insta-genius pills a lot of folks seem to have gobbled up lately—maybe I was too busy surfing—and so remain a simple heavy metal singer who knows he's clueless about the highly specific intricacies of ductal carcinoma, asymmetric conflict in faraway lands, and the seemingly limitlessly climbing-into-the-stratosphere levels of the United States debt ceiling. (This last one is particularly baffling to me because I don't spend money I don't have—does our national economy work like a college student with too many maxed-out Visa cards? Just endlessly borrowing from one credit company to pay off another. Can someone please explain this to me?)

So as not to lose my mind, I have to shift my embattled attention to matters I have some agency in. These, of course, are few because I have precisely zero control over other people—nor should I because I would make a *horrible* dictator. I suppose I could create some sort of cult and install myself as the ridiculous divine figurehead (in fact, on more than one occasion I've had fans say, "Dude! You are a god!" I always tell them they need to pick a better deity because I am a moron), but I would be way too annoyed by anyone foolish enough to follow me to put in the hang time required to bilk them of their cash.

So, without becoming a morally bankrupt apathetic asshole, I have to turn my focus to the only thing I have control over—myself. As Epictetus, an ancient Greek Stoic philosopher, said, "The chief task in life is simply this: to identify and separate matters so that I can say clearly to myself which are externals not under my control, and which have to do with the choices I actually control." To my knowledge, *everything* but my own choices are externals beyond my control, so I better brush all that outside stuff aside and get busy controlling myself and making the best choices I can.

Today, I believe the best choice I can make is to focus on fixing my own bullshit—God knows, I have enough of it.

Chapter Five
I'LL FLY AWAY

Tuesday, August 3, 2021

4:30 p.m.

Franklin, Va.

I am sitting in an old wooden chair beside my grandmother, waiting for her to die.

I have been here every day for the last ten days, except one, when my brother Mark drove up from North Carolina to sit with her and say goodbye.

Today is the first day Grandma has not spoken in my presence. She's mostly been asleep, thank God, due to an increase in morphine. She just now had a coughing fit, so I stopped writing this and held her hand until she calmed down. After the coughing fit passed, she did not say a word, merely made painful-sounding noises of exhaustion—short and high-pitched gasps, like a small bird winded after a long flight. Her breathing is slow and ragged, fighting through the rattle deep within her chest that tells me she is not long for this world. Her hurting so has repeatedly shattered my heart over the last few days, and I feel so helpless in the face of it.

After I calmed her down, I sat watching her breathing. It is so shallow. Her breaths are coming so slowly now that a few times I thought she had died—it is an awful thing to sit here and write this, but that would make me very happy right now. Grandma is one hundred and a half years old, and she does not want to be here anymore. She is suffering, and there is nothing I can do but sit and hold her hand and type this with the other after another coughing fit. I can only be present. I can only let her know I am here. I can only look at her and whisper:

"It's okay, Grandma. You can let go."

My grandma has told me since I was a child that life can be hard; she was, after all, raised during the Great Depression. But watching her now, she is showing me that dying can be hard, too—she is ready to go, but her heart simply will not stop beating. Her hands and feet have grown mottled from where her body is directing blood away from her extremities, carrying it to her vital organs in a last stand against the Reaper.

Grandma was built too well. She is just too tough to die easily.

This is what I come from.

Some grandmas are soft, fluffy, malleable creatures, all sweetness and sugar cookies and on-demand trips to the toy store. Many don't start out this way, but the second their adult children pump out a few kids of their own, their primary function immediately shifts from responsible parental-type figure to spoiler-rotten-in-chief. Suddenly, they are perfectly willing to feed four-year-olds ice cream for breakfast before taking them into town to blow some retirement money on whatever those grubby little grandchildren's paws snatch up in the store aisles. (I'm not a grandma, so I can't say for sure what causes this startling shift, but in my opinion, it's mostly revenge on their own kids for all the hell they put them through.) I'm not putting these sweet old ladies down, because this breed of grandma is amazing and cuddly and a ton of fun (especially because you can get away with almost anything around them), so God bless them. What's not to like?

But *my* grandma? Well, she was cut from a different, rougher, cloth.

Grandma was a short woman, and as the decades went by she became even shorter, shrinking with age as old people do. She was at most four and a half feet tall by the time she died, but she cuts a towering figure in my mind. She may have been small in stature, but Grandma was no weakling or pushover. I remember her in an almost geographic way, an immutable feature of the countryside of my youth, but she was not like the cane reeds growing by the creek bed I played in as a child, gentle and bending in the breeze that whispered over the tea-colored water. No, she was like an old oak tree, standing alone in the middle of a fallow peanut field, weathering blizzards and hurricanes and tornadoes without so much as leaning an inch to one side, instead soaking in the blazing sun of the hot Southern summer days for so many seasons that the wood almost petrified. She was solid, sturdy, tough as nails, unyielding, and I always felt safe around her. You could have built a house from my grandma and it would have *never* fallen; in fact, as the years went on, I began to wonder if perhaps she was actually *immortal*. "She's never gonna die," I joked many times, "she's just going to keep getting shorter and shorter until she disappears and we can't see her anymore, only hear her hollering at us to come in for supper."

Grandma was born in the upstairs bedroom of a farmhouse in Isle of Wight County, Virginia, in the early winter of 1921, the youngest of four siblings. For the first twenty-three years of her life, she lived in that same house, one owned and inhabited by members of my family to this day. At age twenty-three, she married my grandfather and made the lengthy journey fourteen miles down the road to his house in the next county over, Southampton, where she would spend the next seventy-two years. Finally, at age ninety-five, when her eyesight got so bad she could no longer be trusted to cook for herself without burning down her tiny house, she agreed to move into The Village, a wonderful assisted-living facility exactly five miles down the road—she didn't want to live out her final years any farther away than necessary from what she had always known. For over a hundred years, the entire span of her long life, Grandma lived within a fourteen-and-a-half-mile radius, and that is where she chose to die.

And Grandma was marked for death from the second the good Dr. Bradshaw and a country midwife brought her into this world in that farmhouse bedroom. She was born with spinal meningitis, almost totally blind and extremely sickly. Dr. Bradshaw was so convinced that she would not survive that by sundown of her first day on earth, her parents had already chosen and laid out the tiny clothes she would be buried in. "But I survived somehow or the other," she told me when I interviewed her about her life over the course of two days during her ninety-second year, "I don't know how."

"Because you're a tough lady!" I said.

"I must be," she replied with that impish grin I loved so much. And make no mistake about it: she was a very tough lady.

The world my grandmother was born into and grew up in is one that no longer exists, at least not in most places. The family house did not have electricity until a year after she graduated high school, not because of economics but rather because electrical lines had not yet reached that area of rural Virginia. She lived in a house without running water until she got married, and even then, for the first year, there was no indoor bathroom, only an outhouse for a toilet and an old zinc tub in the backyard for bathing. Toilet paper did not come in twenty-four-roll economy-size plastic-wrapped packs from a grocery store; it was a page ripped from the Sears and Roebuck catalog. Hot water for bathing did not appear like magic from a faucet with the twist of a chrome-plated knob; it was pumped by hand from a well, then heated over a wood fire. Even the soap they scrubbed themselves clean with was not store-bought but made by her mother and sisters from lye and rendered hog fat. Their house was heated by a wood-burning stove, and food was cooked that way, too. Any sort of comfort was *worked for*.

One thing I heard Grandma say again and again whenever I would complain about something was, "You think you have it tough, huh? Well, brother, you don't know what hard times are." As a child, I used to blow this off as one-upmanship, but as I grew older and learned about history, I knew she was right. Grandma grew up during the Great Depression. She was just eight years old when it started in 1929, and by the end of that terrible decade millions of Americans would be unemployed, homeless, and suffering from malnutrition. But luckily for Grandma, she lived on a farm in the green and fertile lowlands of Virginia. Her family grew their own vegetables, kept chickens for eggs and cows for milk, and raised and slaughtered their own hogs for meat. They smoked their own hams, canned their own vegetables, and lived in relative comfort out in the country. My ancestors were spared the awful starvation that so many in cities and the drought-stricken Dust Bowl of the Great Plains experienced.

But just because Grandma and her family didn't starve to death during the Depression didn't mean they had it easy. Food did not arrive on the table after a quick trip to the grocery store; it was raised or grown, and that required a lot of sweat. Farming is very hard work, and it was even harder back then. My great-grandfather plowed his fields walking behind a mule, not sitting atop a gas-powered tractor. By the end of the Depression, all Grandma's immediate family had moved in together, and she shared a bed with her two older sisters—nine people crammed into that small house in the fields, and all of them labored to keep the farm running. Her older brother and sisters toiled in the fields, but Grandma couldn't see well in the bright sun, so she stayed inside and did housework. She kept their home clean, did laundry and other domestic tasks of that nature. Everyone pitched in, everyone did their bit, and the family survived.

Money was scarce—*very* scarce. "During the Depression, you didn't go out and buy anything unless you had to," she told me. For Grandma, this did not include situations like "This old dress is threadbare and full of holes. Time to break open the piggy bank and go buy a new one." There was no budget for store-bought garments, so her sisters sewed their clothes, and when the clothes got dirty, they washed them by hand. One luxury item the family eventually splurged on was a hand-cranked wringer washing machine. These were also known as "manglers" because of their long and gruesome history of doing precisely that: mangling or even killing a careless washerwoman or curious child whose fingers, arm, or hair got caught up in the machine. "Oh, it was wonderful when we got that wringer washer, *just wonderful!*" Grandma enthused when I asked her about doing laundry as a child. *Wonderful?* I thought, remembering stomach-turning pictures I had seen online of old-school washing machine injuries. *Something called a mangler was your idea of "wonderful" as a child?*

The Great Depression ended in America in 1939, and my grandmother married my grandfather five years later. By then, the United States had been involved in World War II for three years. In 1944, the economic situation was much better than during the Depression, but that didn't mean it was time for everyone to go on a shopping spree. Wartime rationing was in full effect, and cash or no cash, spending was limited to the number of stamps in your government-issued ration book. In January 1942, just weeks after the attack on Pearl Harbor, the government began rationing products, the very first of which was automobile tires (additionally, a national speed limit of 35 mph went into effect, and all forms of automobile racing and sightseeing driving were banned to conserve fuel and rubber for tires). Rationing of tires was swiftly followed by rationing of personal automobiles, gasoline, fuel oil, coal, firewood, bicycles, sugar, flour, jams, jellies, juices, coffee, beef, pork, veal, lamb, canned fruits and vegetables, butter, margarine, lard, cooking oil, canned fish, cheese, canned milk, paper, nylon hosiery, silk, and shoes. Even if you did have the ration stamps to buy what you needed, many times these items were in very low supply. "I remember one time your Aunt Bertie heard about a grocery store that had just gotten in a shipment of five-pound bags of sugar," Grandma recalled, "so we drove into town and got in line with everyone else to wait a few hours." I think about this whenever I see some whiny jerk being impatient in a coffee shop because their fancy latte doesn't instantly appear.

There was a black market, of course, but the penalties for buying and selling goods on it were severe. And most people seemed to abide by the rationing system simply because it was the right thing to do, trying their best to help one another out—there was a sense of duty, a willingness to engage in collective sacrifice for the greater good. "Your Aunt Annie had three little boys at that time, and little boys do need shoes," Grandma told me, remembering her older sister. "I was an adult and didn't need that many shoes, so I would let her use my ration book." Grandma did not speak of this in a bragging way, like some sort of footwear martyr, but as a simple matter of fact: if someone needed something more than you did, you gave it to them. If someone needed help and you could provide it, you did. This pragmatic, helpful mentality was present from her very first memory, which was of visiting her father in the hospital. "He was laid up sick, I can't remember with what," she said. "I was sick too and unable to walk, so I remember my older brother carrying me up the stairs of the hospital to visit him. This was in the fall, during harvest time, so all the area farmers got together and took in the crop for my daddy." From the very beginning of her memory, there was hardship— but there was also a willingness to help others during those hard times.

For my grandmother, so many things we take for granted today simply didn't exist at her birth and well on into her adulthood. Things like thermostats, leftover Chinese takeout, vacations, $100 tennis shoes, cell phones, kitchen accent LED track lighting, air conditioning, indoor toilets, microwavable snacks, hot showers, instant messaging friends in Finland, fancy hair care products, taxi cabs and Ubers, movies on demand, shopping mall pedicures, home espresso machines, and whatever other luxury items strike our engorged fancies and get delivered the very next day (if not sooner) to our front door. All this extravagant abundance would have seemed absurd to her as a young woman, yet somehow she managed to survive without all these things and still lived a very good life. "I need to get away from it all!" is the angst-riddled refrain of the sensory-overloaded and world-weary modern sufferer. We need to get away from what? Our ridiculously soft and privileged lives?

I think perhaps so.

Most younger people today could not even imagine living the way of life I grew up hearing about from my grandma, and many of us middle-aged and older people are so habituated to getting whatever we want whenever we want it that we have forgotten things weren't always this way. I feel lucky my grandmother told so many tales of an older way of life, and some of them I've even lived out a tiny bit myself. I remember many times sitting in the backyard next to Grandma, shelling butter beans or shucking corn I had picked from the garden (oh, how I *hated* picking corn—so itchy!), listening to her laugh and tell stories of the old days. I didn't know it, but I was learning with my hands and ears at the same time.

And for a good period of my youth, I, too, lived in a house heated by a wood stove, just like Grandma. I learned to swing a maul and split logs, and I have neatly stacked many a cord of firewood in the spring to lay and season for the dark winter's chill. When I would groan and complain about having to do this while other kids were out goofing off and riding their bicycles, my father would say, "Do you like having heat in the winter? Well, you better stack that wood then," before turning back to blindly sling another massive piece of oak from the pickup bed he stood in, causing me and my brothers to scatter as log after log flew at our heads.

Wood-stacking day in the Blythe household resembled a game of high-consequence dodgeball played with lethal objects, and I don't know how my brothers and I never suffered a concussion or had our teeth knocked out. Pops wasn't *trying* to hurt us; he was just getting the job done and didn't have time to waste on silly things like worrying about caving in his sons' skulls with a chunk of hickory. On the bright side, stacking wood taught us to remain alert and be nimble, fast moving, and responsible for our own well-being. This is why I always crack up when I see some helicopter parent's histrionics over the skinned knee of their wailing eight-year-old who took a digger in the drugstore—I honestly have to restrain myself from laughing out loud. *Kid, obviously you have never had a near-death-by-firewood experience, I think. You had better start ignoring Mommy—she ain't doing you any favors. Learn to rub some dirt on it and walk it off, because life is only gonna get harder.*

My dad used to say, "You can tell a lot about a man by the way he stacks his woodpile." Pops never explained what that meant to me, but it makes total sense now. There is a method and order to properly stacking firewood, and a right and a wrong place to locate your woodpile, and neatness is key—a sloppy, haphazard jumble of uncovered logs rotting away on the dirt in the shade won't season for burning, and when winter comes, you'll wish you had put in the time and done things the right way. A well-stacked woodpile says, "I'm competent. I'm handy. I know what I'm doing, and I am well prepared for the bitter days ahead." My father was trying to teach me something much larger than merely how to keep the house warm, but like all young boys I was hardheaded, obstinate, and didn't want to listen most of the time. Our physical woodpile was well-ordered (the old man wouldn't have allowed anything else), but because the greater metaphor was lost on me for many years, many hard lessons about delayed gratification waited in my future. Today I'm trying to learn to stay focused, take my time, and stack my woodpiles the right way—my life seems to run much smoother when I do.

I am lucky to have lived with my grandmother as a child. I learned just as much from her as I did my parents, and only now do I grasp the depth of the continual sacrifices she made for her family, even as she began her golden years. When my parents separated at the end of my third-grade year, my dad, two younger brothers, and I all went to live with my grandmother for a couple of years. When we moved into Grandma's small house, there was a bit of an adjustment period for her, to put it lightly. This was in no small part because her previous child-rearing experience was limited solely to my father, who (from what I can tell) was one of those most annoying of specimens—a perfect child. My brothers and I, to put it mildly, were not. At an age when she should have been relaxing and preparing to retire from her secretary job at a local plant farm, suddenly and unexpectedly there were three extremely rambunctious boys ripping through her previously quiet household. This was not exactly easy on Grandma, a rather reserved, no-nonsense woman known to have a bit of a temper from time to time.

In short, we drove her nuts.

When the tornado of Blythe boys invaded her domicile, Grandma was fifty-nine years old. She had been living entirely by herself since her husband had died twelve years previously. Although she loved her three grandsons dearly, Grandma was accustomed to living peacefully alone with her AM radio, antique furniture she'd refinished, neat book shelves, and well-ordered kitchen. She was settled nicely into her solitary way of life out in the fields of Southampton County, but we three heathens arrived and slowly but methodically disassembled whatever serenity she had built for herself. Grandma did not take our wild ways lying down— whenever we misbehaved in public (which was always), she would threaten to spank us with the dreaded fold-up paddle, a portable and deadly disciplinary device she kept in her purse at all times. No one ever actually *saw* the fold-up paddle, so its existence is suspect, but much like the doctrine of mutual assured destruction, it kept us in line most of the time.

Around the house, when we would do things that displeased her, she would start by calmly but sternly telling us to quiet down and stop raising so much hell (or raising Cain, as she would put it). Obviously, we would ignore her and carry on destroying her new set of venetian blinds or whatever else of value happened to catch our eye. "Boys!" she would holler, kicking up the volume a notch or two, "Y'all stop that right this instant!" Nope. Eventually, she would boil over to the point where her voice would erupt in a high-pitched whoop, hollering out an elongated "WELL, GWOOOOON!" This sounded kind of like a cross between an air raid siren and an infuriated Minnesota lake loon. (For those of you who don't speak Southeastern Virginian, that translates as "Well, go on!" which means "y'all had better knock it off and get out of my sight immediately or I will kill you little monsters dead with this cast iron frying pan.") If that didn't work and we willfully continued making mayhem, or if we had committed some particularly egregious act of savagery that had ground her last nerve down to its final frayed edge, she would truly lose her cool and let fly with the only curse word I ever heard her utter: *shit*. She wouldn't just *say* "shit," though; it was part of a command: "WELL, GO DO SHIT!" Once we had been told to go do shit, we knew we had truly crossed the line—the party was over, and it was time to scram before she blew a gasket.

To this day, whenever my brothers and I are together, in Grandma's honor, we command each other to go do shit… whatever that means.

On the day we finally drove Grandma completely over the edge, she didn't curse or even yell. We were in the backseat of her car, a silver four-door Chevy Nova that I wish I had today. We were returning home to the country after a trip to the grocery store in the nearby paper mill town of Franklin. I'm sure we had been ill behaved in the grocery store, as was our standard operating procedure, but at least there we could GWOOOOON! for a little bit and stay out of her hair while she did her shopping. But, sadly, in the car Grandma had no escape, and on that fateful afternoon, we broke her.

I don't remember exactly what set her off—it could have been one of a million different exceedingly annoying things that we loved to pass the time doing—name-calling, insulting each other, arguing viciously over something incredibly insignificant, wrestling, picking on each other, pinching each other, stabbing each other with pencils, punching each other, or maybe even our ultimate favorite car-ride activity of all time: the Junior Wally Spitball Fight. We'd put little bits of the paper wrapper of pilfered fast-food drinking straws into our mouths, then shoot them at each other as well as every available surface in the car that a slimy piece of paper would stick to—windows, dashboard, steering wheel, Grandma's hair, and so forth. (The reason we called this foul game the "Junior Wally Spitball Fight" instead of just "a spitball fight" is lost to antiquity.) Whatever it was that we were doing, I can guarantee we weren't doing it quietly, and finally...Grandma snapped.

Taking a hard left onto the narrow blacktop country road we lived on, Grandma didn't make a sound—but the car did. The Chevy's straight-six engine suddenly roared to life as she punched it, stomping the accelerator to the floorboard with her sensible shoes. The Nova lurched forward like a racehorse kicked in the ass, and we began to rocket down the road. As the world outside the window blurred by, I looked up front and saw Grandma, her tiny body hunched forward, bony hands bloodless and white in an iron death grip on the steering wheel. I couldn't see her face, and she wasn't saying a word, but when I remember that day, I picture a tiny black storm cloud of rage roiling above her head, miniature lightning bolts erupting all around her tight salt-and-pepper curls. That stretch of road was pretty straight—country boys in souped-up muscle cars liked to race the quarter mile on it on weekend nights, but Grandma (who normally drove like, well, a grandma) would have left them all in the dust that day. She left the starting line at an impressive clip, zipped past our neighbor Allie Mae's house at the end of the road with her annoying peacocks, aggressively picked up the pace as we cleared the long stretch of peanut fields immediately before she really gunned it through the slight downhill at our cousins Rosa and Carey's house and then roared past the pond where we went catfishing. We were already almost home, having closed the gap from the turnoff to our house in record time, and Grandma was still steadily picking up speed, with no signs of letting up anytime soon.

By the time we reached Uncle Larry's house, which was right next door to Grandma's, we were *flying*. Grandma was so mad, so singularly focused on gunning that car forward, that I figured she was going to just keep on driving until she had a stroke or we ran out of road or we ran out of gas, whichever one came first—but she didn't.

Instead, right as we reached her house, she wrenched the wheel hard to the left, slinging the Nova into her half-circle gravel driveway like a Hollywood stunt driver at the end of a big-budget car chase. Regrettably, unlike a highly trained and precisely calculating Hollywood stunt driver (who would have performed a spectacular fishtail maneuver, drifting the car sideways completely around the driveway before sliding to a perfect predetermined stop mere inches from the side-walk leading to the front porch), Grandma was in control of neither (1) her emotions, nor (2) where the car was going. As we hit the driveway at a velocity normally reserved for NAS-CAR races, not grocery store trips, the Chevy's wheels failed to find purchase on the loose gravel. Immediately, the car slid off the driveway and onto the crabgrass-covered side yard. For fifteen or twenty deliciously terrifying high-speed feet, we skidded sideways across the yard, gouging four long tire-shaped trenches in the sandy Virginian soil the whole way, before coming to an abrupt stop by crashing into a young loblolly pine.

Hol-y shit!

We were home.

Inside the car was so quiet you could have heard a mosquito fart.

Grandma turned to us and said, "Well, I reckon you'll be quiet now!" Then she snatched up her brown leather old lady purse and lurched out of the car, slamming the door behind her as she stomped off on her short legs across the yard and into the house, leaving us in the car still crunched against the tree.

We let out the breaths we had been holding, looked at each other, and like the little savages we were, immediately burst into uncontrollable laughter.

I'm still laughing about it today.

We did our best to drive that poor old woman crazy, but she always took care of us, no matter how much we got on her nerves. Grandma certainly had a stern side, but we had a lot of good times together, too; she loved to laugh, and I remember sitting up in bed with her giggling so hard that our sides hurt and neither of us could hardly breathe. She had a quick wit and found humor in a lot of things. But in many ways she was a hard woman, because she had grown up in hard times, and she certainly did not spoil her grandchildren. Instead, she tried to help prepare us for life, and for that I will be eternally grateful—the things I learned from her are gifts that have served me far better than any stupid plastic toy I tried to weasel out of her at Christmas (which, as far as I remember, never worked anyway—Grandma's

Christmas gifts were always socks and sweaters and things of that unglamorous nature).

My grandmother was not a fan of bellyaching and whining, to put it lightly. "Some people would complain if you hung them with new rope," she once said. Being a Southern woman, she had a tendency to say all sorts of funny things, most of which didn't actually make any sense. Anytime someone uttered the phrase "curiosity killed the cat," she was quick with the rejoinder "but satisfaction brought him back." *By what means?* I always wondered. *The cat is* dead—*is curiosity some sadistic feline necromancer, cruelly slaying and resurrecting the inquisitive?* Another thing I never figured out was her weather-conditional calendar. If I were to ask her, "What day of the week is it, Grandma? Tuesday, right?" without fail she would reply "All day long…unless it rains." To this day, I have absolutely zero idea of what that means, but if you ask me whether it's Friday, you'll *never* get a "Yes, it is! TGIF!" out of me.

Nope. It's gonna be Friday, all day long…unless it rains.

As we both grew older, I learned to appreciate my grandmother more and more. She had lived so long and was so precious to my heart that for a while I refused to imagine life without her—she had just always been there, and it simply didn't seem feasible that this woman would ever die. Ignoring her own mortality was not her way, though. One year on her birthday, I said, "Grandma! You're ninety-three years old!"

"Yes, I am," she said with a smile.

"That's amazing! I hope you live to be a hundred!" I said.

"Well, I don't!" was her quick reply in a matter-of-fact voice, no trace of a smile any longer on her face. I grimaced. I knew she meant it, too. *Well, crap, I guess it's not about what I want.* It made sense to me, though—as she moved into her nineties, Grandma could no longer do all the things she loved to do, and this was distressing for her. "I'll tell you, Randy, I can't do like I used to," she told me many times. "This old age thing is for the birds."

Yet even as she approached a century of life and her body began rapidly breaking down, her disdain for laying around and wasting away was resolute. "I reckon I better keep on walking, or one day I won't be able to," she would say when I visited her, then we would go outside and take a walk. Her will to keep on moving was incredible. Ninety-seven years old and she would get behind her walker and start pushing it, and I could see the momentum coming from deep within her heart, driving that tiny ancient body forward, unstoppable, unbreakable...my iron ancestor.

As Grandma grew older, her hearing grew worse and worse. By the end of her life, Grandma was deaf as a stump (as she would say), and you had to yell to make yourself heard. Her eyesight wasn't much better, reverting back to the same state as when she was born. She moved through the world with greatly diminished senses, but for the most part kept a good humor about it. One of my favorite memories of her later years is the last Christmas we spent all together at my father's house; Grandma was ninety-eight then. I was walking out of the house to drive back home and found her in the den, pushing her walker along. I leaned down and gently wrapped my arms around her in a hug, kissing her on the cheek and saying directly into her ear, "I'm going to drive home now, Grandma, but I'll see you soon. I sure do love you!"

"Well, honey, I love you too," she replied, then paused. "Now which one are you again, sugar dumpling?"

I told her, and we both had a good laugh, but... I knew right then we wouldn't have too many more Christmases together.

In her final years, Grandma never slipped into full-blown dementia—she never became convinced she was the Queen of England on a cruise ship bound for Tasmania or anything bizarre like that. She remained cognizant of who and where she was, but her memory rapidly and progressively worsened. Each time I made the hour-and-a-half drive south to visit her, I dug for jewels from her past, stories from times long ago, but these gifts appeared less and less frequently. Questions that used to get quick answers befuddled her, things like "Do you remember what you and Granddaddy did on your first date?" More and more often she would silently consider a query I put to her, and I could see her searching through the halls of her memory for an answer (and those must have been vast halls, built over the course of a hundred years), then she would say, "No... no, I'm sorry. I just can't remember."

I stopped asking her such specific, direct questions because, even though she never complained or acted annoyed with my prying, I did not want to frustrate her. To be unable to connect with your own past through the act of memory must feel like you are losing a connection to the building blocks of your very identity. If we are the sum of our experiences, what do we become when those experiences vanish from our minds? Do we ourselves eventually disappear? So I began taking an indirect route into her past. Instead of asking questions, I relayed commonplace memories from my own childhood, things like my first day of school, or I would mention stories from her childhood that she had already told me. Sometimes my recalling these things triggered a recall of her own, and another previously unheard memory came rushing out of her with surprising clarity.

For example, one day I was telling her a funny story about being scolded by a school bus driver, and she suddenly said, "Oh, my first school bus driver was a red-headed boy named Curtis Hines. He was a high school senior who lived across the road." I asked her how old she was then. "Six years old." Then she proceeded to tell me about Miss Prosise and Miss Duncan, her first- and second-grade teachers. Aside from the fact that I was astounded they let high school students drive their own school buses back then, I was in awe of how sharp Grandma's mind was, even as it began to fail her—I mean, apologies to anyone who ever drove me to school or taught me as a young child, but I cannot remember a single one of my school bus drivers' names, nor do I remember any teachers' names until fourth grade, when the terrifying Miss Simmons came into my life. On that day, Grandma could not remember what she had for lunch two hours earlier, but she could still dig out names from ninety years ago.

As her memory went more and more, she began repeating things, mostly in the form of questions. I paid attention to what she asked, because I felt it gave an insight into her emotional state, perhaps painting an unconscious picture of what was truly important to her. She would ask, "Have you talked to your dad or your brothers lately?" I would answer, and then five minutes later she would ask me the same thing. It never frustrated me, and each time I would answer the question as if it was the first time she had asked it. She was the reigning matriarch, and in repeatedly asking this question about my father and brothers, I believe that she was reassuring herself that the family unit was still intact. She also asked me over and over what time it was (a very common question from elderly people), and once again, I would answer as if it was the first time. *Why is knowing what time it is so important to her?* I wondered. *It's not like she's running late for a job interview.*

I thought deeply on this and came to believe that, in knowing what time it was, she was reaffirming her existence to herself—time was passing in a measurable way, and she was still here. We chart the maps of our existence on earth through various measurements of time, not just the passing minutes and hours, but through the seasons, periods of war, marriage anniversaries, and birthdays of grandchildren (or in my case, through tours—"Wait, when did we first eat at this restaurant? Oh yeah—second leg of the North American Metallica tour"). We mark the calendars of life through our experiences until we die and enter the timeless realm. At the end of Grandma's life, there were no more truly significant occurrences in her day-to-day existence. It didn't really matter what time it was, but she wanted to know, and so I told her. She was shifting into the timeless realm, when it is always only ever *now*, and I wanted Grandma's *now* to be as pleasant as possible. "It's 3:17 p.m., Grandma," I would say, five minutes after telling her it was 3:12 p.m. I wanted her to know that at that particular 3:17 p.m., her grandson loved her and was oh so happy to be with her. I wanted it to be the best 3:17 p.m. it could be, because it was all that existed then, all that had ever existed before, and all that ever would exist in the future.

And it is all that exists right now.

For the last three weeks of her life, Grandma was in hospice, and friends and family all gathered by her side to say goodbye. During a visit about a week before she died, I asked her how she was feeling. By this time, she was totally bedridden and could not get up by herself anymore. "Well, not too good, I guess...but it could always be worse," she replied. *Um...how?* I wondered. *You're* dying—*ain't that about as bad as it gets?* I had forgotten that until just a few months ago, because of the COVID-19 pandemic, assisted-living facilities and rest homes across the globe had gone on strict lockdown in an attempt to protect their vulnerable elderly residents. I worried constantly that Grandma would finally begin to die, whether from COVID or just old age, and that she would die without anyone she knew by her side to see her off—the thought of that happening was like an ever-present knife twisting in my gut, by far the worst part of that bizarre time period for me. No one—family or friend—had been allowed to visit her or touch her for over a year. She had been separated from *her people.*

For Grandma, *that* felt worse.

When I'd interviewed her eight years earlier, I told Grandma that most people my age had no frame of reference for anything even remotely like her childhood. "No, there's been such a change," she said, "some of it for the better, some of it for the worse."

"What do you think is the biggest difference between today and when you grew up?" I asked, and Grandma did not hesitate to answer. But she did not talk about laptop computers or rechargeable cars or large-screen smart TVs. She did not discuss the state of modern politics, the information economy, or large-scale social reform movements. She kept it to what truly mattered most, on an individual human level.

"Well, I really don't think people are as close as they used to be. Community used to be real close—people don't come and visit like they used to," she said.

For all our advanced communication technology and multiple social media platforms that link us to people across the globe, the fleets of fast-moving airplanes and highways crammed with speeding cars, despite all these things that were designed to bring us together but that mostly keep us *busy busy busy* ... we are a much lonelier world than we used to be. How many of us know our neighbors? Where is our community? Who are *our people*? Do we even know anymore? Maybe this is why things are so divisive right now—people are disconnected, lonely, and desperately searching for something, anything, to belong to. They are searching for a place to call home.

So maybe we should slow down, stop frantically *doing doing doing*, and try going for a visit next door.

The last night of Grandma's life on earth, it was just me and her. I told my family to go home and get some rest, that I would take the evening shift. Grandma had suffered hard for a few days—the doctors and nurses were magnificent, doing everything they could to minimize her pain, but there is no escaping the fact that a hundred-year-old body just *hurts*. But on her final evening she rested peacefully and was feeling no pain. I sat up with her until the wee hours, staring at her sweet face, holding her hand, speaking softly, and singing old gospel songs to her.

> *I'll fly away, oh, Glory*
> *I'll fly away*
> *When I die, Hallelujah, by and by*
> *I'll fly away.*

Sometime around sunrise, very soon after I dozed off in a chair right beside her, Grandma's body finally let her soul go, and she peacefully flew away. She did not leave this world alone, without family by her side. I woke up and saw that she was gone, and I was so happy and honored to have been by her side. I owed her that, and so much more.

In our modern society, we seem to have lost touch with death and how to deal with it. Far too many old folks are locked away in homes and left to die alone. This is an abomination. So I say to you now: If you have any old ones left, go visit them as much as you can, and when they begin to die, be there with them until the very end if you can. At times it will be difficult, and your heart will hurt, but this is your duty. Honor that duty. This is the correct way.

Do not be scared. Do not look away. Help them to die well.

This is how you help an elderly loved one die: sit beside them and hold their hand. Tell them that you love them and are grateful for all they have done for you. Speak softly, telling them that you and all the rest of their family are okay. With gentle words, tell them that it is okay for them to leave, that they can go be at peace whenever they are ready. Let them know that you are there, that they are not alone, and that you will not leave them. Quietly fill the room with your support and love.

Be patient, be kind, be present.

Sit and wait.

You will not regret it.

Chapter Six

SOUL CRAFT

A s I sit here typing this in the back lounge of my tour
bus, there are many things that weigh on my heart and
head. A member of my family is waiting for her appointment
to get a potentially cancerous mass in her breast analyzed.
There was yet another mass shooting in America three days
ago, this time in Minneapolis at a punk rock house show, of
all places. A friend of mine has been evicted from his apartment after being out of work for just two weeks and is now
living in his car with his one-eyed cat. And on the island of
Maui, in Hawaii, the death toll just keeps on rising after wild-
fires burned down the old town of Lahaina, and I am trying
to figure out how to help these people. The news is all bad,
it seems, especially the actual news. I'm only two weeks into
this tour and already every morning when I drag myself out

of my bunk my body feels like someone worked me over with a baseball bat.

I need to go surfing, dammit.

When I started writing my last book, I took some of my advance money and rented a small house on Oak Island in the Cape Fear region of North Carolina, right next door to a friend of mine. At $650 a month, one block away from the ocean—the price was unbeatable, and I needed solitude and quiet to write. I kept that house for five beautiful years, long after I was finished writing the book, until my neighbor called to inform me that my ninety-six-year-old landlord had decided to start renovating it without my knowledge while I was on tour. I wasn't mad about it because I knew it wouldn't last forever. The house was small and run-down and weather damaged from years of salt air, and with the increasing frequency of hurricanes it will inevitably be blown away. Easy come, easy go. But I have extremely fond memories of my time in that little beach shack, and several major life events happened while I was there: I wrote my first book and became a published author. I curated my first-ever photography exhibit. I wrote a movie script. I wrote and recorded music that was used by the Richmond Ballet.

And I became a surfer.

Surfing came to me late, at age forty-three. Before surfing, I was a skateboarder. It started when I was a child in the 1970s with a messed-up homemade haircut (thanks, Dad) and a yellow plastic banana board pushing down what seemed to be a very long driveway. (I know now it was very short.) Then in the 1980s, I got a real skateboard for Christmas one year—a black and green Vision Gator that I eventually snapped in half acid dropping off the back of an abandoned van in a parking lot—and I got serious about the process of injuring myself. I was pretty good in my early teenage years, then quickly reached the limits of my abilities—I am not a graceful skateboarder. No one has ever watched me skate and said, "Man, that dude has a smooth style." I am a tall, lanky caveman, and I go as fast as I can, trying by brute force and sheer willpower to do things that other skaters make look effortless. I fail spectacularly most of the time, and regrettably I somehow never learned to bail, so I have hit the bottom of a ramp like a bony sack of meat more times than I can remember. When I do manage to pull off a trick, it always looks like an actual miracle has occurred. Skating, I have broken all the toes on each foot at least once, most of them twice. I have put my bottom teeth completely through my lip. I have rolled my ankle so badly that I have to wear an ankle brace every time I take the stage. I have a torn meniscus in my left knee from a wall ride gone wrong in Toronto. My shins are covered in scars, and my knees are a disaster. I wake up every day in pain from this full-throttle life I have led—some aches come from skateboarding, some from stupid things I did while drunk, and some from stupidly skateboarding while drunk. (I used to think I was a *ripping* skater after five or six beers—clearly, I was not.)

My skateboarding came to an almost complete halt in my late twenties as my alcoholism progressed. I took out my board only every now and then to eat drunken shit on the concrete of whatever city I was in on tour. Then I got sober at age thirty-nine and started skating hard again for another couple years. I went skateboarding on my fortieth birthday and felt really good about myself. But I discovered very quickly that being a forty-year-old mediocre skateboarder is a very, very different experience from being a nineteen-year-old mediocre skateboarder. It hurts more—*a lot* more. I rarely skate now, and when I do, I try my best to restrain myself from attempting things that will put me in the hospital. But I will always be grateful to skateboarding for all the things it has given me—a bit of balance in a naturally clumsy, lanky body. The ability to jump from high places and not injure myself. (If you've ever seen a picture of me flying through the air onstage... well, those are skateboarding hops, my friends.) Many lifelong friends. The skateboarding community even gave me punk rock music, which without a shred of forethought or really even any desire on my part eventually led to my career as a musician. And finally, skateboarding gave me an intuitive, preinstalled understanding of the basic mechanics of wave riding—this because skateboarding originally comes from surfing.

Growing up in southeastern Virginia and North Carolina, I was never far from the beach. For a while in the 1980s, my mom lived in a house on Atlanta Avenue in Wrightsville Beach, North Carolina, and my brothers and I spent a lot of time there—you turned left out the front door, walked half a block to the end of the street, kicked off your flip-flops, cruised over the dunes, and there was the ocean. I have always felt the most at home by the sea, and since I was a little kid I have swum in her waters. I know how to deal with rip currents, I know how to throw a cast net for bait, and I am not panicked by the sting of jellyfish on my bare skin. I respect the ocean, because I know from experience that she is the boss and the mother "from whence we came," as JFK put it in a famous 1962 speech. And so, having been by the sea as much as I had, one would think that I would have learned to surf earlier. I'd screwed around with surfboards many times, including smashing the nose of my brother Scott's new board in the shore break *immediately* after he expressly told me, "DO NOT SMASH MY NEW BOARD IN THE SHORE BREAK" (I'm sorry, bro), but I never took it seriously until I was writing my first book. I was always too busy skateboarding (which I deemed way more *punk rock,* an extremely important distinction to my snotty little fifteen-year-old self) or chasing girls or drinking. Plus, surfboards cost a lot more than a complete skateboard setup does—I do not come from money, and my parents couldn't afford to kick down the cash for a surfboard. A skateboard was stretching the budget (and thank you, Mom, for that first skateboard—it changed my life). Once I started working, I had better things to spend my money on (or so I thought), things like records, punk rock shows, girls, beer, and eventually drugs. But a few months after I moved into my writing shack on Oak Island, I was walking on the beach one day and stopped in front of a few people surfing. I watched them for a minute, and thought,

You know what? I live at the beach now—I might as well learn how to surf. It looks like skateboarding on the water—how hard can it be?

Very hard, as it turns out.

Although the physical "language" of surfing may be the same as that of skateboarding, and even much of the actual terminology remains the same (goofy, regular, front side, back side, carving, pumping, etc.), the environment you surf in is vastly different from the one you skate in. In skateboarding, everything is static: a twelve-foot vert ramp remains the same every time you drop in on it; it will not disappear and suddenly reappear three minutes later as a four-foot mini half-pipe. A yellow convenience store curb is not significantly different from one slappy grind to the next. You can approach the same obstacle from the same direction and try the same trick again and again and again until you dial it in. All that goes out the window in surfing—even at the most consistent of point breaks, each wave is different from the next. Ocean tides and currents are constantly shifting and moving, pushing you toward and away from shore and up and down the beach, so even on the calmest of days you are never perfectly lined up to take off from the exact same spot, no matter what landmark onshore you use to position yourself. You cannot precisely predict when, where, or which incoming line of swell will produce a surfable wave until right before it happens, so you are in a state of constant alert, observation, and analysis, trying to make the correct judgment call on when to turn and start paddling. And timing is everything, because surfing is all about conserving energy, keeping gas in the tank for when the right wave finally arrives and you need an explosive burst of paddling energy. Constantly chasing peaks (aka "down the beach syndrome") is an exhausting process and will leave you pissed off and with arms that feel like overcooked spaghetti. You have to remain patient, alert, and, oh yeah—extra capable in the water, because you are in the ocean, not a swimming pool.

Surfing can be maddening, frustrating, and even (on bad days) severely demoralizing, especially if you let your ego run the show and don't stop to remember how fucking lucky you are to be *playing in the ocean*. But, for the most part, it is one of the greatest joys of my life. Since I learned to surf, not a day goes by now that I do not think of surfing multiple times, even if I am caught thousands of miles inland. I have always loved the ocean since I was a child, but surfing has turned that love into an obsession. "Only a surfer knows the feeling" is an old saying, but it is entirely true. There is no way to explain what riding waves feels like to someone who has never done it, but I can explain the effect it has had on my life.

I love the ocean, but she is a fickle mistress, uncontrollable, unpredictable, and given to unexpected stormy outbursts. And from time to time, the unexpected days-old echo of one of her distant tantrums will travel hundreds of miles across her fluid surface to the very outer limits of her body, building in force and shape as it goes. Then, if the wind is right, if the tide is neither too high nor too low, if the inner sandbars lining the ocean floor have held enough from the last storm, if that pulse of manic energy heads my way from a specific direction—if all these things line up perfectly— then, and only then, I will enter my church. If it is during the winter months, I will put on my now-thinning wetsuit, grab a long fiberglass-coated plank shaped by my friend David, and run into the cold water. I will gasp as the chilly white water of the gray sea rushes over my head and paddle hard through the breakers to the calmness of the outside. There, I will sit on my board, pointing toward the horizon, facing the shifting emptiness, with the slight wind chill on my wet hair, and I will repeat the same words I utter every single time I do this:

"Thank you, God, for giving me this part of my life."

Then I will say hello to The Landlord. It's really the only polite thing to do—after all, I am in his house, and the highly aggressive bull sharks that are so common in the North Carolina waters I surf most often have tasted more than one of my kind in recent years. So I always let him know I am visiting his home, that I mean no disrespect, and that I will in fact fight for his continued existence against the members of my species who are moronically driving his to the brink of extinction. Then, I look for the wave.

When I see the line of water rising my way on the horizon, I turn my board and paddle to a spot in the sea where I hope and believe that line will rise and begin to pitch. I wait there until I judge it is near enough, then turn and face the shore, lay down on my board, arch my back, and begin digging my arms into the sea, one after the other, propelling me forward. I glance over my shoulder from time to time, increasing or decreasing my paddling speed in an attempt to match the velocity of the wall of energy now almost on top of me. Then, suddenly I feel the wave take me as it begins to break, an impossible sensation to accurately put into words. It pushes me forward, and I begin sliding down its face as the energy that has traveled so far is finally unleashed in a spiraling mass of whitewater behind me. Automatically, I spring up from my board and land in a crouch on my feet.

Then, I ride the wave.

I am not thinking of how I will ride this wave. In fact, I am not thinking at all. Everything is moving and changing far too quickly for that. It is impossible to plan ahead in this unknowable protean liquid environment, so for a few brief seconds my fears, my ego, my wants, my pitiful desires—all that I *think* I am—vanishes and I just *am*.

I am surfing, walking on the water with God.

I am complete.

And because I am complete, I am moving in perfect harmony with the universe. When the waves are good and I am surfing well, the delineation between the ocean, my board, and me disappears. I am not imposing my will upon the face of the sea, attempting to muscle the crude kinetic agenda of a specific direction I wish to go. I am not aggressively riding on top of the wave in a relationship of dominance and submission. Instead, I move *with* the wave, graciously accepting what it offers me and honoring that gift by sliding along in harmony with it for its brief existence. When it is over and I sink back down on my board, I usually cannot restrain myself from giving out a hoot of pure joy. Blinding happiness permeates every fiber of my being.

This is what surfing gives me—perfection. But because that feeling is so elusive, transparent, and temporary, after I ride a wave, I turn my board back toward the ocean and look for another one. Always, just one more wave. I will do this until I'm exhausted, the waves are gone, or it is too dark to see. After, if it was a good session and I am with my friends, we will go eat and talk about the waves we just rode. Some people talk about the news, some about whatever TV program they are watching, some about the latest game of their favorite sports team—we talk about the different waves we just rode, and on the East Coast most of them usually last no longer than five or six seconds, but we discuss those five or six seconds in great detail. It's kind of strange when I think about it. No other activity that is over so quickly takes up so much of my mental real estate. Why?

From an intellectual perspective, surfing is utterly pointless. It accomplishes precisely nothing. Sure, I suppose you could look at it purely as a form of exercise with the attendant physical health benefits—people who surf a lot are generally in pretty good physical shape—but there are much easier and consistently available ways to exercise that don't require (1) an ocean, and (2) the ability to walk on freaking water. But the incredible feeling of rightness with the universe that surfing gives me does wonders for my perspective in a way that

nothing else can. "Leave it on the shore" is another old surfer's saying, and when I paddle into the sea, I do—"it" being
anything bothering me. And after a good session, no matter what difficulties I may be facing, my attitude and outlook
on life are always greatly improved. I am energized, level-
headed, and ready to deal with problems that might have
seemed insurmountable before I caught a few waves. Surfing
is not just good for my body but also good for my soul. A
positive perspective makes me a better person, and surfing
consistently provides that.

It's also just fun as hell.

Like skateboarding, I am at best an average surfer. I will
never surf the fabled left-hand barrel Pipeline on the North
Shore of Oahu, and I am perfectly fine with that. That wave is
far beyond any skill level I could ever hope to attain; besides,
it kills people regularly, and I don't want to die attempting
something I already know I am destined to fail at. However,
unlike skateboarding, which peaked early for me, I *am* slowly
becoming a better surfer—I can catch and ride a decent-size
wave without looking like a total kook and sometimes even
do a little ripping. One reason for this not-so-rapid improve-
ment is that every single person in my crew is a much, much
better surfer than I am, and they do not cut me any slack. I
regularly surf with dudes twenty years younger, and they give
me shit nonstop about being a tired old man, about looking angry when I paddle for waves (I'm not, I'm just *concentrating*), and even about my stance. "Mister Blythe, what do
you think you're doing, riding that wave with your long-ass

skinny arms all spread out like wings? Do you think you're some kinda surfin' bird?" I have to fight for my waves with the boys, and it makes me better—this is good life advice in general. If you want to get better at something, do it while surrounded by people who are already doing it at a much, much higher level than you. Swallow your ego, shut your mouth, then pay attention and learn from getting crushed by these people again and again. There is a friendly spirit of competition among the guys I surf with, complete with lots of shit-talking, ball-busting, and even stealing waves from each other (by the way, this is *not* something you do to people you don't know because it can be very dangerous, because of both accidents in the water and retaliatory violence). No one in my crew is going to sit back and wait for me to *maybe* catch a wave that they could be riding—this is a strict aquatic meritocracy, but it's all love and we have a great time together.

Another cool thing about surfing is that it is one of the only "sports" (for lack of a better term—I think even most pro surfers who earn their living competing don't really think of it as a "sport" most of the time) I can think of where it's not just *weird* to do it with people of a wide variety of ages and sexes. For example, it would be *super* creepy if I were to walk onto a field of middle school girls playing softball, throw on my glove, stroll over to second base, and holler, "Let's play ball, ladies!" But I have been in a surfing lineup that ranged from a seventy-eight-year-old man to a nine-year-old girl, and it's perfectly normal for all of us to be there having fun together. I also have been recognized by fans of my band in the water before, but it's never once been awkward—they paddle over, ask if it's me, then say, "No way, dude—I *love* your music!" and we chat for a bit, but the whole time they are scanning the horizon, looking for a wave. When that wave comes, they don't let it pass—fan or not, they are there to surf, not talk about heavy metal. Surfing is a great equalizer, I love it for that, and every single time I've met people in the water who like my music it's been an absolute pleasure to surf *with* those fans.

It's also an activity that I have done all over the world, and I have made good friends around the globe in the process. Ninety percent of the friends I've made while surfing had never even heard of my band when we first met, and they could give a shit less that I'm a musician—I might as well be a plumber or an accountant as far as they are concerned. With the exception of two or three people, no one I surf with listens to my music; in fact, most of them actively dislike it.

Surfing has its own culture, and in the places where that culture is firmly grounded in its roots, it's a beautiful thing. When I started surfing, I was lucky enough to learn from my friend David, who grew up riding waves in Hawaii. There is a tradition and culture of respect in the water there, with, ahem, "repercussions" for those who do not abide by those traditions. You do not just show up at a serious break in Hawaii and start paddling for whatever wave you want. You wait, watch, observe the locals, figure out the pecking order, and start off slow, picking off leftovers. You show *respect*, and by behaving in a respectful manner, you earn respect.

I do not believe in the stupid and arrogant version of localism that plagues some beaches because the ocean belongs to everyone. But I also do not believe that anyone, no matter how good a surfer they are, is entitled to show up at a strange break full of people who know each other and act like an asshole. Show respect, and generally people will be cool to you. We're pretty laid-back where I come from because surfing is about having fun, not fighting over a piece of ocean that belongs to everyone. If someone is hogging waves, back paddling me, or paddling out directly in front of me, I just shake my head and wait for them to leave, or I paddle over to a different break. I'm a fifty-three-year-old grown-ass man, and fighting in the water is not why I surf. *But . . .* from time to time, someone has to be put in their place.

I've gotten really ugly with someone in the water only once in my life, but it was bad. A total beginner was paddling hard for a wave I was already surfing. This is a pretty common occurrence at this particular break because it is a very easy wave to catch and a great spot to learn surfing. Beginners trying to figure out how to surf are always very excited, entirely focused on trying to get into the wave, and they don't remember to do the most important thing while surfing in a group of people: look down the line to see if anyone is already on the wave. This is very dangerous because surfboards move over the water at high rates of speed, there are no brakes, and you can severely injure or even kill someone if you smash into them with your board (and yes, this happens—surfing can be deadly, especially if the spot is crowded and the waves are big). However, you can't expect a bunch of beginners to not fuck up, so if you get dropped in on at a beginner break, unless you're a total douchebag, you just have to laugh it off and remember the times you did the very same thing— because we *all* accidentally dropped in on a stranger while learning to surf. (FYI, the correct protocol when you do that is to immediately paddle over to your victim, say, "Holy shit, I'm so sorry, man—my bad, I was stupid and didn't look to see you coming." Ninety-nine percent of the time, the person you dropped in on will say, "It's all good, dude—no worries." You will actually gain respect for admitting your mistake, and the people in the lineup will know that, although you may still be a total kook, at least you know it and are trying to get better. This advice is applicable to pretty much any situation in life where you make a boneheaded maneuver—promptly admit your mistake, apologize, and everyone tends to move on a lot quicker.)

But this particular guy was obviously too stupid to be allowed to stay in the water around other people. The waves were perfect that day, about waist high, and I was riding a beautiful brand-new nine-foot-four longboard I had bought from my buddy Jason at Rodanthe Surf Shop on Hatteras Island. At this point break, I get sixty- to ninety-second rides on the regular, and I had already been on a wave for at least half a minute when I saw a dude awkwardly paddling for my wave down the line. He was obviously a beginner, so I gave a big hoot to let him know I was on the wave—no big deal. When you hear someone already on a wave hoot, you stop paddling, lean back to pull out of the wave, and they surf on by, no problem—happens all the time. But this guy heard me, turned and looked at me, then went back to paddling for my wave. "HEY!" I yelled, and he looked at me again. "NO!" He looked at me again, speeding toward him on my huge board, then kept paddling, struggling even harder. *What the fuck?* I thought. *This guy is an* idiot.

I was rapidly closing the gap between us, so I started screaming, "NO-NO-NO-NO-NO!!!!!" and pointing my finger at his face like I was scolding a bad dog. He looked directly into my eyes and then turned and dug his arms into the water even harder. I had never seen anyone on a surfboard act so blatantly suicidal before. It was like someone with two broken legs hopping along on crutches and trying to cross train tracks while a locomotive is barreling toward them, blowing its horn over and over. Clearly, this guy did not grasp the severity of the situation, so it was time to abort mission. I leaned back on my tail, shifted my weight, and started to swing the nose of my board toward the shore, straightening out in an attempt to avert disaster... but I was too close and it was too late. The wave took the guy forward, he (of course) ate shit, flailing in the white water as he fell off his board, and we smashed into each other very hard.

I came up out of the water with my arms crossed in an X in front of my face in case one of our boards was flying through the air toward me, checked myself really quickly to see if I was broken or bleeding anywhere, then yanked on my leash and pulled my board to me. I was already pissed, but when I saw the deep gouge the other dude's fin had cut into my beautiful new board, I *totally* lost my shit.

"*YOU!*" I screamed. "*YOU FUCKING IDIOT!* I told you to stop—I could have *killed* you, you moron—plus look what you fucking did to my brand-new board!" The dude turned white as a sheet. Between our wreck and me screaming at him, he was obviously very shaken up and scared, but I was too pissed to care. "You are going to come with me to the surf shop *right now* and pay for this to be repaired," I said. At this point his buddy, also obviously a beginner, paddled over to investigate. "What the fuck do you want?" I screamed at him. "Are you going to smash into my board too?" Then they both hopped on their boards and paddled toward shore as hard as they could, looking over their shoulders to see if I was following them. I was so mad I just stood there in the waist-deep water, punching the ocean like a lunatic and yelling, "HEY! YOU! Come back here! You are gonna pay to fix this! COME BACK HERE!" I kept screaming for them to come back even when they got to the shore, picked up their boards, and literally *ran* into the woods at the edge of the beach. I had severely frightened them both, and I never saw them again.

Thinking back on it, I must have looked like a total maniac. I had lost almost total control of my temper (I say "almost" because at least I didn't punch anything other than the water). For two full days after that, I felt like utter shit and walked around pretty ashamed of myself. I don't drink anymore, so I don't wake up with the brutal hangovers that characterized the end of my drinking days, but when I do act out now, *particularly* in anger, I get emotional hangovers. These are almost worse; they last longer, and I don't even have the crappy excuse of being drunk when I flip out. I need to remember that *shit happens*, that some people are just, well, *stupid*, and I would do well to act like a grown-ass man, not an infuriated child, when I get sprayed after those people make the doo-doo hit the fan.

I have never acted out like that in the water since. In the end, the most important thing is that nobody got hurt. It was just a surfboard, and it didn't cost me much when my buddy repaired it the next day. Though I still feel like shit when I think about it, honestly that guy got off pretty lucky—people have been beaten down in the water for much less. Hopefully, he will never try to surf again, because someone with that little common sense in the water could very easily get some-one killed. I know this is not a popular opinion in today's world of "everyone belongs everywhere and is automatically entitled to everything they want," but you have to *earn* your place in the lineup. If you don't know what the hell you are doing in the water, you probably shouldn't try surfing; start with swimming lessons, then maybe take a dip in the ocean first so you understand its power. If you don't want to do that and are determined to kill yourself on a surfboard, please… go do it far away from the rest of us. Know that some people just don't belong in the ocean, a fact that is proved at beaches across the world every summer when tourists from inland drown in rip currents. Sometimes, the ocean is not the place to "conquer your fears" or whatever else some self-help book advised you to do.

However, lest you, my dear reader, think I am one of these snobby elitists who wants to keep surfing all to himself, I am also the guy who is always telling people, "Oh, you want to surf? Let's go! I have extra boards—I'll teach ya. You'll *love it!*" Some of these people will actually show up at the beach, I'll do my best to explain the basics to them, then we'll get in the water. Ninety percent of these folks paddle around, have some fun eating shit in the water while enjoying a nice beach day, but the next morning this is the message they send me: "DUDE—holy shit, I am *sore.* It was fun, but that was *hard*— I don't know how you do that all the time." But the remaining 10 percent? They're at the surf shop later that week buying their first board and absolutely frothing to surf again.

For me, very few pleasures match the feeling I get when I see someone I know, or even someone I just met in the water, catch their first wave. After struggling forever, somehow this kook finally manages to stand up and stay up, arms flailing as they teeter wildly on their board, rushing straight toward shore on knee-high mushy white water. Bent over at the waist, legs spread insanely far apart in the stance known as *stink bug,* eyes bugging almost completely out of their heads—they look like drunken toddlers trying to walk. With zero control over their board, they are utterly ridiculous, and it is very obvious that at any second they are going to eat shit. They are the very embodiment of ungracefulness, a living archetype of the word *klutz*. And eat shit they do, falling into the sea after a few seconds of *the worst-looking* surfing possible.

But when they break the surface of the water, emerge after getting tossed around for a bit by the wave they miraculously flailed their way into, there is a huge grin plastered across their face. Then, from the lineup, a huge hooting yell of congratulations erupts.

YEEEEEWWWWWWW!!!!!

We hoot because all of us who ride waves know what is racing through their mind at that second: *Holy shit, holy shit, holy fucking shit I WAS FUCKING SURFING!!!!!* We all know this because at one time, we too caught our first wave, we too looked like idiots on it, and we too had that overwhelming moment of disbelief when we realized we had popped our surfing cherry—it's an awesome feeling, and it makes us *stoked* to see someone else experience it.

When you feel *that good*, in that moment you can do no harm. You move peacefully through the world, so overwhelmed with joy that the head-splitting clamor of bullshit that the modern world daily crams down your throat goes silent. The pieces of your spirit that life has ground into little tiny bits are made whole again, if only for an instant. And, yes, at the end of the session, you will leave the water, and unless you are a monk meditating your life away in some wilderness cave, existence itself will once again begin its relentless assault on your serenity and sanity. But your internal being will be fortified...you have known peace and happiness, even for the briefest of times, and you know that it waits for you again, there in the ocean that birthed us all.

This is why I get cranky if I go too long without surfing. When my gills dry out, I can get pretty irritable—*I need it*, and I am not alone in this. All my friends who surf get this way when they go too long without waves. Surfing is an indispensable part of maintaining some semblance of balance in our lives. It also keeps you young—your body may be tan, wrinkled, and weather-beaten from the sun and salt air, but your soul remains youthful. When the waves are good, it's impossible for me to be the bitter old man I can all too easily become—life is just too good to be a curmudgeon when a glassy waist-high left pulses beneath your feet. You are walking on water, for Pete's sake. How could you possibly be unhappy?

As I've told many people: "Surfing will *change your life.*" It's a crazy, pointless, and at times dangerous activity that can literally take the last breath from your lungs and fill them with saltwater as you sink into a watery grave after dropping in on the wrong wave and smashing headfirst into a coral reef—but I will *never* stop doing it until I am physically unable. Hopefully, that won't occur until I am very old, and by that time, I will have sunk deep into dementia. And when my constant bitching about how much better the good ol' days were has pushed whoever my unlucky caretaker is to the edge of their sanity, when the next big swell comes they can just put me on my board and push me out to sea. The ocean has never failed to make me happy, so as they yell, "Good riddance!" at my gray-bearded, insane self, I'll probably just think I'm paddling out to find a nice left. I'll feel that stoke one last time, and hopefully I'll wipe out quickly and drown without too much of a fuss. (*Supposedly*, once you get past the initial panic, drowning is a pretty peaceful way to go.)

And if Poseidon takes me tomorrow while I'm riding waves, I'm cool with it. I've lived a good life, and though it is far beyond a cliché, if I die surfing, people will be able to honestly say, "Well, at least he died doing what he loved." What more can anyone ask for?

Chapter Seven

MONEY IS NOT OUR GOD (BABYLON DUB)

The older I get, the more I try to structure my life around activities that I believe bring a deeper sense of meaning and purpose to what's left of my existence. Each day I know my time here grows shorter, so more and more I focus on things I do not deem pointless wastes of that swiftly shrinking time. Admittedly, I've previously described one of my favorite things to do, surfing, as pointless, but that's not really true; in fact, in my life it has led to many things that I have found deeply meaningful. Real friendships, opportunities to see new places, learn about new cultures, and absorb as much good as I can from this world so that I can walk through it a better, more balanced man—which makes me more effective at producing a positive change in my environment. I'm even trying to take the gifts surfing has given me and ensure that they will continually make the world a better place long after I am dead and gone. Ironically, one of nature's most destructive forces, the hurricane, caused this.

One hot August day in 2017, I was about to go surfing with my buddy David on Oak Island. While we were waxing our boards, he said, "Have you met the Ecuadorean yet? He's gonna come surf with us in a bit." Ecuadorean? What in the hell was a surfer from Ecuador doing on little ol' Oak Island? I have a lot of love for Oak Island, but it's not exactly what I would call a prime surfing destination. It's a south-facing island, which can make for some fantastic sunsets, but unless there is a strong south swell, most of the time the waves aren't the greatest. In fact, it's normally pretty crappy mush, especially with the near constant southwestern winds that blow in the summer months.

Sure enough, about thirty minutes later a wiry brown-skinned dude paddled out to our spot, gave us a big grin, and David introduced me to Carlos. Carlos's wife, Olivia, was from Ohio, and some friends of hers had loaned the house they owned on Oak Island to the couple for a little vacation.

Over the next week, we surfed terrible mushy waves with Carlos and hung out in the evenings. We had a lot of fun— the dude *loved* to surf, and even in crappy conditions, I could tell he ripped. "Sorry the waves are so shit right now," I told him, "but if you're ever here during hurricane season, it can get really good." Carlos just laughed and said shitty waves were better than no waves and that he would try to come back for the next big swell.

A couple months later, Carlos flew back to the East Coast to surf with us. We had been watching Hurricane Irma develop out in the Atlantic, and it looked like conditions were right for her to deliver us a nice swell. Every surfer on the Southeastern coast of the United States is an amateur meteorologist, especially in September and October (peak hurricane season), obsessively checking weather updates, reading buoy heights, and trying to decipher the spaghetti models put up by the National Hurricane Center that predict the possibilities and potential paths of a storm off the coast of Africa strengthening into something big enough to give us good waves. It is a never-ending learning process detangling the arcane art of swell prediction, much like surfing itself is, and pursuing it has taught me a bit about how the natural world works and reinforced my respect for the sheer power of the sea.

East Coast surfers have a bizarre love/hate relationship with hurricanes. On the one hand, we hate the destruction they unleash on our coastal areas, wrecking beaches, marshlands, and people's homes. Hurricanes kill coastal residents every year as well. On the other hand, we love the big, long-period swell waves they bring us. These are the best waves of the year, and we wait for them eagerly. The ideal situation is when a storm strengthens into a nice-size hurricane but stays miles out to sea, never making landfall but pushing those big, beautiful lines ashore for us to ride. The swell Hurricane Irma sent to Oak Island was one of those; there was no destruction of our beach, and the waves were big, clean, and perfectly shaped.

Florida and various Caribbean islands were not so lucky. By the time Irma was done, 134 people had died. Daily before I went out to surf that swell, I texted my friend and surfboard shaper in Florida, Kane Barrie of Nightmare Shapes, to check in on him. I let him know that we were getting great waves but that I was worried about him and everyone else down south. Kane was safe, but he told me that Irma was causing utter mayhem outside—the sea in Florida was a boiling cauldron of death. "I'm staying inside," he wrote, "but go chase down those bombs for me, braddah…ain't no waves to be ridden down here at the moment! Yew!!!"

It is a strange feeling to be extremely excited for the effects of a monster storm while simultaneously being worried about that storm killing your friends, but if the situation were reversed I know I would want Kane to go catch every wave possible while I hunkered down, so I said a prayer for everyone in Irma's path and then went out to surf. I had just gotten a really good chest-high ride one afternoon and paddled back outside when Carlos said, "Brother, if you like these waves, you should come to my country this winter. I will take you to some spots that will blow your mind."

"Okay," I said, "I will."

Four months later, I was on a plane to South America to hunt down waves.

I had been to Ecuador once before in 2012 when my band played a wild outdoor gig in Quito, the capital city, a huge metropolis in the highlands. We were supposed to have played a festival there two years before in 2010, but unforeseen circumstances prevented that: We were waiting to board a plane in Santiago, Chile, to fly to Quito, when an announcement was made that all flights to Ecuador were canceled—the Quito airport was closed because, apparently, a good old-fashioned coup d'état was underway. Protesting police or soldiers (or both, I think—honestly, I've never quite been able to figure it out) infuriated over pay cuts had seized control of the airport and the National Assembly building (Ecuador's version of Congress). I was watching the news on a TV at our boarding gate when I saw the then-president of Ecuador, Rafael Correa, in a display of high drama and pure South American machismo, literally ripping his shirt open to show his bare chest to an angry crowd while screaming in Spanish and shaking his fists. "What is he saying?" I asked a gentleman standing beside me. "He says something like: 'Treason! Traitors! So you want to kill the president? Well, here he is. Kill him, if that's what you want. Just try to kill him if you have the guts, you cowards!'" the man replied. Then some protesters tear-gassed the Prez, who was hobbling around on a cane after a leg operation, and tried to kick him in the knee.

Well, damn, I thought, *I guess we aren't gigging in Ecuador,* and we didn't. Instead, we slept on the floor of the airport that night and flew to Colombia the next day.

"Ecuador is *raw*, brother," Carlos has told me more than once, and he is right. Like most South American countries, things run a little differently down there. Infrastructure we in the United States take for granted is lacking, institutional-level corruption is high, and there is a level of poverty in some places that most Americans have no conception of. In fact, most Americans these days have zero idea of what the word *poor* really means. *Poor* does not mean you don't have enough to pay rent and the cable bill at the same time; it means your family has built their house out of whatever materials they can scrounge together and the only cable you have is the one you used to splice into a power line. *Poor* doesn't mean you can't afford to buy a new pair of brand-name tennis shoes for your kids to go back to school in; it means you can't afford to buy your kids shoes, period. *Poor* doesn't mean you are living beyond your means as you mire yourself deeper and deeper in credit card debt; it means that nothing resembling a credit card machine has ever existed in your village. *Poor* doesn't mean you don't have the money to pay a plumber to come fix your fucked-up toilet; it means you don't have running water, much less an actual toilet for a plumber to come fix.

Beyond economic circumstances, other aspects of the country also take a little getting used to. Driving in Ecuador is a test of skill, endurance, and sheer nerve. The roads are a nightmare of giant potholes and suicidal dogs and helmetless families crammed onto a single motorcycle. Malaria is common enough that when I went to a Red Cross blood drive to donate at the beginning of the coronavirus pandemic, I found out I was not eligible because I had been tramping through the jungles of Ecuador a few months earlier. From an American's perspective, one that is deeply rooted in comfort and convenience, almost nothing ever seems to come easy in Ecuador—simple tasks we take for granted in America always seem to take an excessive amount of time (especially when you are traveling with my friend Carlos, because no matter where you go in the country he seems to know *someone* and always has things to discuss with them). Ironically, in a country containing part of the planet's mightiest jungle, there is no next-day delivery because Amazon Prime doesn't exist in the Amazon. Unlike America, you can't have whatever you want whenever you want it, but that's okay— you probably didn't need it anyway.

Ecuador is not unique in its economic issues; I have witnessed the same level of poverty all over South America, in parts of Asia, and in Africa. Although there is nothing romantic or noble about poverty, I can say that I have directly benefited from the generosity of spirit many economically depressed people have displayed toward me and one that I see so very lacking much of the time in my own highly privileged and overly comfortable country. In general, people down there seemed more willing to help each other or even a stranger than are people in the United States. I asked my Ecuadorean friends who had been to the States if this seemed true to them, and they all said yes. Paradoxically, the less a community has, the more its members are required to lean on one another, the more giving they seem to be.

My first surf trip to Ecuador could make for a book in its own right. Carlos picked me up at the Quito airport in his family's battered red Toyota truck, and from there we made our way through the stunning landscape of the cloud forest and out to the emerald coastline. On that first trip, I met his family (whom I now consider family myself—Carlos's mother always greets me with a hug and a smile and a kiss and calls me *mijo*), and many wonderful people I now call friends—Fred and Graciela, Eduardo, Sol, Joao, Chuckie, Mercer, Gallo...beautiful human beings, both Ecuadorean and expatriate, all of whom call that country home. I saw howler monkeys and toucans, ate huge meals fit for a king that cost me three American dollars, slept happily each night beneath a mosquito net, took many gorgeous photographs... and surfed perfect waves until my arms simply could not paddle anymore.

The waves...oh, *the waves*. They were *magnificent*, including one point break that has given me the longest, most perfectly peeling waist- to head-high waves I have ever surfed. When conditions are right, this spot is like a machine. I had never seen anything like it. On a really good day, the majority of waves on the East Coast give you a ten-second ride, max—that's a lengthy ride here in the States. But at this spot down south, I got a few rides that lasted almost two minutes, and a one-minute ride was pretty standard. Sixty seconds is a looooong time on a wave, and more than once I burst into laughter as I surfed, actually saying out loud to no one but myself "This is *ridiculous!*"—it was so, sooooo good. The break was crowded, but nowhere near as crowded as a merely average spot in, say, Southern California. The traffic would make the wave almost unsurfable if it was in California, but this spot is far away from any city and on the edge of the jungle—it takes commitment to get there. It is a magical spot, one I return to as often as I can. And then there is Secrets.

One afternoon our friend, a crazed sixty-year-old French wild man named Fred, called to let us know the conditions would be right to surf Secrets the next day. All I knew of Secrets was that it was on privately owned property, it was not accessible to the public (except by boat, and no one ever took a boat there), and you had to know the land owner, a mysterious man named Sergio, to access the beach. It is called Secrets because its location is, well, a secret (and it shall remain so, so don't bother to ask me). We met Fred at his casa early the next day, loaded up his boards and a picnic lunch prepared by his chef-level-cooking Argentinian wife, Graciela, drove to pick up our friend Eduardo, then headed out into the countryside, traveling dirt roads until we reached a locked gate. Fred got out and unlocked the gate, and we drove a very bumpy five minutes through a gorgeous hilly jungle landscape until the road ended at the top of a cliff.

I got out of the truck and looked down at the ocean and beach below. Except for a single large thatch-roofed wooden house, there were no buildings as far as the eye could see, just an empty stretch of beach at least a mile long that started right where thick jungle ended. Long, beautiful lines rolled in the clear blue sea—even from high above, I could tell the waves were epic...and they were *totally empty.*

This is fucking INSANE, I thought, and we grabbed our gear and walked down a flower-lined path to the beach. The path ended at the house I had spied from above, which was even larger than I thought, two graceful stories constructed of dark wood with an airy top porch and roofed with thatch made from the toquilla palm leaves traditionally used to roof houses in Ecuador. The building reminded me a lot of the graceful seaside open-air-design houses I had seen in Bali, but with a South American flair. A rough-edged bunch of dogs ran out from behind the house barking at us, but Fred yelled at them by name and they gradually calmed down, sniffing our legs and boards, only giving an occasional growl to remind us that this was their beach.

I looked back at the house and up and down the beach but didn't see anyone other than the four of us who had just arrived. "Should we go say hi to Sergio?" I asked. "Are you sure he's cool with us being here?" Fred told me not to worry, that Sergio knew we were coming and was probably taking his afternoon nap—we would say hi later, after we surfed and had lunch. So Fred, Carlos, Eduardo, and I grabbed our boards and paddled out, carefully timing our entry into the sea to avoid waves smashing us into the large rocks that edged the shoreline. We made it outside and then surfed amazing and totally empty waves for a couple of hours.

After we had our fill, we sat on the beach eating a delicious lunch and drinking from a thermos of the brutally strong coffee Fred brewed. I looked around at the empty beach and beautiful jungle and thought, *This is too good to be true.* By this time, the tide had filled in, taking the waves with it, and Fred said in his South American–tinged French accent, "Okay, we go say hello to Sergio now." We left our boards on the beach and walked up the steep and worn wooden stairs to the upper porch of the house, and there was Sergio.

The mysterious Sergio turned out to be a very distinguished seventy-eight-year-old Italian gentleman with an incredible lined face and kind eyes. Sergio had lived and worked all over the world when he was a younger man, and faded photos on the walls showed him in Italy, Egypt, Afghanistan. He had landed in Ecuador, working for an oil company, and had fallen in love—both with a gorgeous Ecuadorean woman and the country itself. He had worked in the Amazon as well, getting to know the native Huaorani tribes there. They had even accepted him to the point that they pierced his ear and stretched it in the traditional manner with a large wooden plug—what is now a fashionable body modification among the tattooed set was a matter of survival that allowed him to travel the Huaorani territory unmolested. The Huaorani were known at that time to kill outsiders, whether by spear, bow and arrow, or poisoned blowgun darts—given the relentless destruction of their home for oil and timber, I do not blame them. Sergio even guided an Italian photographer through the Amazon to shoot photos of these people deep in the jungle. The photos were eventually published as a book, which Sergio pulled down from his shelf to show me.

At some point, Sergio looked at all the destruction the oil and timber industries were causing to the beautiful place he had come to call home and thought, *What am I doing?* He left his job and bought several thousand acres of cleared land on the coast. Then he let the jungle do its thing and take over again. Ecuador lies on the equator, and things grow very fast there—plants flower all year round. The beautiful coastal paradise I had spent the day in had been a bare hillside, ravaged by timber companies, cattle ranchers, and palm oil farmers thirty years before. Now it and adjacent properties owned by people who also had Sergio's conservationist mentality were protected land—nothing would be developed there.

It was an amazing day, and after a nice long chat, it was time to head home. As I was walking back up the hill with my surfboard, I looked around at Sergio's land and thought, *What an amazing place. I wish I had the money to do something like this.*

That was the first of many visits to surf Secrets and talk with Sergio. Every time I visit Ecuador, I make sure to go sit and talk with him over a coffee. He is an amazing and kind man who is doing good things for the planet—but Sergio is also no one to mess with. Once he was driving his old truck through the Ecuadorian countryside when he blew a tire. He pulled over and got out to assess the situation when two young guys rolled up on him, pointed a machete his way, and said, "Hey, old man, give us all your money or else."

"Okay," he replied, "let me get my wallet out of the truck." He reached into his glove box, grabbed his pistol, pointed it at their heads, then calmly told the would-be bandits it was time for them to go to work. Then he held them at gunpoint while they changed his flat tire—*straight gangster. Grande,* Sergio!

I had such a great time on my first surf trip to Ecuador I made it a habit to return whenever my touring schedule allowed so I could visit my newfound friends and ride the amazing waves the country offered. During these trips, I also spent time on the farmland Carlos and his family had bought. Carlos is an environmentalist, and from my very first visit to his country it was apparent that the ongoing destruction of the forests and wetlands by timber operations, monocultural crop farming, the oil industry, and even inland shrimp farming was extremely distressing to him. Ecuador has the highest rate of deforestation in the entire Western Hemisphere, and Carlos often cursed while pointing out examples of this destruction as we traveled from one surf spot to the next. In an attempt to mitigate some of this damage like Sergio, Carlos had bought some beaten-down land

and was letting it restore itself while farming some of it using the concepts of permaculture and leaving the existing forest alone.

Permaculture is a permanent agricultural system developed by a Tasmanian academic and biologist named Bill Mollison and a Western Australian environmental design writer named David Holmgren. The basis of permaculture is working as closely as possible with nature to design an agricultural system that resembles natural cycles, using specific plants in a symbiotic manner that nurtures the earth rather than strips it of nutrients the way monocultural farming methods do. Endlessly planting the same crops over and over, crops like oil palms and pineapples (which are grown almost exclusively for the export market), depletes the soil and destroys the living ecosystems; permaculture restores them.

I became familiar with the basic concepts of permaculture after my friend Cody Lundin, a well-known survival and primitive-living skills instructor from Arizona, showed me how he used permaculture principles to build his amazing self-heating and -cooling earthship home out in the desert. Carlos and his family were using these same concepts in a much more fertile region, and the results were impressive. With each trip to Ecuador, I watched his land grow greener and greener, and he always had a different new and delicious fruit for me to try fresh off the vine. Other people we know, both Ecuadorean and expatriate, owned land adjacent to his farm and were doing the same thing, letting the jungle take back over. My friends were building an ecozone that stretched from Carlos's land to Sergio's coastal paradise, trying to save what they could. It was beautiful to see.

In January 2020, I was back in Ecuador, surfing epic waves with Carlos and visiting my friends. During that trip, Carlos pointed out a piece of beaten-down cattle-grazing land across the road from his farm and Fred's house. "It's for sale, you know. You should think about buying it," he told me for what seemed like the millionth time.

"Yes, yes—I know. Maybe one day," I replied, and then we went over to Fred's for dinner.

At the end of that trip, I received some very distressing personal news, and I returned to the United States in February with a heart full of sadness and confusion. My life had been turned upside down, and I did not know what to do with myself. Then, in less than a month, the coronavirus pandemic that had been swiftly spreading across the planet hit the United States, and *everyone's* lives were turned upside down. The pandemic was in full swing, killing massive numbers of people across the globe. I was reeling from all the chaos, both personal and global, when Carlos sent me a text message.

"Hey, *hermano*, I know right now is not a good time for you or anyone else. But I need to tell you that the people selling the land I showed you have dropped the price. Now would be a very good time to move on this before someone else does."

Jesus Christ, dude, now is definitely not *the time for this*, I thought. *My life is exploding and the world is falling to fucking pieces.* I was overwhelmed and teared up in frustration.

Then I sat and thought about it for a second.

You know what, dude? Fuck it, I thought. *Now is the* perfect time *to do this*.

So I texted Carlos back and told him I was in. Two days later, I took a large chunk from my savings and wired the money to Ecuador, and Carlos's family began the process of purchasing the land, land I hadn't even ever set foot on. In the midst of all the sadness and chaos, I had found a bit of happiness—I was doing something good for the world instead of sitting around on my ass crying and feeling sorry for myself. I felt good about buying the land. I would let it return to its natural state, and this would benefit everyone. And, yes, it was expensive, but fuck it. My band had just recorded a new album, it would be coming out soon, and I would make the money back when we went back on tour to support the record. This pandemic had to be over soon, right? *Right?*

Wrong. The pandemic stretched on, the record release kept getting delayed, and we continued to not go on tour. In fact, *nobody* was going on tour—cramming a bunch of people into an enclosed space is how I make my living, but pretty much every venue on the planet had been shut down. I couldn't complain, though. I live simply, and I had enough money saved to last me a couple of years if I watched my budget. But millions of others were not as financially stable as me; many people fell behind on their mortgages and lost their homes. I watched beloved local businesses, some that I had patronized for decades, shut their doors forever. I felt particularly bad for touring-crew personnel and folks working in the service industry—the guitar techs, lighting directors, bus drivers, merch guys and gals, cooks, bartenders, and waitstaff were all struggling to make rent and feed their families. These were my people because for most of my working life I have either been onstage or in a kitchen. When concert venues and restaurants are empty, these people don't make money, so I did what I could to help out with a few charities for them, and I felt lucky to be in the position to do so. As well, many sober folks relapsed—the stress overwhelmed them, and they turned to the only thing they knew for relief: the bottle or a baggie of drugs. A record number of deaths from drug overdoses occurred during the pandemic (over 93,000 in 2020 alone), so I focused on staying sober myself and being available to those who needed help. (By the way, shout-out to all the folks who got sober during the pandemic. I don't know how in the fuck y'all did it. You're stronger people than me.)

I was okay, even grateful at times for how the world had slowed down a bit. But as the pandemic stretched on and on and tours kept getting endlessly rescheduled or canceled altogether, I began to worry as I watched my bank account balance steadily shrink. *Fuck, dude—you need to figure out how to make that cash spent on the land back,* I thought. *This COVID bullshit might last longer than we think.*

Then I remembered Cameo.

Cameo is a service where people pay "celebrities" of all sorts to record a video greeting. Most of the time it's something like a husband wanting his wife's favorite actor to wish her a happy birthday or parents who get their kid's favorite guitar player to congratulate him on graduating high school. The people at Cameo had contacted me several times in recent years, telling me they thought I would be good at it— that I could actually make money with my cell phone instead of merely doom-scrolling the news (a horrible addiction I struggle with to this day). Several musician friends were on Cameo, and they indeed made decent cash for just playing with their cell phones. It had been tempting, but I do not consider myself a "celebrity"; it seemed like just another pain-in-the-ass thing I would have to deal with, plus I was riddled with punk rock guilt at the thought of signing up for it.

Punk rock guilt is a very specific kind of guilt, rather hard to explain if you don't come from the punk scene. Rooted in the antiauthoritarian, anti–mindless consumerism, and (ahem) anti–rock star mentality historically prevalent among members of a subculture that consciously rejects societal definitions of "success," punk rock guilt is a sort of self-imposed combination of tall poppy syndrome and Catholic guilt (but without the threat of burning in eternal flames if you fail to say enough Hail Marys or whatever). In this case, punk rock guilt was the harsh and judgmental voice in my head saying, *Dude, there are starving children in war-torn Syria, and you actually want to take someone's hard-earned money for singing their girlfriend "Happy Birthday"? There was a massive earthquake in Indonesia the other day, thousands are dead, and you are going to let a hard-working single mom with two jobs pay you to congratulate her son on graduating high school? That's criminally selfish,* dude. *Oh, and by the way, just who in the flying fuck do you think you are, Elvis Presley? Are you some kind of* rock star *now—is that what's happening here? It sounds like you've forgotten where you came from and what you're supposed to be about. Just look at the website—"celebrity video greetings"—what the fuck? Black Flag never sold their ass and sang anyone "Happy Birthday" into an iPhone, you egomaniacal douchebag.* And so I always blew off the Cameo people— it just wasn't my style, and the punk rock guilt always raised its spiky head the second I thought about it.

Frankly, I think the entire world could use a massive dose of punk rock guilt from time to time. People might not be so goddamned selfish and egotistical then. But left unbridled, my punk rock guilt can also get out of control, causing me to lose sight of reality. My reality was that I had just slapped down a large amount of my savings to buy land in a country I couldn't even currently visit, my primary form of income (touring) had totally disappeared, I had no idea if and when it would ever come back, and rent was still due at the first of every month. I knew I had enough money left to be okay for a while, but after spending most of my adulthood in a drunken haze of financial irresponsibility, I had finally begun to understand the fable of the grasshopper and the ant. For years I had bounced around like the reckless grasshopper, blowing an obscene amount of cash on useless things: stuff like booze, drugs, and chintzy remote-control robots that caught my eye when I wandered into truck stops on tour, higher than an eagle's nuts on said booze and drugs. Now that I had stopped drinking, I wanted to be more and more like the ant, saving up provisions for the hard times and winter ahead. Winter had indeed arrived, and though I was fine for the moment, I would be a complete idiot if I counted on something as already precarious as the music business suddenly returning to normal. I didn't regret purchasing the land at all, because it was simply the right thing to do, and I will *never* regret doing the right thing—but doing the right thing can definitely come at a cost.

The land was bought, but we still needed money to fence it off so cattle would not destroy the new vegetation we hoped would grow. We needed money to pay for heavy machinery to break up the barren and compacted earth, hard as brick after decades of being trampled by grazing cows, in order to plant that vegetation. We needed money to have a scientist test the soil, to have a surveyor survey the land, to buy seedlings, to pay people to plant those seedlings—we needed *money, money, money* . . . and I wasn't making any.

So I thought about it and realized that I'd better start singing some happy birthday songs if I wanted to try to save the planet and still be able to pay rent. Though we were already planting trees, money didn't grow on any of them. So I kicked the ol' punk rock guilt in the balls, made a Cameo account, explained what I was doing and why on my social media account, and started getting paid to wish fans a Merry Christmas, Happy Father's Day, and congratulations on finishing up parole without any violations.

From the beginning, I have done nothing but act like the ridiculous buffoon that I am, and most of the time it's actually a lot of fun. I've even gotten to meet some of the people who have supported the project by ordering a Cameo, and they have all been lovely folks. I don't know if I will do it forever, but so far I've been able to make back my initial investment and then some, money which I have promptly spent on buying more property adjacent to my existing land, expanding this ecozone even farther. I started off buying nine hectares of land, then bought one more hectare connected to that, then four more hectares connected to that. As of this writing, I have managed to buy fourteen hectares, or roughly thirty-five acres of land—this translates into approximately 26.5 football fields, all paid for by singing "Happy Birthday" to fans of my band. Connected to my land is another thirteen hectares that Carlos, his family, and a couple of his other friends have purchased, bringing us up to twenty-seven hectares total—or almost fifty-one football fields of land that we have planted with indigenous trees and fruits while preserving existing forests. The land is green again, and when I walk it my heart swells with happiness.

But why should people far away from this land, folks who will never see what we have done there, even care? Well, if they enjoy breathing, that's a good enough reason. Trees and rainforests make about 28 percent of the planet's oxygen;

microscopic plants in the ocean produce the rest. As for me, I know that maybe what we are doing won't ultimately make a difference, maybe humanity is too far gone already, but at least I'll go down swinging. When I die, this land will be my final gift to the planet, wild and savage and untamed in its beauty, a lush and verdant green middle finger to the ever-encroaching concrete.

In the meantime, Carlos and I have been trying to figure out how to make this project sustainable in an economic sense, not just for us but for the local people in the area. My code of ethics will not let me be just another gringo buying land, fencing it off, and smugly patting myself on the back for taking an environmental stance. Some of the land we will farm in a sustainable manner, and to do this we need to pay local people a fair and livable wage. Saving the environment is not a top priority for most people who live in poverty—feeding their family is. Poverty directly impacts the local environment in ways most of us don't think about because we don't see it. But because the planet is one huge interconnected ecosystem, there's really no such thing as a "local environment"; there is just *the environment*, and what affects one place eventually affects all places.

Those of us who live in affluent nations must remember this when we look down our pampered noses at poorer countries and judge them for things like high crime rates, poor environmental conditions, and lack of infrastructure. A few years ago the president of the United States famously referred to some of these places as "shithole countries" during a meeting with congressional leaders and cabinet members, but Americans and people in other prosperous nations would do well to realize that all our convenience and luxury always, always, *always* come at a cost to someone else. The materials used in the manufacture of all the goods made to meet our incessant demand for whatever we want, whenever we want it, delivered to wherever we want have to come from *somewhere*. Guess where that somewhere is? I have seen evidence of this all over the world in the form of depleted natural resources. In Ecuador, friends of mine have received death threats for organizing locals to take a stand against the illegal mining of a beautiful black-sand beach. The sand contains high amounts of titanium, a mineral that is used in countless objects that sit in my house and around yours as well, things like my iPhone and the iPad I type this on as well as a million other things that I can order online without a second thought using that iPhone, some of which will arrive overnight on an airplane constructed of titanium as well.

Natural beauty and resources valuable to local people in these "shithole countries" are constantly being destroyed for an endless parade of *stuff* we don't really need, but we don't ever see the actual cost of all this *stuff* because it's only immediately affecting people who are far away, out of sight and out of mind. Activities that are destroying the environment like the illegal mining my friends received freaking death threats for standing up to wouldn't be so prevalent in the first place if everyone were informed enough to sit back and think about the consequences of their actions. We are consuming ourselves to death. In the span of our lifetime, this is occurring at what seems like a glacial pace, but in the span of humanity's existence, it's happening at warp speed. I am trying my best to help arrest that process of decay with our reforestation project.

Aside from environmental destruction, the thing I fear the most for this tiny emerald nation I love so much is the increasing presence of narco traffickers and the inevitable gang violence that accompanies them. Ecuador is bordered by Colombia and Peru, two of the world's top producers of cocaine, but was previously known as South America's *isla de paz* (island of peace). For decades, it had one of the lowest homicide rates in all South America. But international drug traffickers have moved in, turning Ecuador into a hub on the export route of cocaine to the United States and Europe. A plague of violence, often directed from the gang-controlled prisons, has exploded onto the previously peaceful streets of Ecuadorean cities as rival organized crime groups fight to control the drug trade. As of this writing (2024), the homicide rate in Ecuador has more than quadrupled since 2018, and headless bodies have been found hanging from bridges. Such scenes were previously unthinkable, the province of Mexican border towns like Juarez and Tijuana. But the Mexican drug cartels, Colombian crime groups and paramilitary organizations, and even the Albanian mafia have established strong footholds in the country, both physically and politically. Car bombings, extortion and protection rackets, police assassinations, kidnappings, the public execution of a presidential candidate who spoke out against narco violence, and most recently the armed takeover of a television station by masked members of a drug gang who warned Ecuadorean politicians against interfering with their business have left a terrifying stain on the people of this once peaceful nation, and there has been a surge of people leaving the country as it becomes a cocaine superhighway. In a few short years, Ecuador has become one of the most violent countries in South America.

Again, this is due to consumers in more prosperous countries. Various European nations, the United Kingdom, Australia, and the United States lead the world in cocaine consumption. In the law of supply and demand, we are the demand. Although local drug use is becoming more and more of a problem, the vast majority of cocaine that passes through Ecuador goes straight up the noses of consumers out for a fun evening thousands of miles away from the jungle compounds where it is produced.

I do not have a clean conscience in this matter. Before I got sober, I snorted enough lines of Bolivian marching powder to keep the population of a midsize city up for two weeks straight. If I am honest with myself, my drug use fueled the violent deaths in Mexico, Colombia, Peru, and other places. No, I didn't chop off anyone's head and hang them from a bridge, but I was part of the equation. During the crack epidemic of the eighties and nineties, I disassociated myself from the problem because I didn't smoke crack—I just snorted coke if it was that kind of party. *Hey, everyone does a little blow from time to time, right?* But crack comes from coke, and coke comes from South America, which was a loooong way away from Richmond, Virginia. I did not think about the broader human cost of my good time because I did not see it—I was blind. But I have seen it with my own two eyes now.

If you've never seen the body of an executed man lying lifeless on the road beside you after the top of his head was blown off by a shotgun, you might not think about this too much. But that's what I saw the last time I was in Ecuador, and it's not a pretty sight. I have done more drugs than most, so I cannot judge anyone, but if you are reading this and like to party, the next time you decide to do a little toot, you should know the true cost of that baggie of white powder is violence of a scope you have only ever seen in horror movies. People will die violent deaths just so that you can stay up later spouting all sorts of pathetically sincere nonsense that you will not act on the next day when you come down and feel like death.

Regardless of how you feel about the legalization of drugs, the undeniable current reality is that our appetite for a good time is contributing to death, poverty, and the destabilization of an entire country. Most people out for a night on the town don't ever think about this because it is far removed from their current chemically enhanced reality, but this is hard, cold truth, like it or not: our actions get other people killed. When the big tobacco companies were finally called to the carpet after years of misleading advertising, they paid out billions of dollars in lawsuits. But who is going to sue a Mexican drug cartel? Or the Albanian mafia? So, ask yourself, is staying up way too long and grinding your teeth to bits worth perpetuating this shit? On an ethical level, the answer can only be no.

Carlos's childhood friend Vico was shot and killed in March 2023 near the border of Ecuador and Peru while heading out on a surf trip. He and another surfer named Rody from Argentina stopped at the wrong place at the wrong time, and now they are both dead from narco gun violence. Vico was a funny guy, and a great surfer—I caught my fair share of waves with him, and we had many laughs during my visits to Ecuador. He was also a conservationist and first on board to help Carlos when Carlos began our reforestation project. When Carlos went home to Ecuador for Vico's funeral, even in his sadness and grief he took the opportunity to plant seven hundred more plants on our properties. We cannot stop. Vico will be there in the barrel during low, mid, and high tide with us when we surf, telling us that this work must continue.

And violence or no violence, we *will* continue it. This planet, our only home, demands it.

All this was set in motion because one afternoon I looked to the sea and decided to try doing something that looks pointless. I never would have met Carlos otherwise, much less bought a bunch of messed-up land in Ecuador and started returning it to a healthy state. Surfing took me there, and while surfing I saw a problem.

Surf tourism has gotten bigger and bigger as flights get cheaper and technology causes more and more previously isolated spots to get mapped out. Beautiful resorts are built directly in front of some of the finest breaks on earth. People can fly in, stay at the resort, surf incredible waves, enjoy very affordable chef-cooked meals, then fly home full of stoke. But the locals who live in these areas still struggle to survive. If we as a surfing community want to truly respect the ocean and the land connected to it, we must remember this and find viable ways to share our wealth. The law of supply and demand cuts both ways: there is an inexhaustible supply of waves to meet our demands, so how can we help supply these people's basic needs? It's great to go to faraway countries where the waves are excellent and the living is cheap, but it's wrong to just show up, take advantage of the waves, and leave without giving anything in return. As surfing tourism grows, this aspect of the culture must grow with it.

As for me and Carlos, we're just two dudes trying to figure it out on our own the best we can with what resources we have. We'll keep on talking and dreaming and planting trees and hustling because that is part of the mentality as well—we don't wait for someone else, we do it ourselves. If we don't, who will?

But we will damn sure take plenty of breaks to go surf Secrets when it's firing.

What will yeeeeewwwwwwww do?

Chapter Eight

YOU'RE NEVER ALONE

For a few years now, I have been periodically experiencing the return of an emotional state that characterized much of my youth: a feeling of not belonging or fitting in anywhere. Although the world is (in theory) becoming more and more "connected," as of late whenever I open my computer or pick up my phone to read the news, answer a call, check a text message, read an email, or look at the posts of people I follow on my lone social media account, paradoxically, I immediately feel a need to *detach*. All these supposed connections are overwhelming me, and it's become too much to keep up with.

Each day when I plunge into the swirling sea of chaos that is the internet, I swim along beside millions of other disembodied minds, all voicing a million different opinions on a million different issues, and many of those opinions are increasingly expressed as dogmatic screams. I do not enjoy being screamed at, even in a virtual space. I am drowning in this turbulent and deafening electronic ocean, and every time I try to grab ahold of something solid to keep me afloat, the current violently switches paths with the storm surge of the latest tragedy or outrage, ripping from my hands whatever bit of stability I had. I try to employ critical thinking, searching for varied reputable and academically credentialed sources of information in order to examine current issues from different perspectives, but it's a hard slog through a nightmarish swamp of angry opinions, bizarre conspiracy theories, politically motivated misinformation, and the endless parade of distracting ads for things I don't truly need fed directly to me by algorithms optimized to drain my bank account one bright and shiny gadget at a time.

In my attempts to stay both connected and informed in this vast digital sea, I struggle daily to reach a solid bit of informational land where I have enough space to maintain friendships and walk the ground of empirical truth. But the sea is vast, the shoreline keeps receding into the horizon, and the longer I swim in this chaotic crowd, the more alone I feel. How can I feel so isolated surrounded by all these people?

Of course, I'm not actually surrounded by "all these people," and I don't "belong" *anywhere* on the internet. I belong here, in the physical world, where there are actual people, friends and family I can hug and smell and look in the eye and laugh with until my sides ache after they make a hilarious joke at my expense (my favorite variety of joke). I'm feeling isolated because I am isolating myself, not actually experiencing life; in reality, I'm just sitting here looking at my phone.

The illusion of connection is a powerful narcotic, and like the tastiest narcotics, it's highly addictive. And just like those narcotics, if you mess around too much, you'll wind up strung out and alone, endlessly hitting the refresh button on the hunt to cop just one more cheap endorphin hit from the glowing screen. If you think I'm being dramatic about this, just take a walk through any city and note how many people are shuffling along like zombies, lost in their own little world, eyes glued to their smartphones as they move through the physical realm utterly oblivious to their surroundings. It's a completely batshit-crazy way to exist, but of course it is by design: welcome to the attention economy, dude.

However, once I put down the phone and take a drive to visit my family or go surfing with the homies or just have an actual in-person conversation with some friends at a house party barbecue, the illusion of isolation vanishes like a cheap parlor trick. Regrettably, I can't spend all my time visiting my mom, surfing with my buddies Patty and Andrew, or grilling chicken wings in my guitarist Mark's backyard. My various jobs and the logistics of merely existing in this modern society dictate the use of a cell phone, email addresses, and computers, but the addictive design of these tools consumes way too much of my time beyond their necessary functions.

So, like a compulsive overeater, I periodically put myself on digital diets, only to eventually wind up bingeing again and again on the endless supply of mental junk food that cyberspace lobs my way in relentless volleys of distraction grenades. Inevitably, informational bloat leaves me isolated and confused, not informed, not connected, and I feel like that outsider teenager again until I reengage with the real world.

It was often quite unpleasant being that outsider teenager, but at least things were much simpler back then. Of course, that is the inherent nature of youth itself, but I do believe that in a very quantifiable way, today's world is shifting and changing at a much more rapid pace than at any other time in history, including during my teenage years. The incessantly negative 24/7 news cycle moves so swiftly that it is almost impossible to grasp the true impact of any current event with any form of big-picture clarity before the next tragedy is thrust onto our overloaded consciousness. With so much constant data being blasted our way, we are not given the time to mentally digest anything. Technological advances are moving forward at such blinding speed that the very same people responsible for the invention of things like artificial intelligence are freaked out—they do not understand their own creation or how it is behaving and are issuing public warnings about the potential existential threat facing the human race from our carelessly rapid and unregulated adoption of AI. Modern human beings (*Homo sapiens sapiens*) have existed for roughly 150,000 years, and during that time the human brain has evolved and advanced in functional cognitive ability, but mental capacity has improved at a glacial pace compared to the very recent evolution of communications and information technology.

It took our brains approximately 144,000 years to invent the wheel, but in a tiny fraction of that time, computers have evolved from apartment-size behemoths to the smartphone. ENIAC, the first fully programmable electronic general-purpose computer, was completed in 1945. It cost around $500,000 to build (over $8 million in today's money), was eight feet tall, a hundred feet long, and weighed more than twenty-seven tons. ENIAC required an entire crew of programmers to make it function—six brilliantly skilled and highly educated women proficient in conceptualizing and solving complex mathematical equations. Less than a century later, ten-year-old children effortlessly operate portable tablet computers, a flat piece of seven-by-ten-inch plastic and glass less than a quarter inch thick that is literally millions of times more powerful than ENIAC.

The ramifications of this ever-quickening techno-acceleration are (and have been) manifesting in troubling ways.

Once again, to put things in perspective: it took the human race the vast majority of our existence, well over *one hundred thousand years*, to arrive at the conclusion that riding in a horse-drawn cart was more efficient than walking. Conversely, in less than a century, computers transformed from

(1) a single primitive school-bus-size number cruncher that only six mostly unsung genius-level women possessing advanced mathematics skills could operate into (2) ubiquitous pocket-size devices with godlike computational power that a high school boy can use to instantly manufacture and distribute fake pornographic images of his fourteen-year-old female classmates, as recently happened in New Jersey.

The fact that teenagers have ready access to tools that can instantly create highly realistic photos of any warped version of reality their hormone-addled brains can dream up tells me that it just might be time for us to slow way the fuck down and ask a few questions before blindly embracing every new technological advance touted by all those slick Silicon Valley PR firms. Adults think with the prefrontal cortex, the segment of the brain that controls rationality—you know, that stuff that concerns itself with things like evaluating the potentially damaging long-term consequences of our actions. In teenagers, the prefrontal cortex isn't fully developed, so they tend to filter information primarily through the amygdala, the part of the brain that deals with emotion—you know, the stuff that makes you instantly lose your shit when someone cuts you off in traffic. The synaptic bridge that connects the two isn't fully developed until around age twenty-five, yet over one billion of the young humans who tend to process the world with the road-rage section of their noodle are handed these reality-altering tools as a matter of course. The end results are, and will continue to be, painfully predictable.

There's a *very good* reason you often hear people of my generation and older say "THANK GOD there were no smartphones or social media when I was in high school."

When I was a child, I had a pen pal in Japan. (Shout-out to Isao Tsuchihashi, wherever you may be.) We would send each other actual handwritten letters through the mail, detailing the small events in our lives. It was almost magical whenever I received one of his letters—the oddly different style of envelope, the strange *katakana* postmarks imprinted on beautifully artistic stamps, even the smell of the vellum stationery his incredibly precise penmanship marched across in orderly black lines. We wrote each other about once a month, but to place an actual phone call to him never once crossed my mind, as it would have certainly resulted in my death—my father would have murdered me the second he saw the long-distance phone bill. Today, I can choose from a multitude of apps on my phone to instantaneously send a text or even call Nami-san, my tattoo artist in Osaka, and I can do this practically for free. Our ability to instantly connect with other people anywhere around the globe (thus, theoretically, building "community") is often touted as one of the best aspects of the internet, but this connection carries a heavy cognitive load as well. Despite what cell phone company advertisements try to sell us ("Get connected to anyone, anywhere, *faster!*"), you simply can't "connect" to everyone everywhere all the time. In fact, science has shown that we are simply not built to maintain relationships with so many people.

Dunbar's number is a principle named after the British anthropologist Robin Dunbar, who studied the relationship between the brain size of nonhuman primates and the average size of social groups. He then took his findings and compared them with different human social groups. Dunbar was trying to find a number that represented the upper cognitive limit of how many stable social relationships a person could maintain. In his research, he examined communities from many different eras and areas, from Neolithic farming villages to twentieth-century hunter-gatherer societies such as the southern African San to modern textile companies. Again and again, the average number of sustainable stable social relationships he arrived at was 150. In his 1998 book, *Grooming, Gossip, and the Evolution of Language*, Dunbar writes, "The figure of 150 seems to represent the maximum number of individuals with whom we can have a genuinely social relationship, the kind of relationship that goes with knowing who they are and how they relate to us. Putting it another way, it's the number of people you would not feel embarrassed about joining uninvited for a drink if you happened to bump into them in a bar." The scientists H. Russell Bernard and Peter Killworth disagreed with Dunbar, so they did their own research, eventually arriving at an estimated mean number of 290, almost double Dunbar's sum. Two hundred and ninety different people is *a lot* of folks to be knocking back a few friendly shots with at the bar (although I'm positive I easily exceeded that number in my drinking days).

Looking in the contacts section of my phone, I see that I have 2,130 entries. As an experiment, I scanned my entire contacts list, doing a quick and sloppy count of all my musician friends. With each musician, I envisioned their face and imagined their voice as I looked at their contact details. These are my friends, people I know, and I could very easily tell an amusing story about hanging out with each and every one of them. After thirty minutes of counting, I realize that I personally know over 350 musicians—*just musicians*. That number doesn't include all the guitar techs, tour managers, lighting designers, record producers, bus drivers, record label execs, sound engineers, radio DJs, merch sellers, music video directors, and concert photographers who populate that part of my world—I have phone numbers for all those people, too. Obviously, I don't talk to each of these folks every day (except backstage during the summer Euro festival touring season, when every single band on earth arrives on the Continent at the same time to play together—it's freaking nuts), but when I consider the number of people I know from the music world alone, it seems *crazy*. I love all my friends and wouldn't give a single one of them up, but it gets rough trying to stay in touch with so many people. Thank God I despise talking on the phone (I'm a let's-have-a-good-conversation-when-we-actually-see-each-other-in-person kinda guy) or I would never get anything done at all.

If a human being can effectively maintain only 150 (or even 290) relationships in the real world, then no wonder I feel so goddamned crazy every time I look at social media.

I mean, I don't run down the streets of Richmond, Virginia, approaching random strangers to tell them they could afford to lose a few pounds, and I don't get embroiled in a screaming match over their political views or seethe aloud with envy at their "perfect" vacation or explain to them that science isn't actually real or even yell at them that their favorite band *fuckin' sucks, duuuude*. That is *lunatic* behavior, but it is the norm online, and more and more, people simply accept all this craziness, saying, "Oh, that's just the internet." That may indeed be so, but apparently a sizable segment of "just the internet" is a gigantic steaming pile of useless crazy-making *shit*. Obviously, I am not a Luddite, as I use the internet all the time, but let's face it: mentally, we are still Stone Age humans stumbling around in a virtual Space Age world, *and it shows*. It's like putting a toddler behind the wheel of a Ferrari—that's just way too much power for a baby, baby. Bad shit is bound to happen.

More and more, I've been getting the feeling that I was not built for these times, and even as a fifty-something man who has developed some adult coping skills, it makes sense that I often feel lost in them—it's just way too much of everything, all the time. All this to say that when I stop being a grumpy old man long enough to really consider it, in so many ways the youth of today face far more complex difficulties than I could have ever imagined when I was a kid. My teenage years were confusing enough—I did *a lot* of stupid shit, and I wasn't surrounded by an iPhone-wielding mob just frothing at the mouth to document my every fuckup. I've been alive for over half a century. If I'm still confused by today's world, how in the hell does a fifteen-year-old feel?

As a child, I always felt a little different from my peers. As a teenager in the mid-eighties, this morphed and solidified into feelings of anger, isolation, and general other-than-ness. For a very short period, I tried to "fit in," but I just couldn't seem to make it work. I wasn't interested in the things most people my age were, and I caught a fair amount of grief because of that. I was far more interested in reading books, skateboarding (and back then, it wasn't *cool* to be a skate-boarder like it is now), and trying to grasp the intricacies of Cold War geopolitics than in playing sports, showing off my new sneakers, or riding around in muscle cars and jacked up pickup trucks cruising for chicks who didn't want to talk to me in the first place. I was *a nerd*, and I couldn't have afforded to do most of that "cool guy" stuff anyway—my family didn't have that much money, we didn't live in the "right" neighbor-hood, and I didn't wear the newest name-brand clothes.

I didn't understand why any of that stuff mattered (I mean, I was a good person—wasn't that supposed to be the important thing?), but some of the boneheads I went to school with made it their mission to remind me on a daily basis that I was somehow not up to their petty standards. As well, it can be difficult being a bright kid, and though I'm not claiming that I was some sort of child genius, in my first year of high school I had a Phys Ed teacher mock and ridicule me in front of an entire class because I read too articulately from a health sciences textbook (he was a massive meathead who loved to remind us that he was once drafted to the NFL but got dropped after blowing out his knee during the first week of training camp—he was great at teaching dudes how to be offensive linemen, but not so great at the whole "reading thing," which is kinda important for teachers). When you finally make it to high school and the *fucking teachers* publicly humiliate you for being too well-spoken, pretty quickly you begin to feel disconnected from everyone who surrounds you. You observe the behavior of the people around you and begin to see how shallow and inane much of it is. Inevitably one thought begins to dominate your consciousness:

FUCK ALL Y'ALL—I gotta get outta here.

That's what happened to me, and it shaped my personality. I am fascinated by humans in general, I love talking with all varieties of them, and I can almost always find common ground in conversation with any *reasonable* person, no matter their background. I do not walk around with some ridiculous childhood chip on my shoulder against people who have always felt accepted from birth because I am a grown-ass man who finds that sort of long-term reactionary emotional state embarrassing and infantile. But, ultimately, I know I am still the most comfortable around those who grew up feeling like oddballs simply because some perceived *difference* was often deemed unsavory by the larger social group they moved through during their youth. These are my people, my tribe, and in our shared past inability to feel like we fit in much of anywhere, we can usually relate to each other almost effortlessly. This nerve-wracking social pressure to "fit in" is still being applied to outsider kids everywhere because life and society and young people tend to be cruel and savage, with an ugly tendency to do their best to break down the weirdos among them.

Tragically, in 1999, almost exactly ten years after I left high school, two weirdo outsider kids armed themselves with guns and homemade bombs, marched into Columbine High School in Littleton, Colorado, and began executing their teachers and classmates before blowing their own brains out in the school library. Although there had been school shootings before, an unprecedented and staggering amount of in-depth media attention was given to every single minute detail of the premeditated and methodical savagery that unfolded at Columbine. This global news blitz inadvertently provided a template for future members of a student assassin association that has only grown in numbers during the years since. Because they are both dead, it is impossible to accurately psychoanalyze either of the Columbine shooters, but after decades of examining the available evidence, it is generally accepted by mental health experts that one of the shooters was a psychopath and the other was a suicidally depressed kid who was pulled along—these were not merely bullied outsiders. Regardless, whether the result of severe mental illness, negative social stressors, or some combination of both, the Columbine shooters' actions provided a violent blueprint for disaffected kids yearning to release their rage at the world, a blueprint that continues to be followed with deadly results (over two decades later, many school mass shooters have been infatuated with Columbine). Columbine-inspired school shootings inspire other school shootings, which inspire other school shootings, et cetera, et cetera, ad nauseam, and the cycle continues as the mythological pantheon of vengeful outcast legends grows. Broken and deeply disturbed kids see how much attention school shooters get, and when they have run out of ways to deal with their pain, they emulate what they see on the news and internet and become murderers. Then they go to prison for the rest of their lives or (more commonly) are shot by police or die by their own hand.

Regardless of what anyone feels is the root cause of these tragedies—overly permissive gun legislation, misinterpretation of the Second Amendment, unenforced red flag laws, lax methods of parenting, inadequate mental health care in the United States, the breakdown of the nuclear family structure, a lack of armed security guards or even armed teachers, violent movies and video games, drug abuse, social media, the internet in general, or even heavy metal bands such as my own (and all these things have been repeatedly blamed for school shootings over the years)—the facts are that somehow kids keep on obtaining guns, school shootings keep on happening, and these shootings happen almost *exclusively* in America. And whichever side of the gun debate you sit on—whether you're marching down the street in a Don't Tread on Me tactical leisure suit and toting an AK-47 and waving a sign that reads FROM MY COLD, DEAD HANDS or making plans to super-glue yourself face-down nude to the NRA president's car hood with "Blood on your hands" spray-painted across your ass cheeks (and I fall somewhere in the middle of these two extremes), when you look at the historical data you cannot deny the irrefutable fact that there has been a horrifying paradigm shift for the worse, and this shift has occurred recently, during my lifetime. From a young age, kids today are accustomed to active shooter drills, but if a teacher had walked into a classroom when I was in the seventh grade and said, "Okay, class, today we are going to go over what we will do if someone comes into school with a gun and starts shooting," I would have been utterly bewildered. *Why on earth would anyone do that?* This sort of thing just didn't happen when I was in school.

To make things even weirder: I spent most of my school years in a rural community. Often guns were on school property, and those guns were openly brought there by students. Many times I saw muddy pickups pull into the school parking lot during fall hunting season, a 12-gauge shotgun or two cradled in truck cab gun racks, with the occasional field-dressed deer carcass laid out in the pickup bed. A student who had been in a tree stand hunting since dawn would get out with bits of forest floor still stuck to their boots, lock their truck, and walk into school. You could see the guns sitting in the parking lot all day long—yes, as inconceivable as it is today, there were loaded firearms out in the open and easily accessible *on school property*. It just wasn't a big deal. (Of course, we also had a smoking tree on the side of the school where students were allowed to go burn a quick cigarette between classes—different times indeed.) However, *not once*, not even during my wildest fourth-period algebra daydreams, did I *ever* imagine that someone would march into class and start randomly shooting us. I certainly never imagined doing so myself, not even to the redneck jock bullies I despised. Engaging in that level of violence was inconceivable to me.

What has happened to our youth? I do not know. I just know that *something* has changed. Although school shootings are not everyday occurrences, and statistically it's still highly unlikely that any student will be the victim of a mass shooting, it is a matter of empirical fact that these shootings have increased in both frequency and body count. We as a nation have become numb to these events, internalizing them as a terrifying yet unavoidable aspect of living in our country, akin to natural disasters like hurricanes or tornadoes, the environmental collateral damage of twenty-first-century America. Sure, every time someone snaps and then kills a bunch of kids in a school—whether the shooter is a student, a former student, or a random outsider—there is an immediate expression of outrage. We wring our hands and call for change and offer thoughts and prayers on social media for a week or two…and then we move on until the next group of students gets slaughtered like fish in a barrel. I remember very clearly sitting in the back of my tour bus on December 14, 2012, and weeping uncontrollably as I read the news of the shooting at Sandy Hook Elementary School in Newtown, Connecticut. Twenty children died that day, all between six and seven years old. *Surely something's got to give,* I thought. *Enough is enough—they were first-graders, for God's sake. We can't just keep on going on like this.*

Nope—obviously, we can. A little over a decade later and I can't even keep all the school shootings that have happened in two years alone straight in my head—I won't even mention all the "regular" mass shootings that have happened in nonscholastic settings because that's too depressing to even contemplate. It's wild we live this way, because just in case you didn't know: the rest of the world thinks we're *fucking crazy.* I know this because I tour the world for a living and I've talked about our school shootings with people on every single continent on the face of the planet with the exception of Antarctica. (I haven't been that far south yet, but I'd bet good money that even the penguins think we're nuts.) No wonder mental health professionals have documented a marked rise in anxiety among children and adolescents. I'd be anxious, too, if I was a kid today. Possibly getting blown away just wasn't part of the deal when I climbed on the school bus in the 1980s.

Regardless of the *why,* the *how* is painfully evident, and that is what we must deal with in the short term, as in *right now.* In my opinion, Pandora's box was waiting to be opened, and once it was at Columbine, the murderous plague inside attached itself to the super-spreader that is the internet and mass media and took us to where we are today. As a pragmatic, reality-based person, I am sick of all the handwringing and thoughts and prayers. Although empathy is obviously important, it isn't bulletproof. Employing said empathy, I've tried imagining what it would be like to be in high school now, to put myself in the modern-day student's shoes, and the outcome has been grim. Way back in 1986, long before all this shit started happening, fifteen-year-old Randy was already pissed off that he had to get up and go to school every morning. A fifteen-year-old Randy today? The very next day after a bunch of kids got shot, he'd have some choice words on the topic.

"You want *what*? You want me to go to *school*? Nah, I'm good—in fact, why don't *you* carry *your* ass to school, okay? *You* can go get shot the fuck up, since *you, the adults who are supposed to be keeping us safe*, can't seem to get your shit together. Have fun sitting at your desk in that murder box. I'm going skateboarding. At least then I'll be a fast-moving target."

Thinking about how scary it must be to walk into class the day after yet another school shooting, I truly do feel for the kids today—I never had to wonder if any of my classmates were planning to murder everyone in the room. The fact that these kids do hurts my heart and brain. But almost as jarring, when I really think about it I realize that in many ways, *at least on the surface level*, a lot of these kids who wound up as school shooters, well, they resembled *me* when I was a teenager.

In the wake of Columbine and the massacres that have happened since, both the FBI and the Secret Service branches of the Department of Homeland Security have published school shooter threat assessment reports in an

attempt to provide educators with a sound methodology for
evaluating the severity of verbalized threats and identifying
students who might be about to make good on them. (And
I think it's safe to say things are *way beyond fucked up* when
the branches of the US government usually concerned
with safeguarding the president from assassination, foil-
ing domestic terrorist plots, and catching serial killers who
enjoy making tuxedos out of human skin have both issued
official guidelines for teachers that could basically be summarized as "This is how you tell if that one fourteen-year-
old in your homeroom class just might be serious about
blowing up the school.") Those papers are *very careful* to
warn that there is no definitive "profile" for school shooters;
that's a good thing, because the amassed evidence shows the
truth of that and profiling innocent kids just because they
look or act a little weird is damaging and sucks. But I also
know damn good and well that had Columbine occurred
back when I was still in high school (and probably if I was
still there today), I would have been profiled faster than a
combat-fatigue-wearing Black Panther at a Ku Klux Klan
homecoming dance. After all, I wore the stereotypical uni-
form and attitude: the combat boots, the black T-shirts, the
weird hair, the strange aggressive music, and a complete dis-
interest verging on disdain for the standard extracurricular
activities that defined normal teen social life in my small
town. ("A football game? Why on earth would I go to one of
those? I don't give a shit about that stuff—also, by the way,
there are no cute punk rock chicks at a high school football

game.") I'm just grateful the mass-shooting era didn't kick off while I was still in school because, as the teenaged owner of a thrift store trench coat and military-surplus bullet belt, I would have caught absolute hell.

And beyond stereotypical external appearances, looking at the government literature on the topic and reading about some of the psychological and background traits that seem to repeatedly pop up across a broad spectrum of school shooters, then comparing my younger self... well, I can still check off a lot of boxes. These include the following: male, history of depression, small social group, substance abuse, outsider status, anger at real or perceived injustices, anger at the state of the world, feelings of rejection, divorced/separated parents, victim of bullying, and (naturally) disdain for authority. A less-than-discerning school shrink (not that we had a shrink in my school back in the eighties) might have taken a look at all that stuff, noted my Misfits "Bullet" T-shirt with the bloody JFK front print, got the sense that maybe I wasn't exactly overjoyed with my surroundings, and been a little nervous. *Hmm... maybe we ought to keep an eye on this one.*

Of course, there are many other traits a lot of school shooters seem to possess that did *not* apply to me back then. The saddest and most common one seems to be some form of severe early-childhood trauma, abuse, or neglect, and I suffered none of that, thank God—my parents didn't always understand me, and we certainly had our share of stormy moments, but I never once doubted that they loved me more than life itself. I also was not consumed by self-hatred (that came a few years later after becoming a full-blown alcoholic), suicidal urges (ditto), poverty (I certainly didn't grow up rich, but I never had to worry about food, clothes, or shelter), an obsession with violence (I enjoyed a good kung fu movie from time to time, but who doesn't?), extremist racial or political views (that stuff always seemed painfully stupid to me), or narcissistic tendencies and feelings of superiority (okay, okay, so I *was* a smarmy condescending little jerk sometimes, but I didn't think I was God's gift to teenagers or anything like that), "leakage" of plans to commit violence (I didn't have any plans to leak), bully others (I only got mean if you messed with me first), obsess over evil figures like Hitler or Satan (my great uncle died in the snow fighting the Nazis at the Battle of the Bulge, so fuck Hitler, and Satan isn't real, so fuck him too), or lack empathy for others (I was—and I proudly remain—a big fat softie).

I'm sure there are kids out there who could check off *all* those boxes (and more). Although they *definitely* need some help, that in *no way* means any of them are destined to become school shooters or are in the slightest bit inclined to even think about doing so. Things have to go severely, severely wrong in a kid's mind and spirit for them to reach a point where they start planning to execute their classmates, and that doesn't just happen overnight. There is a pathway to violence, and this is what ultimately interests me. How can we help at-risk kids not embark on that pathway, and how can we get the ones already on it off?

I am a writer, musician, and photographer by profession, not a child psychiatrist. But I am also a weirdo who sometimes still doesn't feel like he belongs anywhere, and I can trace this feeling of being *other* all the way back to my childhood...but I never considered *killing* anyone over it. And as a former ostracized high school student weirdo and a current artist, I believe I am more than qualified to ask *myself* some questions of a darker nature. (That's part of what we artists do, by the way—dig around in the deep, dark, and uncomfortable places inside our heads.) So, instead of just accepting myself and my past at face value, thinking, *Dude, you just didn't have it in you to be that violent*, my question to myself is, *Why not?* It is true that I was a very gentle child by nature, not aggressive at all. But after the world had beat on me for a while, I did become angry—*very* angry. And when I look into the darkness of my young soul, I can definitely see ugly potential—all the isolation, angst, and rage were there, boiling away within the cauldron of a very clouded and limited teenage perspective. It's horrible to think about, but I wonder if a few things had gone differently, if I had taken just a few wrong turns down a darker path...well, the clay to sculpt the monster existed, and the kiln to harden it was all around me. Maybe I was just too soft-hearted. Maybe I hadn't suffered sufficient damage. Or maybe, because I was long gone from school by the time Columbine happened, I just didn't have a model to follow.

But kids do today—*the model is there.* The evil genie has left the lamp, and we need to remember that. I'm just grateful he was still locked up when I was angrily slogging my way through the bewildering swamp of my teenage years. Although I'm sure it's *deeply* uncomfortable for parents to sit down and ask themselves, "Is my kid capable of that sort of violence?" obviously it's become necessary in today's world. After all, every school shooter was *someone's* kid. And because I don't have kids, in an attempt to understand what drives these tragedies, I can only ask that disturbing question of myself.

To be clear, I am not a pacifist. I believe in the inherent right of human beings to defend themselves. Even as a sober and sane adult man, I am fully aware that I am absolutely capable of extreme violence, but *only* in defense of myself, my loved ones, or innocent people around me and *only* as a matter of last resort. Because I detest violence, I will do my best to avoid it whenever possible, however possible, until it *isn't* possible. I may still be confused by the world sometimes, but I am definitely of sound mind and in full control of my mental faculties, so like any sane person, the thought of shooting someone, even in self-defense, is awful to me. I do not romanticize using deadly force, and I have seen the toll it has taken on others. Several friends are combat veterans, and in sobering private conversations about some of the horrifying situations they lived through as warfighters, *not one* of them has ever said to me, "Bro, lemme tell ya something. You *gotta* shoot someone one day, homie! You just don't know what you're missing until you try it! It's *fuckin' awesome, dude!*" Putting a bullet into another human being is something I have zero interest in, and I will do my utmost to avoid it like the plague.

But I can easily remember times when the younger me was definitely *not* in full control of myself or my emotions, when I did *not* behave in a rational manner, when I did not possess enough experience-based perspective to understand that all the things that were so upsetting to me did not have to permanently define my reality. Thinking back, I remember being mad, just *so goddamned mad*, at the closed-minded knuckle draggers who kept fucking with me, at the petty power trips I saw hypocritical adult authority figures go on, at the stupid cruelty, violence, and greed of the world, so overwhelmingly mad at *everything* that I wanted to scream. I didn't know how to sort through all this anger or where to put it; furthermore, I had every right to be mad about most of those things. In fact, I still get pissed off when I witness them today, because sadly the crappier aspects of human nature haven't seemed to change since I was a kid. I still don't like bullies, I still don't like petty power-tripping hypocritical assholes, and I still despise cruelty, violence, and greed—but I don't let my anger consume me like I did as a young man. I can process my emotions, filter them through the rational part of my brain, and even refocus that negative energy into something positive, using it as fuel to do something good with my life.

Even before Columbine, psychologists, psychiatrists, criminologists, youth law enforcement officers, security experts, social scientists, anthropologists, and other academics of various stripes have studied school shooters, analyzing the available data about their backgrounds and mental states, searching for what went *wrong* in the lives of that 0.01 percent of kids, while trying to figure out how to prevent others from turning out the same. Although the work they do is invaluable and highly necessary, for the most part their analysis (by its very nature) must come *after* the oh-so-sad facts. I am not an expert of any variety, so I will leave the questions of *what went wrong* and *why* to those better qualified to search for those answers—and because I wasn't a school shooter, I can't even supply researchers with a case study. But as an authority on my own (thankfully non-mass-murdering) experience growing up, I have come to the conclusion that the only effective approach I can take in trying to figure out this awful riddle is to ask myself a different question: *What went right?*

Once when I was in high school, I caught a pretty decent ass kicking in front of almost the entire student body from a group of dudes who let me know in no uncertain terms that they didn't like me or the way I looked. This wasn't the first fight I'd ever been in because I was different, but it was still fairly humiliating at the time. The day I went back to school after being suspended for fighting (even though I didn't start it), a teacher asked me to stay after class. I don't remember his name (and even if I did, I wouldn't print it here out of respect for his privacy, so let's just call him Mr. Goodfellow), but I definitely remember what he said to me:

"Randy, I need to tell you something, and I want you to listen to me carefully, okay? First of all, there is nothing wrong with *you*. It's absolutely okay to look different, to *be* different...but you need to know that it comes *at a price*." This was rock-solid advice that I needed to hear at the time, but after thinking about that little talk many times over the years, I've come to believe that he wasn't just doing his job as an educator or telling me this merely out of the kindness of his heart. Remembering the serious tone of his voice and the understanding look in his eye, I'm fairly convinced he was trying to pass on some hard-earned wisdom obtained from harsh personal experience.

I could be wrong, but in retrospect I'm pretty sure that Mr. G was a closeted gay dude. The cliché signs were there, but at that point in my life I hadn't been around enough gay people to read them. This was also the late 1980s, and homosexuality was not nearly as accepted by society as it is today. The AIDS crisis was still climbing to its awful peak, and gay men in particular were openly viewed with fear and revulsion. An openly gay teacher in my school would have been about as welcome as Ted Bundy at a sorority house sleepover, so I can't blame Mr. G for not just coming out (pardon the pun) and breaking it down for me in plain language, like, "Believe me, dude, I get it. I mean how do you think *I* feel? I sleep with men, for Chrissakes—you think I don't catch a bunch of shit around here?" And even if he wasn't gay, the dude's voice was pretty soft and effeminate. I would bet every penny in my bank account that Mr. G caught more than one ration of shit during that era from redneck shitbirds for being a *"fuckin' faaaaaaag, dude!"*—that's just the way things were back then, and though things ain't perfect now, trust me when I say it used to be worse, *a lot* worse. For fuck's sake, *the only thing* I could think about at age sixteen was *girls, girls, girls, girls, girls*, and how maybe, one day, if I was *super lucky*, I would get into their pants…but I *still* had to duck beer bottles tossed at my head from grown-ass men in passing vehicles who had somehow deduced that my combat boots and Corrosion of Conformity T-shirt were a sure sign that I was out cruising for some man ass. As anyone else who was in the scene back then will tell you, the internet meme that reads "I was punk rock when it was called *HEY, FAGGOT!*" is 100 percent reality-based—every single time I left the house, I had to mentally prepare myself to deal with potential violent conflict because of this ignorant bullshit. Sadly, even in the face of it, I wasn't immune to this moronic societal conditioning, and as I grew up I had to unlearn some ignorant ways of thinking about homosexuals, especially gay men.

To be fair, I never hated gay people or was mean to them—hell, I never knowingly saw any gay people *to* hate, because back then they were all still hiding in the closet so they wouldn't get their asses kicked. But I came of age in small-town Virginia in the 1980s, not the Castro in San Francisco or Greenwich Village in New York City, and so the prevailing notion was that there was something *wrong* with gay people. As someone with some very dear gay friends now, it's embarrassing to remember how ignorant I was, especially because I had assholes constantly lobbing f-bombs my way. I should have known better. But I'm not making excuses here, just putting things in historical perspective for readers who have grown up seeing rainbow flag bumper stickers on cars and hearing words like *Pride* and *inclusive* and *gay marriage* used in regular conversation. That stuff simply *didn't exist* in my neck of the woods back in the eighties, so it took me a few years and some growing up to figure out *why* it felt like Mr. G somehow understood what I was going through as an outsider.

Regardless of his sexual orientation, I've never forgotten Mister Goodfellow or what he said to me. He was kind, he showed empathy, and he reassured me that it was perfectly okay to be *me*, but he didn't bullshit me about what that would entail either. He let me know that I couldn't and shouldn't expect the world to accept me, because the world, well, it contains a rather sizable contingent of assholes. That compassionate honesty served me a whole lot better than some sugary and unrealistic pep talk full of empty platitudes like "I know you're upset now, but hang in there—tomorrow's another day! I bet if you ignore them, they will leave you alone. Heck, maybe you could even try to be friends with those guys—maybe if they could get to know you, they will see *blah blah blah*." Give me a break—that's not *the truth*, and I don't think it's going to help anyone. I know it wouldn't have helped me. After all, I wasn't a little kid upset at a playground scuffle over whose turn it was on the swing set; I was approaching the age when I would have to register for the draft in case my country needed me to go catch some bullets. Mr. G was trying to help me understand the way of the world so that later on I wouldn't be wandering around asking myself, *Why do these people keep on fucking with me? Why can't we all just get along?!?* I prefer the truth, and with a few simple but kind words, Mr. G gave it to me. I've never forgotten it.

I wish I could sit down with every confused, angry, sad, messed-up, weirdo outcast of a kid and have a talk with them before they let things get so bad they pick up a gun and aim it at someone else to try to end their own pain.

Or before they take that razor blade to their own skin.

Or before they simply become so bitter and filled with hopelessness that they waste the rest of their years hating themselves, everything around them, and the only life they get to live. What would I say to them?

"It's perfectly okay to be different, to be yourself, but know that there is a price tag attached."

Mr. G blessed me with that jewel over thirty years ago, and the truth of it shines even brighter today than it did back then. Because I've paid that price again and again in my fifty-plus years on earth, and for me, it can never be too high. I can't live as anything other than myself—I just can't. I've got to be *me*, warts and all. And despite the fact that I've often felt out of step with the world, and that even now I still have days when I feel like a goddamned space alien, well, I'm the only *me* I've got, so I might as well get used to it. If *anyone* else doesn't like my nerdy, skinny, glasses-wearing, strange-ass goofball weirdo self or the way I choose to live, if they are offended that I don't fit their definition of "normal" or "cool," well, that's not my issue, so *fuck 'em*. Because I know I'm a good and decent person, and their opinion isn't going to change that fact. Today I'm perfectly satisfied with being me—in fact, *I like me*. Why wouldn't I? No one controls me, so I can choose to view myself however I wish. I'm free as a bird, baby.

I'm free.

You're fat. You're poor. You're ugly. You're too skinny. You're awkward. You're an immigrant. You have crooked teeth. Your dad's in prison. You're gay. You have a speech impediment. You're covered in horrible acne. You're a nerd. You're weak. You're the only kid your color in your school. You have a weird birthmark on your face. Your parents are alcoholics. You're crippled. No one likes you and you can't get a boyfriend or girlfriend like everyone else. You feel so alone, you don't even know what you're supposed to be yet, and people are already telling you that you aren't good enough. So you're angry and sad and confused and you hate the world and you don't know how in the hell you are going to make it to the end of the day, today, *right fucking now*.

Ahhhhhhhh...*there you are!* Hello, my young friend. I recognize you, because you are one of *my people*. And, kid, I'm here to tell you, whether you believe it yet or not, you can be free, too.

Yes, *you*, kid. In case you haven't figured it out yet, *you* are the person I've been writing this for all along. YOU. Not all the adults, the teachers, the parents—they all have their own problems, I'm not a frickin' advice columnist, and besides, I don't know them...but you? Whether you believe it or not, *I know you*, my friend—because I was just like you, and I'm telling you that you can get through this, even if it doesn't feel like it sometimes. So I'm reaching out to you to let you know that no matter what is happening in your life, no matter how bad your present circumstances are at school or at home (and, yes, it may be *rough* right now), no matter what some bully or crappy teacher or even your drunk and abusive parent says or does, only one person on the planet has control over your actions, and that person is *you*. You are steering the ship here, *no one else*.

So, will you let all the bullshit in your life drive you to do something that will only make you hate yourself? Will you let all those assholes who put you down and make you feel bad about yourself live rent-free in your head, jerking you around like a puppet on a string while you waste time dreaming about getting back at them? It doesn't even matter if the most popular kid in school has mounted a massive campaign of lies against you and every single sniggering one of their little kiss-ass acolytes is chiming in to say hurtful shit. You can choose to respond with *dignity*, not react with *stupidity*. Because that is what letting what other people think of you determine how you view yourself or how you conduct yourself is—stupid. And if you've made it this far, sorry pal, I just don't believe you're stupid. So, don't let anyone else make you act that way.

Right now, *this very instant*, you can stand up straight and start walking with your head held high, because, trust me—one day my friend, you are gonna walk right the fuck on outta there and leave all this behind. You may not have control of much in your life right now, and I know you feel weak and scared and sad and angry—*so goddamned angry*—but that doesn't mean you are a cheap toy robot that anyone else can control with the push of a button. It's natural to be upset when people mistreat you; something would be wrong if you weren't. But it's what you *choose to do* with that anger that is going to decide your fate.

You might be reading this and saying to yourself, "That all sounds great...*for you*, Mr. Rock Star. But hey, old man, in case you haven't noticed, things are *different* now. You didn't grow up with the internet or dealing with social media trolls or having to worry about the entire world being able to gang up on you anonymously back when you were in school and dinosaurs still roamed the earth."

Guess what? *You're right*—things *are* very different now, and I'm super grateful that stuff didn't exist when I was a kid. Furthermore, I think it totally blows that any anonymous coward with an internet connection can instantly spread rumors or publicly insult and demean others for no good reason, and they can usually do so with zero repercussions. But guess what else? Though it's true that all that stuff sucks, especially if you are on the receiving end, I've dealt with worse—*much worse*. But I'm still here, and I'm standing tall.

I already told you I was *free*, little homie, and I meant it in more ways than one.

You think high school is bad? Try going to prison in a foreign country for a little while. (If you don't know what I'm talking about, read my first book, *Dark Days*, or just google me.) During that joyous little period of my life, I had more bullshit thrown on my name online (not to mention in actual *printed* newspapers) than the loading dock of a fertilizer factory, but in the end, guess how much all that shit-talking has affected me in real life? Answer: zip, zilch, *zero*. And I don't particularly enjoy having my mental space invaded by some whiny jackass making smart-aleck comments from their mom's basement in Jerkwater, USA, so I have a solution for that: I don't allow them to open their stupid mouths inside my head. It's amazingly easy to accomplish this: I just don't read what any of those idiots say. Because they can't *force* me to read any of their bullshit, *they do not exist in my universe.*

It's like the old philosophy riddle: "If a tree falls in the forest and no one is around to hear it, does it make a sound?" Maybe...*but who gives a fuck?* Social media? Pfftt. *Please.* Why on earth would I waste my time paying the slightest attention to ding-dongs talking smack online? That's *crazy.* Look, getting upset over what some jerk thinks of you on social media is like standing beneath a huge tree chock-full of millions of tiny screeching birds and getting all pissed off as you wonder why it's constantly raining shit on your head.

You can choose to remain there and turn into a human toilet, or you can simply walk out from beneath the tree, grab a quick shower, and go do something better with your time. And, oh yes, the birds will still be there, yapping and crapping away, but who cares? That's just the nature of little bitch-ass birds. But that's not your problem, because you're not in their zone and you're not playing by their rules anymore, so you can do and think about whatever you want—I suggest concentrating on doing something you actually *enjoy*. Doesn't that sound a whole lot more pleasant than standing beneath the ol' idiot tree with turds raining down all around you and wondering why it feels like you're drowning in shit?

In other words, put down the phone. Get off the laptop. Go do something else—*anything else*—with your time, because sitting on your ass like a sponge soaking up all that noise and negative nonsense is nothing more than slow-motion suicide. You are throwing away the only life you have, murdering yourself one wasted second at a time, and you can never get those seconds back. This might convince some of you that I'm completely insane, senile, or both, but I've got a little secret to share with you: um...mean people leaving you shitty comments? *It doesn't matter.* Anonymous assholes turning you into a meme and plastering you all over their fucked-up message boards so that you become the laughing-stock of their smelly little corner of the internet? *It doesn't matter.* Even (gasp!) social media itself? *It doesn't matter.* It's all just noise, and paying attention to that crap, much less actually worrying about it, is a *complete waste of time.*

Look, I'm not saying that the pressure you're feeling isn't real or that it's not upsetting, because I know that *it is*. I'm just trying to let you know that shifting your focus away from the digital chaos is one way you're going to get through it better. If people are physically bullying you or harassing you face-to-face, that's an entirely different matter, and you need to deal with that in a different way; talk to an adult who can help you. But no matter what is going on, what you absolutely cannot do is allow these assholes (or anyone or anything else) to control your emotions, to make you so mad and upset that you give away your power or even do something drastic that will destroy your chance to get out of this situation in one piece and go live a good life.

You gotta trust me on this one because I'm living proof. I've been living a pretty awesome life for quite some time now, but I can remember what it was like to be a very, very angry young person. And the basic nature of anger hasn't changed since I was young, just as it hasn't changed for thousands of years before me, all the way back to the times of ancient Rome and beyond. If you don't believe me, just read a few pages of Marcus Aurelius's *Meditations* or Seneca's *De Ira* (*On Anger*) and you will see that there truly is nothing new under the sun. You feel anger the same way I felt anger the same way the emperors and philosophers of old Rome felt anger, et cetera, et cetera, all the way back to the very first time some Neanderthal got pissed at the dude in the next cave over for stealing his favorite club. People have *always* experienced anger, but the finest of them have tried to conquer their rage.

Those who do conquer it tend to enjoy much more fulfilling lives than those who stay angry over things from their past that they had zero control over. Folks who fail to control their anger, who don't learn how to channel it into something positive and move forward, who just sit and stew and dwell in the unfairness of it all...well, they usually die alone and miserable. Nobody enjoys being around the angry guy, much less invites him to any parties. Don't be that person.

Remember, it ain't your fault you don't have the money to buy all the things the cool kids have. It ain't your fault that you were born missing one arm. It ain't your fault that your parents are fucked up on drugs and can't get their shit together. It ain't your fault your brother committed suicide after his girlfriend dumped him. It ain't your fault you're growing up in a society that's about to explode from the constant pressure emanating from every screen to look perfect, to buy perfect things, to live a flawless and perpetually happy perfect life like the completely full-of-shit social media influencers are desperately *pretending* to have just to get free shoes and maybe another lousy dollar or two in their bank account. All these external problems have been loaded onto your young back through no choice of your own, they are crushing your soul, and you feel even worse when you look around and it seems like everyone but you has their life together—*none of this* is your fault. And it sure as hell ain't your fault that some people are such lame jerks that they see your pain and then make fun of you for it—but those people are a waste of skin, so *fuck 'em.*

You have a choice to make here, my friend. You can either let these douchebags cause you to waste your time and ruin day after day after miserable day by allowing them to live in your head rent-free... or realize that this is such a short and ultimately inconsequential period in your life, get through it the best you can, then leave all those motherfuckers in the dust and go live your life. There's an old saying: "Living well is the best revenge," and I believe that is broadly true. But I'm pretty sure I can do better: the best revenge is not thinking of revenge *at all*. If you stop letting other people and their small-minded opinions of you scamper around freely inside your dome, raising hell and causing havoc like the annoying little rats that they are, eventually revenge will be the last thing on your mind. In fact, you'll be embarrassed to even think about such pettiness. Once you start concentrating on the only truly important thing—your own life and what you want to do with it—well, one day you'll be so busy moving *forward* that the thought of getting *back* at some moron who messed with you in school will seem like the absurdly pathetic waste of time that it is. Trust me, you'll have *much better* things to do.

But that doesn't mean life is ever going to be easy, much less perfect. To this day, I still get confused about what in the hell is going on, what I should do with my life, and how I should do it. Sometimes I feel as if I am just stumbling through this existence, periodically coming to a complete and painful halt as I bang face-first into a brick wall of mistakes that I should've easily avoided but didn't see coming, all because I was too busy fretting over the million distracting inconsequential things that this fucked-up modern society has crammed into my peripheral vision. So I don't have any easy answers to your problems, much less mine—sorry. If I did, I'd share that wisdom. But somehow, for over fifty years now, I've dealt with being such a ball of confusion, and somehow, against all odds, it's worked out pretty well for me so far—I have to admit, I live a pretty freaking rad life. And when things *aren't* awesome and life just *sucks*, when I am sad and lost and don't know what to do, well, I have some amazing friends who are there to pick me up and help me get back on my own two feet. These friends are my community, my family—I need them, because I belong with these people. Where do you belong? How do you fit in?

Well…you *don't*. At least not within a society that constantly tells you you have to toe the line and be "normal" (whatever the fuck that means), to look a certain way to be attractive, to own certain things to be "cool," to chase after some commonly accepted and asinine definition of "success" (which these days seems to center around two things: making a ton of money and being famous in some weird way on the internet). You do not have to "fit in" *anywhere* in this boring, boring, boring *oh-my-God-it's-so-fucking-boring* cookie-cutter schematic. In fact, in case you haven't figured it out yet, you *can't* fit in. But that doesn't mean you are going to be alone forever, that you will never belong anywhere.

One of William Shakespeare's most famous lines comes from his play *Hamlet*: "This above all: to thine own self be true." That, my friend, is the key to finding your place in the world—staying true to yourself. Do not let the world and this time in your life brutalize you to the point that you turn into something else, transforming into something *actually* ugly, something hard and bitter that you are not. Eventually, if you are patient and keep your eyes and heart open, you will meet your people. These folks will gladly accept you for what you are, and because they are not idiots, they could give a rat's ass about the petty and superficial crap that all the narrow-minded jerks have used so many times to try to make you feel bad about yourself. Trust me, your people are out there—I've met a ton of them, because they are my people, too. These are my friends, and they are rock stars, scientists, comedians, best-selling authors, computer engineers, chefs, world-champion martial artists, state senators, poets, Tier One Special Forces warriors, professional skateboarders, college professors, survival instructors, Buddhist monks, psychiatrists, photographers... and *every single one* of them was that weird kid who didn't fit in, just like me, just like *you*. So be proud of who you are, of *what* you are. Kid, take that feeling of being *other*, of not fitting in, of being a goddamned freak, and *own it*. Make it work for you. It will be such a waste if you don't. That thing that makes you feel so different, whatever it is, is a superpower if you use it *correctly*. If you use it incorrectly, if you try to deny it, if you don't *own* it—your pain will never end.

So, in closing, I want you to know that *I see you*, my young friend. It's like staring at a mirror that shows my past.

Thanks for reminding me of what I am and where I come from—I never want to forget that. And I'm in a much better place these days, but you have to remember I didn't get here overnight, and you won't either. And, yes, it's still true that what you are going through *sucks*, it's true that it isn't fair, and it's true that you shouldn't have to deal with this bullshit. But it won't last forever—nothing ever does. You have to stay patient, remain in control of yourself, and stay focused on moving forward. If you play your cards right and just hang in there a little longer, well, everything that seems so over-whelming right now won't matter anymore. Eventually, you can choose to let go of the crap you are going through, and the echo of it won't hurt any more than a mosquito bite. Trust me, a ton of us out here know how you feel, and we are wait-ing for you to catch up to us. It might take a little while, but if you keep pushing forward, sooner or later you will find us, and we will do some *great shit* together.

In fact, you *have* to make it *because we need you*, us old weirdos. One day when we get too old and frail and tired to lift it anymore, you are going to have to pick up our bur-den and carry it for us. What burden, you ask? Why, being a light in the darkness for the ones who come after us, of course—that's what we are, don't you see? *Somebody* has to stand tall and proud, to show the next generation of odd-balls and rejects that despite the whole world trying to knock them down just for being themselves, there can be no sur-render and there is no giving up—that somebody might as well be *you*. As painful as it may be right now, this life could *only* happen to *you*—*you were built for this*. One day in the future, you're going to notice another messed-up kid walking all alone with trembling hands and tears in their eyes, looking like they just can't take it anymore, looking like they are about to break into a thousand little pieces. You're going to look at that kid, and it's going to be like looking into a mirror that shows your past. Then you will give them a smile, say, "Hey! *I see you*," and reach out your hand to lift them up, just like I'm trying to lift you up right now.

This is your responsibility. Do not fail in it.

Can you see us? We're the weirdos, the ugly ones, the rejects...*the wild and free ones*, and we're waving our freak flag oh-so-high for all to see, partying our asses off way out on the outer edges of "normal." This is where we've always been, and this is where we always will be—living free outside the stupid, suffocating box the world tried to shove us into. We wouldn't have it any other way, and we're waiting for you to come join us, so start marching, kid. You just gotta keep putting one foot in front of the other, because there is a better life waiting for you, but there is no express train to salvation. You're gonna have to walk through some crap to get here, but it's going to make you stronger by the time you arrive.

You *have* to make it. In fact, we're counting on you to do so. Remember: we need you.

Don't let us down.

To thine own self be true.

Chapter Nine

BONZO
GOES TO
BITBURG

I t's the day after Thanksgiving and I'm writing this sitting at a small marble-topped table in a New York City hotel room; specifically, room 5A of the Hotel Chelsea, an establishment with a long and storied history of sheltering writers, musicians, and artists. Arthur Miller, Dee Dee Ramone, Jackson Pollock, Larry Rivers, Mark Twain, Bob Dylan, Jack Kerouac, Patti Smith, Robert Mapplethorpe, William S. Burroughs, Thomas Wolfe, Janis Joplin, Leonard Cohen, Mark Rothko, Tennessee Williams, Jimi Hendrix, Herbert Huncke, and Arthur C. Clarke are just a few of the names on an impressive and lengthy list of brilliant creatives who have slept and toiled here. Although now a luxury boutique hotel, the Chelsea also has a long but not quite so illustrious history as an affordable place for hard-core alcoholics and drug addicts to crash, but quite a few of those disreputable sorts who paid rent here over the 140 years of the building's existence also just happened to be said brilliant writers, musicians, and artists. Great artistic talent and addiction don't always accompany each other, but they have been known to frequently skip hand in hand down West 23rd Street and into the Chelsea together.

In 1953, after supposedly downing eighteen shots of rye whiskey at the White Horse Tavern in the West Village, the great poet Dylan Thomas returned to his room at the Chelsea (no. 205), fell into a coma, and died two days later. Thomas is far from being the only resident of this hotel who did not go gentle into that good Manhattan night, and I've heard legends of the place since high school, starting with the most infamous death in punk rock history. In 1978, Sid Vicious, the twenty-one-year-old junkie ex-bassist of the Sex Pistols, was arrested and charged with murder after his twenty-year-old also heroin-junkie girlfriend Nancy Spungen was found dead from a single stab wound to the abdomen in the bathroom of room 100. Sid pleaded not guilty and was released on bail but died four months later of a heroin overdose while awaiting trial, so the truth of the matter will probably never be known. There have been multiple deaths from murder, suicide, alcoholism, and drug overdose in the Chelsea over the years, earning it a reputation as one of New York City's most haunted buildings. I've been wanting to stay here for over three decades, so I've finally come to sit and write and listen for the ghosts of some of my creative forefathers roaming the formerly shabby hallways and still iconic staircases of this one-time bohemian mecca.

No, not the drunken, drug-addicted, and stabby aspect of those ghosts' nature—the artistically inspired side. Thankfully, I left any idiotic romanticizing of addiction behind long ago, so I'm hoping to catch an echo of relatively sober (or at the very least *coherent*) genius gone by.

The great irony of me staying at the Chelsea is that the willingness to pay the exorbitant nightly rate I have decided to splurge on this holiday weekend in a fit of punk rock history nerd-induced fiscal irresponsibility is also the main reason almost no artists sleep here now—well, except for ones like *me* who can afford to blow a decent-size chunk of cash on a few nights of high-thread-count nostalgia for a time and place I never knew. Starting in 2011, the Chelsea underwent an extensive eleven-year-long multimillion-dollar facelift, and during the ensuing disruptive renovation process and multiple court battles with existing tenants, most of the long-term residents who maintained cheap rent-stabilized apartments here for decades were driven out. When I first became a touring musician, I couldn't afford a single night at the Chelsea, not even during its shabbiest and stabbiest junkie-filled era (my band slept on people's living room floors or in our van, not hotels). But after decades of grinding it out on the road, I have somehow transformed from being a broke-ass dude hoping for a quiet corner to put down his grimy sleeping bag into precisely the kind of person the developers hoped would come to this place—a nostalgic creative type enamored with the hotel's low-rent artistic past but financially secure enough to indulge in a few nights of its high-rent present.

Furthermore, I am well aware that the presence of people like me (actual working artists with a bit of fame, however negligible) only adds to the aura of cool that helps draw the much larger clientele the new management *really* wants: monied hipsters lusting after social media photos of themselves looking glamorous and distracted on the art-covered staircases of the hippest hotel in Manhattan. The cultural cachet endowed by the artists who once lived in the Hotel Chelsea has made it a very desirable destination for the see-and-be-seen crowd, but no *new artists* could possibly afford to live and create here now (not that the hotel offers long-term leases anymore anyway). Hell, these days no new artists can afford New York, *period*, and many of the old ones have been forced to leave by skyrocketing rent hikes. A city's artists are the beating heart that pumps invaluable cultural lifeblood through its streets, and when the very last of New York's paint-splattered lofts falls beneath the real estate developer's axe to be chopped into luxury apartment units for the stockbrokers, tech start-up entrepreneurs, and venture capital bean counters, something irreplaceable will have been bled dry here.

All this hurts my heart and even makes me feel a bit guilty being here because I hold an abiding respect and deep fondness for the history of the underground art, music, and literature that defined this city for so many, but I also know that this is just the way of things. After all, the only constant is change, and I'm just grateful I got a gloriously gritty taste of the last of the old days before they were completely swallowed by the ever-ravenous and culture-leveling jaws of capitalism. One example being CBGB, the legendary music venue and hallowed birthplace of punk rock that is now an obscenely expensive clothing boutique owned by the high-end fashion designer John Varvatos. I'm not hating on Varvatos, because apparently he's preserved a bit of the club's history inside, and I've heard that opening his store saved the building from being razed and replaced by a fucking bank or some other insult. I've even peered into the store's darkened windows several times as I've walked by at night, and for a split second I was almost able to smell the perpetual stink of stale beer and sweat that was *eau de CB's*. Although I'm honestly glad that the building is still there, I haven't been able to bring myself to walk into a place that meant so much to me but now (according to the website) sells $148 T-shirts that say PUNK OFF. I am old enough and lucky enough to have visceral, intense sensory memories of the place as it was before, and that's enough for me—to this day I get choked up when I remember the first time I stepped onto the club's battered stage with my band.

Holy shit! This is it! We're here! I'd thought. *This is where punk rock was born, where the fucking Ramones and Blondie got their start! I can die happy now.*

Maybe, one day, somehow, I will get to play CBGB... that was the biggest and wildest I had ever allowed my musical dreams to get, and by eight o'clock on that wonderful evening in 1997 that dream had been realized. (We were the first of seven bands on the bill that night.) We would return to CB's several times after that, even selling it out as the headlining act, then go on to play much bigger venues in New York City, including the ultimate goal of many a musician: Madison Square Garden. But for me, no stage since has held greater emotional significance than the legendarily splintered and sticker-covered mountaintop I ascended while playing CBGB for the first time. Standing in front of the crowd in that moment, I knew that my band had just been written into the noble and smelly history of that club, and no one or nothing could ever take that from us. By having the guts to step up there and do our thing, we had marched ourselves straight into a glorious musical lineage, one I had revered for so long. That day I became a tiny part of the much larger myth, and I always will be—this is a memory I cherish immensely, something that money simply cannot buy.

And by the same token, no matter how much I am paying to stay in this hotel, I have to accept that the legendarily sketchy glory days of the Chelsea are long gone and that I totally missed them. That was made glaringly evident to me within five minutes of checking in last night. As I stepped from the elevator on the fifth floor, a beautiful and perfectly made-up twenty-something decked out in designer clothes descended the staircase in front of me, stopping periodically to whip out her phone, strike the exact same well-practiced and studiously unfocused pose, and snap a glazed-eyed sultry selfie (God, how I *detest* the word *selfie*). This ridiculously self-absorbed process was repeated several times as she teetered down the stairs, until, finally satisfied, she wandered away with her nose buried in her phone, grinning idiotically as she posted her latest bit of well-curated artifice. *Fucking gross—an influencer*, I thought. *Oh Sidney, where are you when we need you, mate?*

The Chelsea has changed and so has New York, but this was never my town anyway, so I can't complain. And I still love this grand old dame of a city. New York and her people have always been good to me, and I've done a lot of solid work here over the years. There is no other town like New York City in the world, and influencers be damned, I sleep in her legendary Hotel Chelsea tonight, so my heart is full.

I didn't hand over my credit card at the Chelsea's front desk in an attempt to buy my way into its history anyway—I came here to respectfully *listen* for it, and outside my room's double French doors, I can hear the iconic neon sign buzzing as it glows red over West 23rd Street, right beside my balcony and so close I can almost reach out and touch it. The wild graffiti covering the subway cars during my first deliciously terrifying rides as a teenage country bumpkin lost in the New York of the 1980s has long been scrubbed clean, but the squealing train wheels still echo in the tunnels, the brake lines still hiss, and the giant rats still scurry along between the tracks at Canal Street Station. And even though the streets of the fabled Lower East Side where I once copped dope from fast-talking Puerto Ricans now seem to have been completely overrun by shiny-faced chai-latte-sipping undergrads (none of whom look even the slightest bit worried about possibly getting stabbed), I can still walk into a bodega to buy a steaming plate of chicken and rice and hear the owner argue with a Dominican customer in rapid-fire Spanish. So, I walk through these places in New York, a city with a manic energy all its own, and I can still hear the magic hanging in the air, just as I can in the noisy Café du Dôme on the Left Bank of Paris, in the salted wind blowing through the canopy of Spanish moss that covers the streets of Beaufort, South Carolina, and in the deafening silence of the exquisitely appointed hillside rooms of La Chascona in Santiago, Chile—I just have to be quiet and *listen*.

Because I am an incurable romantic, I am convinced that creative energy lingers in the places where great artists struggled to bring their genius to life. I have made pilgrimages to many such locations all over the world, always looking to tap into that leftover ethereal current to power my own work. And who knows? Maybe one evening years from now, long after I am dead and gone, a writer or musician will walk the cobblestone streets and alleyways of Richmond, Virginia, straining to hear a ghostly whisper of my voice on the night wind, just as I have listened for Edgar Allan Poe's while roaming the humid darkness of our mutual home-town. I can only hope that whatever energy I put into the work I leave behind will add to that mighty pool of inspiration, that someone will reach out to grab a piece and use it in their own creative process. When Hippocrates said, "Life is short, but art is long," he was referring to the time it took to master a craft or a skill ("an art"), not to aesthetically pleasing objects. But one only has to listen to Beethoven, Hank Williams, Marvin Gaye, or the Ramones to know that, although no artist is immortal, a great song transcends the grave. All those dudes have long turned to dust, but their voices ring eternal in my ear, pushing me forward and telling me to *create, create, create*.

So that is what I am doing here in the Chelsea, looking and listening for inspiration so that I may continue to throw my hopefully beautiful somethings into the world until I myself disappear into the great nothing. I do this because this is what I was born to do, because this is what I am: a treasure hunter stalking eternity, endlessly fumbling for the key to unlock the jewel-filled chest that sits in plain view right in front of everybody's face. I have come to understand that this is my function, the function of the artist—to simply notice what is already there and shine a light so that others may see it. I do not fear the darkness of death, for I am infinitely comfortable in the dark, and I well know the Reaper is coming for me whether I like it or not.

But I am utterly terrified of dying in a state of regret over unfulfilled purpose, of listlessly fading away with the painful knowledge that I did not perform my function. For me, the only method I have to allay that very real anxiety is to perpetually stomp along in my clumsy search for a meaningful life via the artistic process, and I will do this in one form or another until the day I die. I will never "retire." Because after the songs are recorded and mixed and the album's release date is set, when the photos are all signed and framed and hung neatly on the gallery walls, once the final draft has been edited and the book's manuscript has been sent off to the printers, I will feel a brief moment of great satisfaction...then the creeping dread of emptiness and lack of purpose will begin to grow, knotting itself up into an anxious ball within my stomach, and I will become increasingly restless, irritable, and discontent until I bend myself toward my next project.

This is the only way I know how to move through the world without falling into despair, the only way I can navigate its chaos and ugliness while retaining some sort of belief that all life is not merely a meaningless slog toward extinction. I do not want to stumble through this world wearing tear-soaked blinders, hopelessly trudging along the bitter, narrow path of nihilism. So I remain engaged in the creative process, forcing me to keep my eyes open and my heart wide as I move forward to my inevitable end. I do this because I want to see *everything* until I can see no more. What a gift it is to be able to see!

Admittedly, my eyesight *sucks*. I've worn glasses since I was in the third grade, and I well remember being called

"Four Eyes" by other kids the first day I walked into class with those hideous brown plastic frames perched on my nose. But these days, "Six Eyes" would be more appropriate, because in addition to my two slowly failing retinas and the endless pairs of spectacles I've broken over the years, I've come to view everything in the world through two additional lenses—and I do mean *everything*. I suffer from an existential myopia, and so far, these two corrective points of view have been the only way I can make sense of anything, the only perspectives that have brought any clarity, focus, and sense of purpose into my life.

The first and most important corrective lens is sobriety. I can have zero clarity in my life if I am drinking or drugging. If you don't suffer from alcohol or drug addiction (meaning that you are one of those strange people who can have one or two beers every now and then without winding up in jail/divorced/knocked out cold/suicidally depressed/financially destitute/in a mental ward/permanently uninvited to the family Christmas celebration/waking up covered in your own blood in a cheap hotel room two states away from home with no memory of how you got there), then you don't need to put on the sober goggles, so cheers to you! Congratulations, and by all means, please go enjoy your glass of champagne on New Year's Eve. You are a normie, and trust me—you should be *stoked*. But if you *are* an alcoholic or drug addict (or both), then you might be interested in how I learned to better deal with life. It was very simple:

One day, I put down the drugs and alcohol, and I simply didn't pick them back up. No matter what problems the world threw my way, I stayed clean and sober, because hard experience had taught me that drinking and drugging always made things worse, never better. I focused on my sobriety, life slowly began to make sense, and things eventually got better.

That's it. That's the only solution I have found to my problem with drugs and alcohol—complete abstinence. Because once you are an addict, things will never, ever get better until you stop. *Ever.* By "an addict," I mean your life looks something roughly like this: you can't seem to prevent yourself from starting to drink and/or use drugs, and once you have started, you can't stop. You spend a lot of time doing this stuff, and even when you aren't doing it, you are *thinking* about doing it. Partying may have been fun in the beginning, and may even *still* be fun on occasion, but now it has become increasingly detrimental to your mental, physical, and emotional health. Signs that your substance intake is problematic are popping up more and more frequently, yet you ignore them and continue on because you cannot function *without* whatever your particular poison is. But in those rare moments that you are honest with yourself, you know that you aren't functioning all that well *with it*, now are you? At some point, if you still have any people in your life you haven't driven away, you will start hiding your drinking and drugging from them. Some part of you knows that this sneaky behavior is not normal, that you should quit, but you have lost control over your "partying." Therefore, in a very real way, this bullshit controls your life. Addiction has made you its little bitch, because if you weren't, you could just put down the bottle of booze or drugs and forget about it, not immediately start scheming and dreaming about how and when you are going to get more of that stuff and then get away with doing it again. You are a slave to a substance—that's precisely what addiction is: slavery wrapped up in a liquor bottle, pill, or little baggie of powder. Eventually, that slavery will kill you, one way or the other, just like it killed so many denizens of the Chelsea. Alcoholism took Dylan Thomas, Jack Kerouac, and Jackson Pollock. Jimi Hendrix, Mark Rothko, and Tennessee Williams ate one too many barbiturates. Sid Vicious, Janis Joplin, and Dee Dee Ramone died under the lash of heroin. Drunks, pill poppers, junkies...slaves to alcohol and drugs. All of them dead.

One day I had a moment of clarity and realized that I was a slave. I decided that I didn't want to die as one, so I went to some sober dudes I knew and said, "I have a problem with drinking—please help me." Then I shut my big fucking mouth and listened to what they had to say. If you are like me, then I would advise you to do the same, because I've got bad news for you, my friend—until you quit getting fucked up, your life is going to be *fucked up*. In fact, *you* are a *fuckup*, and until you own that fact and do something about it, things are only going to get worse. Find some sober alcoholics or drug addicts (we aren't hard to locate—try the internet), ask them for help, then physically hang out with these folks instead of your current drinking and drugging buddies (if you have any left), because those "friends" probably have the same problem you do and aren't going to improve your situation any. When you stop fucking up your life with booze and drugs, being around positive, sober people is like hanging out at the beach on a beautiful Caribbean island—it may seem a little bright at first, but eventually you're gonna get relaxed and catch a little tan. Conversely, being around negative, fucked-up people is like squatting in a Boston alleyway dumpster in February—pretty quickly you're gonna start stinking and catch a cold, maybe even develop pneumonia and die. So, try getting sober and see what it does for you. What do you have to lose by trying? Don't worry—if it doesn't work out, it's not like they are going to stop making booze and drugs. You can always go back to your currently failing method of dealing with life: hiding from the sad reality of your existence inside a fog of liquor and drugs until it chokes you and you die.

Once I had been sober a little while, that awful fog began to clear, and reality came back into focus. Sometimes that focus was so sharp it hurt. I could clearly see the mess I'd made of my life for the first time, and I had no one or nothing else to blame other than myself. When I was still caught in active alcoholism, one thing that made it very easy for me to justify my drinking was the fact that the rest of the world refused to behave in a manner that I deemed appropriate. The sad reality of my existence was a state of being consumed by impotent anger and crushing depression at the sad reality of the world, because drunk or sober, when you look at the world with any level of objectivity, well, it's a pretty fucked-up place. Sober, I could no longer escape that reality by diving into a bottle, I could no longer drink *at* the world. I was thirty-nine years old, and I had to figure out some way to deal with my emotions, to make sense of this existence—or at least learn to function within it without being crippled by depression or going completely insane.

I had been in my band for fifteen years by the time I got sober, and I wasn't good at much other than expressing myself creatively through music, and by the end of my drinking, I wasn't even really good at that anymore. My creativity had been dulled along with every other aspect of my true self, and the new ideas I did manage to come up with were really just dark and tiresome refrains of things I had already said to death. But very soon after I quit drinking, the ideas started coming, and they came so fast I could barely keep up. The fire of my creativity had almost been extinguished by the buckets of booze I kept throwing on it, but deep beneath the soggy, blackened wreck of my life, an ember still glowed, fighting to stay alive. When I cleared away all that burnt, drunken wreckage I had piled on top of myself, oxygen got to that ember, and it burst back into flame. A fire needs three things to burn—a spark, oxygen, and fuel. The spark was still there, sobriety was the oxygen, and the rest of reality was the fuel. Without consciously trying, just by getting sober, I had taken a fresh cloth and wiped clean the other smudged and soot-covered lens I had almost destroyed, and once again I began to view reality through the eyes of an artist. What does that mean?

It means that I look at every single situation that occurs in my life, everything that happens in the world around me, everything that enters my consciousness as creative building blocks for a potential song, a potential story, a potential picture. I look at *everything*—the proverbial good, bad, and ugly—as fuel for artistic expression, and I do this automatically and without consciously trying. That's how I process my life and navigate reality, and once you begin viewing the world this way, things begin to appear very differently, in the same way a skateboarder views the urban environment very differently from how a nonskater does. The regular person looks at a shiny new marble bench on the edge of a city park and sees a fancy if uncomfortable place to sit. The skateboarder looks at that same bench and sees endless kinetic possibilities to express himself. That is what the artist sees in the totality of life: the possibility for expression. That possibility is in the sad feeling you get on those strangely empty days between Christmas and New Year's Eve, it is in the slick of motor oil shimmering atop a rain puddle beneath the buzzing lights of a rooftop parking deck after midnight, it is in the intricate spiderweb of veins covering the paper-thin skin of your grandmother's folded hands as she lay on her deathbed, it is in the flash of light reflecting off the bared teeth of a German shepherd as it lunges for your leg, it is in the dappled golden beams flickering through the leaves of the blurred tree line on the highway's edge as you drive south at sunset to visit an old friend, it is in *everything, everything, everything*—you only have to *look* to see it.

Then, once you've seen it, if you are an artist, you turn it into *art*.

What is art? There is an age-old debate around this, and as for all the biggest, deeply philosophical questions that continue to plague mankind ("What is the meaning of life?" "What happens after we die?" and "Who has better pizza, Chicago or New York?"), I don't have the answer. A simpler question for me to wrap my head around is, What makes a person an artist? That's a much easier one to answer—here come the hurt feelings, so get ready.

Despite the flaming load of feel-good horseshit that some suspiciously self-helpy books about creativity try to sell you, not everyone is an artist. Sorry. It's just *true*. And that's okay. Not everyone *has* to be an artist. I will say that a nonartist may become an artist *at any point* in their life, but it's not a magic, instantaneous event. Just waking up one day and saying "I'm an artist" doesn't make you an artist. That's a crock of shit—I know it, and you know it, too, no matter how many affirmations of impending creative bliss you say to yourself in the mirror every morning. "*Living a beautiful and authentic life*" does not make you an artist. A Zen Buddhist monk who sits and meditates eight hours a day on the nature of reality and periodically dispenses insightful pearls of wisdom to an enraptured audience of enlightenment-seeking pilgrims gathered at a gorgeously austere monastery in the Kyoto hills may indeed live a beautiful and authentic life, but that doesn't make him an artist; it makes him a Zen Buddhist monk who meditates a lot. This doesn't mean a Zen Buddhist monk *can't* be an artist. In fact, I have a friend who is a bona fide Zen master who received dharma transmission in Japan with all the fancy ceremonial trimmings and who is also an artist. He sits his ass off with his legs in a pretzel for hours and has some pretty deep insights into the nature of reality—but that's not what makes him an artist. Having children and raising them to be good people, though important to society, doesn't make you an artist; it makes you a standard-issue decent human being who has fulfilled the entirely pedestrian biological imperative sequenced into every living organism's DNA to ensure the continuation of their species. And for God's sake, assembling a carefully curated social media page full of nothing but beautiful pictures and videos of yourself "living your best life" sure as fuck doesn't make you an artist; it makes you a narcissist and (at best) a visually creative liar. So, what *does* make a person an artist?

The answer is quite simple: an artist makes art.

That's it. If you don't make art, you're not an artist. *Period.*

And when I say "an artist makes art," I'm not talking about someone who wrote a poem once in ninth grade for a girl they wanted to date or someone who still has their portfolio of nude charcoal sketches from the two semesters of figure-drawing class they took in college fifteen years ago before coming to their senses and switching to a business major or even someone who picks up a guitar and painstakingly learns the entire Led Zeppelin catalog note for note and practices to the point that they can play "Ten Years Gone" so perfectly that Jimmy Page himself would sit and weep upon hearing the flawless reflection of his own genius. No, I'm talking about someone who consistently sits down, bends their head toward whatever art form they so choose, and, by engaging in that process, creates something from nothing.

That person is an artist. They may be a shitty artist, but if they are creating art, then they are an artist. And most artists are compulsively *driven* to create art (I know I am). I believe this compulsion exists because it is within the often-painful experience of the artistic process that the artist attempts to understand both themselves and the world around them. Art is the outwardly manifested expression of the artist's search for meaning.

I said I wasn't going to define art, but now I've hauled off and written myself into a corner, so fuck it. What is art? Some people will vehemently disagree with me here, including some of my friends who are respected professional artists. Luckily for me, this is my book, not an internet comments section, so they are just gonna have to yell at the page instead of leaving me a snarky comment. (And by all means, please—go ahead and scream your head off at this book. Fuck it. Throw it across the room. Feel better? *Good.* Glad to be of service.) To me, as an artist (and *I am* an artist— once again, I may be a shitty one, but I create art all the time, so I get to claim that title), art is an expression of imagination perceptible via our senses that conveys a truth of some sort about the human experience as interpreted through the eyes of the creator. As well, art is capable of being witnessed by others; it can be viewed, read, heard, touched, even smelled or tasted, or some combination of all of the above, by someone other than the creator. Furthermore, someone other than the creator can have their own experience with the art, run it through the filter of their own perceptions and experience, internalizing and interpreting it through that filter, and then assign their own meaning to it, even if that meaning is not the same as the creator's original intent. This, of course, is one of the hallmarks of *good* art—it kickstarts the imagination of the viewer/listener/et cetera, perhaps even inspires their own artistic ideas.

But an idea is not art until it is manifested in the world, and that manifestation occurs through an artist engaging in the artistic process. Therefore, merely having a great idea for a book you're going to write one day doesn't make you a writer. *Writing* makes you a writer. I know this because I was a writer when I was younger, churning out a few issues of a self-published fanzine full of roughly written but amusing anecdotes from my life as a punk rock kid, line cook, and budding alcoholic. Then, watered with copious amounts of beer, my alcoholism eventually grew from "budding" into "full-on raging" status, and I stopped writing. Sure, I managed to scrawl out some lyrics for my band over the years while thrashing drunkenly about in the depths of my alcoholism, and some of them were even halfway decent, but beyond that I wrote very little. Yet I still *talked* about "being a writer." I had some *great ideas*, you know? I was a *writer, maaaaan*. In fact, just like every other angst-riddled young American macho wannabe writer dude I knew, I emulated the worst stereotypical traits of the supremely male canon of writers we all invariably read (Hemingway, Fitzgerald, Bukowski, Hunter S. Thompson, etc.). So I did a lot of drinking, a respectable amount of womanizing, even a little brawling here and there—yep, I was mastering all the stuff the greats I loved to read did, with the exception of one crucial component: *writing*. I wasn't a writer anymore; I was a drunken poseur. Then I got sober and wrote a book and some other stuff. Now I'm writing this one. Guess what? I'm a writer.

Writers write. Painters paint. Dancers dance. Photographers photograph. Actors act. Sculptors sculpt. Musicians make music. Directors direct.

In other words, artists *art*. That's what makes them artists. *That's it.* You don't agree? So you're one of those people I mentioned earlier who's been convinced by some life-affirming book or social media "creativity guru" that anyone who declares themselves to be an artist is an artist? *Fine*—let's unpack that seductive little gem.

I have a lot of *great ideas* about finance and money, most of which the government would hate, but I would *never* wake up one day and say, "I'm a banker," any more than I would wake up and say, "I'm a brain surgeon" or "I'm a fighter jet pilot" or "I'm the Queen of England." I don't perform craniotomies, I don't crank out barrel rolls in F-14s, and I don't do Queen shit (whatever that is). I don't even engage in the process of *banking* that often, beyond depositing the occasional check, and that's okay; I'm not suited for that stuff. Even if I cashed out my whole account entirely in pennies, stuffed them all by hand into those nifty little cardboard sleeves that hold fifty cents each, neatly arranged them on the shelves in my study, and then hung up a sign that said BANK OF RANDY, I still wouldn't be a banker; I'd be an idiot with hands that smelled of copper who was losing out on the interest that a high-yield savings account in a real bank provides.

So, I trust bankers (okay, maybe *trust* is the wrong word here) to do my banking stuff, not me, because...*I'm not a banker*. I mean, would *you* trust me to hold all your money? I hope not—I suck at it. Furthermore, my customer service would be terrible. You would call me all upset after your account balance was suspiciously low, and if I bothered to pick up the phone, I would reply with something along the lines of "*What?!?* What do *you* want? Oh, you're missing money? Well, that *sucks*, but let's look at it this way—when you think about it deeply enough, money doesn't really exist, now does it? It's really just a mutually agreed upon conceit, a fantastical abstract lie that we as a society somehow keep accepting and perpetuating in order to convince ourselves that everything isn't truly falling apart. I mean, ask yourself this: What *is* money these days? The vast majority of it is not paper bills or silver coins or even stacks of wampum but unseeable and ultimately meaningless strings of ones and zeros floating along like ghostly turds in the digital sewer of cyberspace, swirling around among all the cat videos, weird stepmother porn, and those relentless spam email ads for penis enlargement pills...and isn't money just more of the same? Do you really *need* that stuff? I didn't think so. *Think about it.* Okay, have a good one. Peace."

And, yes, there *are* those people who wake up every day and proclaim that *they are bankers*, but they usually do this via email or over the phone to unsuspecting and easily misled elderly folks. Regrettably, for those particular "bankers," when their "banking activities" are brought to the attention of a judge by their very dissatisfied geriatric clients, that judge invariably disagrees with their self-appointed status as the employee of a viable financial institution, then proceeds to hand down a lengthy prison sentence. These "bankers" are more commonly known to the rest of us as *scam artists*, a highly ironic name given the context of this chapter. Although there is no career-encompassing retrospective of the amazing swindles pulled off by the most beloved scam artist of the Italian Renaissance on display in the Louvre, there *is* the *Mona Lisa* hanging in those hallowed halls, and each year more than ten million people go to gaze at her and be moved by her enigmatic smile. Leonardo da Vinci didn't wake up one fine Florentine morning five hundred years ago, decide to call in sick to his job at the local bakery, look in the bathroom mirror, and say, "Leo, you handsome Italian son of a bitch, you know what? *You are an artist*, by God!" then proceed to sit down on his marble balcony and bang out the most famous painting of all time before lunch. No, from the time he was a teenager, da Vinci completely immersed himself in the artistic process, always painting, drawing, sculpting, sketching out studies for his next commission, always *making art*. That is why we revere him as one of the great masters to this day: he left behind beautiful *works of art*, not half-baked spiels about how he was an artist.

No art = no artist. Deal with it.

And people seem to be more and more confused about how to go about being an artist or even what being an artist really means these days. It's bizarre to me, but I've definitely witnessed a shift in the way people, young people in particular, view what the *purpose* of being an artist is. (I suspect that reality TV probably has something to do with this, but I can't be sure.) "What advice do you have for young musicians just starting out?" is probably the number one question I've been asked over the years, but I've noticed that the question has changed, getting oddly more specific as of late, but in all the wrong ways. (By the way, the answer to the original question is always the same old boring thing: practice, practice, practice, and play as many shows as possible to anyone, anywhere that will have you—that's how we did it.) I have to stop myself from melting down in front of these kids when they ask me the updated version of the question with increasing frequency over the last few years. The new version goes something like this: "I am thinking about starting a band. What advice can you give me that will help me be successful in the music industry?"

NO, NO, NO. STOP. *Wrong question.* You don't even have a band yet, and you're already worried about getting ahead in the music industry? You're doomed, and my advice to you is

to become an accountant, a computer programmer, a proc-
tologist, a mortician, an auto mechanic, or any other profession with a pretty clear career path forward and at least *some*
sort of probability of making a decent living, because music
ain't that. Plus, you don't really want to be a musician in the
first place; you want to be *rich and famous.* I have zero advice
on how to achieve those dubious goals because, statistically,
they appear to be pretty much unobtainable for the vast
majority of people on earth; plus, I've never been interested
in that stuff anyway.

A musician wants—no, *needs*—to *make music,* and a
real musician makes music whether people like it or hate
it, whether they ever get invited to some stupid televised
awards ceremony show, whether anyone ever gets their
band's logo tattooed on their body, and even whether they
ever make a single penny from their songs. Musicians make
music because *this is what we do.* We have a burning desire
to express ourselves through our chosen instrument, and yes,
all that other stuff may be nice, but in the end, it doesn't matter because it's not the reason we picked up a guitar or pair of
drumsticks or a pen and notebook and started writing songs
in the first place.

I am able to make a very comfortable living as a member of my band, and that is a real blessing that I do not take
for granted, but it's not what causes me to pull over to the
side of the road and jot down an awesome idea for new lyrics
when it suddenly pops into my head on the way to the store
to buy toilet paper. (For some reason, driving is often when

lyrics just come to me.) I'm not thinking about all the nonexistent streaming services checks I'm going to cash when that song gets a placement on the soundtrack of the top-grossing movie of the year, nor am I imagining a flood of adoration from fans across the globe when that tune goes to the top of the charts. In fact, I'm not thinking *anything* in that moment other than, *Hmm . . . this might just work for a song!* That's all that matters to me—*the song*.

"What would you do if you won the lottery tomorrow and never had to work again?" is a common and amusing thought exercise. I've thought about this, and though my band *is* my job, I know *exactly* what I would do: keep on writing and playing music with those dudes until we decided as a group that we were done. Then I would pick up a pen and notebook, scribble out some ideas, make a few calls, and start working on different music with other musicians. *What else* am I supposed to do? Buy a bunch of expensive designer bullshit until I die? I am *an artist*; this is my function in life. And sure, some musicians daydream about becoming rich and famous and adored by all the bands that influenced them in high school, but if they are real artists, the music part always comes first—*always*. If the art is not the most important thing to you, if you don't feel that burning need to express yourself, to let out something *real* before you explode, then go do something else, because you are wasting your time.

I don't give a shit who this upsets, and I don't want to spare anyone's feelings. I'm simply trying to save the "Give me advice on how to become a rock star" crowd a lot of future grief and disappointment when their misguided dreams don't pan out. Because even if you *are* a truly gifted artist, you still might never be able to pay a single lousy electricity bill with your talent, because no matter how great you may be, there are no guarantees in music or any other form of art. This is a pirate's life, and the only thing you can be sure of is that you will be sailing into stormy seas, so if you don't love the wind and salt air, if you don't enjoy a bumpy ride, if you can't deal with all the emotional blood and thunder of constant rejection and the never-ending lack of certainty about your future, then this life is not for you. But do I hope that it is? *Fuck yes*, I do. And if you have the *cojones* to put your ass and future on the line and try to make it as an artist, do I want you to succeed? Oh, *absolutely*—I'm behind you, and I'm rooting for each and every one of you. I'm just letting you know that there is no free lunch, so be ready to hustle.

Some will read all this stuff and think I'm just being a negative gatekeeping asshole out to keep the playing field clear by crushing young people's artistic dreams, but nothing could be further from the truth. I'm not gatekeeping here because *there are no gates to keep.* Either you are going to be an artist or you are not, and there is nothing I or anyone else can say or do that will make that happen or not happen for you. There is no "secret to artistic success" to withhold from anyone, because unlike some members of the United States Congress who always seem to make freakishly lucky moves on the stock market to the tune of millions, in artistry there is no insider information to trade in. Anyone trying to shill some surefire secret method guaranteed to turn you into a successful artist is a goddamned liar, a snake oil salesman, a con man, and I will gladly tell them so straight to their fucking face. You want to be an artist? Start making some art, like *now*. Don't think about it, don't talk about it, don't sit around agonizing over whether the imaginary art you haven't made yet is gonna be any good, just start *doing it*. That's all there is to it, and I hope that you do, because *I love art* in all its forms. I don't think there can ever be enough art made; therefore, there can never be enough artists. I also truly believe that the more working artists there are in the world busting their asses in the search for truth and beauty, the better off we will all be, so why on earth would I discourage anyone from trying to become one? I'm just not going to bullshit anyone about this life, because the artists I respect never bullshitted me.

One cold February night in 1996, when I'd been in my band a little under six months, we played a particularly bad show at a local club called Twisters. We were opening for two out-of-town acts, Sheer Terror from New York City and Napalm Death from Birmingham, England. This was a big show for us, the biggest we had played yet, and I was super excited to open for Napalm Death because I had been a big fan for years. When we went on early that night, there weren't many people in the club yet, and even though it filled up while we played, it was obvious no one in the audience was paying attention to our set. Not a single person gave enough of a fuck to even heckle us; they just stood there talking to each other and ordering drinks at the bar, like we didn't exist, and I felt very demoralized by the end of our set. Sweaty, pissed off, and extremely bummed out, I was pushing one of our guitar cabinets through the now jam-packed club when I heard a distinctive voice yell out from the crowded bar, "HEY, RANDY!"

I looked up and sitting at the bar a few feet away was Dave Brockie, singer of the legendary Richmond group GWAR. Dave was flanked by two extremely attractive punk rock women, both of whom were hanging on his leather jacket and vying for his attention. He untangled himself from these enchanting creatures, sat up straight on his barstool, raised his drink to me in a toast, and then, looking for all the world like some sort of goddamned underground lord, gave me a very valuable bit of advice.

What did he say? "Hey, man, good on you for trying—ya got guts, kid," or "Don't worry about it, you'll get 'em next time," or "Bro, don't sweat it, we've all played a bad show or two," or even "If I were you, I wouldn't wear that stupid-looking T-shirt onstage next time"? No. He didn't say anything of that sort. Brockie looked me in my obviously miserable eye, gave me a huge shit-eating grin, and said:

"Remember—it's a loooong way to the top if you wanna rock 'n' roll, baby!"

Then he laughed directly in my face, took a huge gulp of his drink, turned his back on me, and immediately returned to flirting with those two impossibly hot women.

FUCK YOU, Dave! I thought. *I can't believe that rock star asshole just quoted fucking AC/DC lyrics at me.* Then, as I angrily shoved the guitar cab through the crowd to the exit, I suddenly realized, *Wait—that dude knows my name!*

Dave would eventually become a dear friend of mine, and his band generously took us out to open for them on our first real tour, even though most people didn't have any clue who we were back then. And I learned a lot about the artistic work ethic from hanging out with Brockie and just watching how he did things, because he was *always* working on something. Dave was a singer, a painter, a drawer, a sculptor, an actor, a writer, a comedic genius, a madman . . . he was an *artist*, and I miss him so very much, because like way too many of my artist friends who are no longer here, he let drugs kill him. Sometimes I still get very mad at Dave over that criminally stupid decision he made, and part of that anger is more than just my heart hurting over missing him (because I genuinely loved the man)—no, I'm pissed off because he robbed the world of all the art he could have made, and I'm mad he's not here for me to learn from by watching him make it. Brockie was the most wonderfully bizarre mentor-type figure any young artist could hope to have, always very generous with his time and counsel to me over the years. I learned some important lessons from him that I carry with me to this day, and I cherish my many warm memories of the times we spent together.

But the first time he spoke directly to me, the first time I knew the singer of the biggest band in town even knew I existed? He gave me the uncut stuff, the cold truth, with no mercy, no handholding, no fucking around. I'll never forget it for as long as I live. *Thanks, Dave.*

So ask yourself: Do you *really* wanna rock 'n' roll, baby? Do you dig what I'm saying?

I wasn't born a musician, a writer, or a photographer—I *became* all these things. I *do* believe I've always had an artistic temperament, a certain way of viewing the world, and a potential ability to communicate that way of viewing the world to others through art. This ability to communicate that view is what we call *talent*, and that's all artistic talent really is: the ability to effectively communicate ideas in a particularly focused specific form. Some of us are natural-born communicators, and some of us have to work very hard at it. Talent is not an absolute, inert, monolithic thing dispensed in precisely equal measures. But no matter how much innate talent one is gifted at birth, *no one* is "born an artist." People *become* artists when they start making art. Furthermore, no matter your original intent, you never know exactly what will happen once you start making art, and that's one of the most exciting parts of the whole thing. The type of art you eventually produce may even be totally different from what you had envisioned at the beginning; for instance, it is a complete *accident* that I am both a singer in a metal band and a photographer.

I never wanted to be the singer of a heavy metal band, probably because I was never a metalhead. I always wanted to be in a punk rock band because punk was mostly what I listened to growing up. In my senior year of high school, I joined my first band, Black Friday, a short-lived blues-tinged punk rock outfit that banged it out for a total of four or five practices in my buddy Alex's garage. Alex played guitar, someone neither of us can remember played drums, and I howled along through a crappy RadioShack mic that Alex had somehow connected to some shitty stereo speakers, making up lyrics as I went along. I have vague memories of hollering something about driving down the highway with a bottle of vodka beneath my seat (I believe this could be classified as *foreshadowing*—I should have paid better attention), but we didn't even have a bass player, and regrettably, because we were more interested in drinking cheap beer than actually working on our music, Black Friday never made it out of the garage to conquer the punk rock scene. (Alex and I are still friends, and supposedly he has boombox cassette recordings of those jam sessions somewhere, so maybe one day we'll have to get the band back together…hmm.)

Anyway, Black Friday and other more punk and weird rock-and-roll-style bands I was in never went any further than a few local shows (with the exception of one glorious trip to play a college party in Shippensburg, Pennsylvania— shout-out Abe, Bryant, and Jim "the Rim"—Stink Hogan lives!). But one drunken evening during my not-so-illustrious career as a local musician, I was screaming along to (well, actually being obnoxious and making fun of) some death metal record blasting from the bar stereo at one of my favorite local watering holes, The Metro, when one of my drinking buddies was like "*Whoa!* You can actually *do* that Cookie Monster voice?" From that evening on, I would occasionally jump onstage with friends in local groups who would say, "Do that metal voice thing!" mostly for a laugh. I kind of became known for it in our small circle, and eventually, I wound up "doing that metal voice thing" in my current band. That wasn't at all the plan, and obviously my half-assed efforts to become the South's answer to Johnny Rotten didn't pan out, but so what? I found something I was good at, I embraced it, and almost thirty years later, I'm still at it. What started out as a joke became a career, a career that has carried me literally around the world several times now. It still blows my mind when I think about it.

Photography came to me in almost exactly the same way. In 2012, I was on a plane while on tour in Australia, sitting beside my friend Jamey Jasta and punishing his ears with my elaborate plan for a book I wanted to write. I was going to completely unplug from the internet for a year, then write some undoubtedly highly caustic and severely judgmental tome detailing my year of magnificent internet-free experience that would confirm what I already knew: that our mentally anemic society was rapidly collapsing beneath the weight of our techno-dependence. Jamey listened to me prattle on for a half hour or so, and when I was done, he looked at me and said, "Okay, here's how we're going to do the movie." Jasta completely disregarded my high-minded literary aspirations, but he did lay out a pretty compelling argument for how a documentary film would be a more effective way to make my point. I was a little upset at first, because I had always wanted to be a writer, not a filmmaker, but soon I came around to his point of view.

I contacted my friend, the documentarian Don Argott, to see if he could suggest a relatively affordable camera I could buy to shoot some B-roll footage for my upcoming film (never mind that I had no plan in place for A-roll footage). I purchased the camera he suggested and even did a couple of interviews for the film, but mostly wound up using it to film myself and my buddies skateboarding. One day I was about to go skating, so I grabbed the camera. I was standing in my kitchen, fiddling with the camera and checking to make sure I had remembered to charge the battery, when I noticed my warped reflection in the rounded chrome lid of the French press coffee maker. *Man, that looks pretty cool*, I thought. *Lemme see if I can use this thing for what it's actually made for and try to take a picture.* I switched the camera from video to automatic mode (aka "dummy mode"), pointed it at the French press, looked through the viewfinder, and pressed the shutter button. *Click.* Almost instantly a photo popped up on the camera's back screen.

Whoa! That looks fuckin' AWESOME, I thought. *Holy shit—I'm a goddamned GENIUS!*

But sadly, as I swiftly learned after researching the work of some *actual photographers*, I was *nowhere close* to being a genius. In fact, I didn't know squat about photography, and that first picture was at best something any average middle schooler about to enroll in a beginner photography class could have taken. Furthermore, for *years* this "genius" had often caught himself noticing things with an artistic sort of eye—interesting street scenes, the intriguing shapes of common everyday objects, the contrast of deep shadows on bright days, and the way light always looked so soft and warm right around sunset. *Hmm, that looks so cool*, I would think. *I really wish I had an image-capturing device of some sort in my mind so that I could take a picture and show others what I'm seeing here.... If only someone manufactured that sort of device. Damn.* Not once in my more than forty years of life did I ever stop and think, *Eureka! I've got it! I'll go* buy a camera *and shoot a photo of what I see!* It's hilarious now when I go back and think about how glaringly obvious the solution to my image-making dilemma was, but I wasn't really interested in photography before—it always seemed like some dauntingly complex, highly esoteric discipline far beyond my limited aesthetic abilities.

But since that first photo, taken without any forethought and entirely on a whim, I am rarely without a camera of some sort when I leave the house. I have shot photographs all over the world during my travels, and those photos have hung on gallery walls in the United States and in museums in other countries, have been used for album and book covers, have appeared in magazine articles, have been utilized as T-shirt designs, and have appeared in printed promotional material for musical equipment companies. I became a photographer entirely by accident, but it has brought so much joy into my life, and I constantly feel the need to learn more about the photographic process so that I may engage with it more effectively, because engaging in the process is the only way to get better. This is the same with any artistic pursuit. There are no shortcuts, there are no exceptions.

You have to *engage in the creative process* to become an artist, and to do that, you have to have the guts and be willing to put a huge chunk of yourself into the work if you want to create something new—this is the only way. There are only twelve notes on a guitar, and since at least 1951, when Jackie Brenston and his Delta Cats released "Rocket 88," a tune that is commonly accepted by musical scholars as the first recorded rock and roll song, untold millions of guitarists have picked up their axe and attempted to hammer out a new rock song using those same twelve notes. How many different chord progressions are there to choose from to build a song structure? How many different ways can there possibly be to combine those twelve notes into a guitar solo? I am not a guitarist, and I do not know. I only know that when I hear certain guitarists solo, I can *immediately* tell who is playing, like my friend Dr. Know of the legendary Bad Brains, my favorite band of all time. Doc is working with the exact same twelve notes as every other guitarist on earth, but it is *his hands* on the frets, and he is pouring himself out through those hands and into that instrument. He is putting all his joy and pain into that solo, and so it sounds like him and no one else, even though I'm sure the exact same progression of notes has been stumbled on a staggering number of times since "Rocket 88" was released. If you hold back from putting yourself into your art, your *entire self*, your art is going to be bland, pedestrian, and forgettable.

In other words, your art is going to *suck*.

Sometimes during the artistic process, things get broken—preconceived notions, cherished ideas, relationships of all sorts, and even sanity itself. Horrible mistakes can and do occur, but you must stay committed to the process until the end, because it is only by seeing a thing through that the conditions for greatness are allowed to bloom. A project abandoned halfway through the process just because things got tough unexpectedly will never go down in history like "Rocket 88" did. And although Jackie Brenston did go down in history for singing "Rocket 88," and he and his Delta Cats are credited on the release, the band was actually Ike Turner and his Kings of Rhythm, a group that Brenston normally played saxophone in. During the drive from Mississippi to Memphis to record at the now legendary Sun Studio, the Kings of Rhythm guitarist Willie Kizart's amp was damaged when it fell out of the band's car and onto Highway 61 while they were changing a flat tire. When the band arrived at the studio, a quick fix was implemented by stuffing the amp with newspaper in an attempt to hold the internal speaker cone in place. Kizart plugged in his guitar, powered up the amp, and a strange noise came out. Sam Phillips, the owner and in-house producer of Sun Studio, liked the way the damaged amp sounded, and instead of switching to a different, "properly working" amp, the busted, paper-filled rig went on the recording of "Rocket 88"...and thus, distortion was born.

Things get broken in this life. Use them.

When you begin engaging in the creative process, you will be absolutely terrible at it. Accept that, and keep going. You will be filled with doubt, insecurity, and probably a healthy dose of self-loathing—this is good medicine, so swallow it and keep going. You will see other art, read other books, hear other music, and you will think, *My God, what I am doing is absolute trash compared to that painter, that writer, that drummer. I will* never *be that good.* Guess what? You're probably right, but that also means you are paying attention to the artists worth learning from—high-quality ones. Deal with it, and keep going. How do you know when you're truly fucked, when you should throw in the towel, when you should just call it quits and go do something else?

When you completely stop feeling all those awful things.

This usually happens after you have attained a bit of notoriety, after you have paid too much attention to flattering compliments and good reviews and attractive people way out of your league who suddenly want to sleep with you. After you have believed some of your own hype, after you think your shit doesn't stink, you can go ahead and hang it up. When you have allowed the fawning opinions of others to convince you of the infallibility of your God-given talent, that talent has abandoned you and you have nothing interesting left to say. You have stopped feeding your talent the only way possible: by giving bloody chunks of yourself to the process. I do not believe in the popular myth that only great suffering produces great art, but if you're doing it right, it sure as hell won't feel good all the time. This is because giving away parts of yourself to anything, whether a romantic partner or the artistic process, *should* be uncomfortable at times, it *should* scare you. This is how you know you are working toward something valuable, something worth fighting and maybe even dying for, something *real*...because you put something *real* into it. Nothing ventured, nothing gained.

This is also why using AI, that terrifying engine of banalization and intellectual decay, to instantly produce an illustration or "photograph," a piece of music, a book, or any other form of "art" doesn't make anyone an artist either—there is no process. An artist *must* engage in process, for that is the only way the artist can insert the only thing of true value they have into a work of art—themself. For better or worse, this book was written by me, and solely me. It is not an algorithmically assembled composite of the sum of millions of other writers' hard work—it is the result of *my* hard work, *my* process, and whether it's a good book or the worst one ever written, anyone who can't say the same about the book or article or song lyric or painting or whatever it is that they are trying to pass off as their own has no goddamned business calling themself "an artist." This book stands on the shoulders of giants, all those writers who came before me who completely gave themselves to their work, work that gave me comfort, broadened my thinking, influenced me, and shaped me into the writer I am. If I am to honor their labor, then I must put myself into my own. Because "AI artists" don't put anything of *themselves* through an actual process and instead use an AI engine to instantly shit out a gold-plated turd, they don't learn anything about themselves, which is perhaps the greatest gift of the artistic life. They didn't grow as a person because they weren't forced to face and do battle with their own limitations, to break through and push beyond the limits of their talent. They just microwaved an idea, ripping off every single one of us throughout history who has actually had the balls to step into the sacred arena of creation, raise our fists, and fight like madmen to make something worthwhile. Either these people are too scared to go through that bloody process or are too goddamned lazy to make the effort. Either way, don't ever for one second be confused about the nature of this type of "art" because there is no such thing as "AI artists"—only a slothful legion of warp-speed hacks employing automated plagiarism machines.

You want to be an artist? Then raise your fists, goddamn it, and step into the arena. Get sweaty, take a swing, and see if you connect with your better self—you might even surprise yourself and pound out something great.

That is what the creative process, *especially* the book-writing process, is often like for me: boxing with myself. There are those rare and blessed days when the words come easily, the muse guiding my hands as I float like a butterfly and sting like a bee, the sentences flowing out of me almost effortlessly and dancing across the page like Muhammad Ali to an early bout knockout victory. Those days actually feel like the romantic sitting-by-the-fireplace-tweed-sweater-wearing-made-for-TV version of the writing life that most people seem to believe in, that I myself used to believe in before I became an author—how I love those lucky days! But the vast majority of the time I put myself in the writing chair? It's a desperate, knock-down, drag-out, completely graceless bare-knuckle street brawl with the empty page to survive all twelve rounds of my allotted writing time without losing too many of my teeth. I swing and I swing and I swing, throwing clumsy haymakers as I try to beat some words that mean something onto the page, and every now and then I'll land a lucky punch. But most of the time I miss, and for my trouble I get repeatedly smacked in the face by frustration over my inability to say what I mean with any sort of grace or style. Most days I approach writing with a sense of overwhelming dread and anxiety, because I have learned from painful experience that I am probably going to wind up on my ass, battered, bruised, and feeling like an imposter, not a contender.

But if I just keep on showing up at my desk every morning with the will to fight, if I commit to taking my lumps and going the distance each day for a few hard hours, I know that eventually my artless jabs will wear down the opponent. This is a war of attrition, and sooner or later, I will see an opening—then I will put this motherfucker to sleep.

There is nothing "magical" about this process, just as there is nothing magical about getting in shape by exercising a little bit each day. Anyone who chooses to get up off their ass and try can engage in the artistic process. You may start off weak and soft, but if you have even a smidgen of talent and you keep at it, the creative muscle *will* grow stronger.

The only way to know whether you have any talent is to try, and yes, you may indeed fail. But in that failure, you might just find out where your true gifts lie, what you are really supposed to be doing with your life, because if the artistic process is anything, it is an act of self-illumination. And just like physical exercise, no matter how painful, disheartening, and utterly exhausting your exertion in the artistic process has been, at the end of the day you will *never* wind up a weaker person. Science has proved that exercising creativity is good for mental health, so start a project and begin exercising. You'll never know what might happen unless you start trying.

If you want to be an artist, or follow any other non-standard path in life, for that matter, you must be cunning, self-sufficient, and willing to suffer. You must learn to think outside the box and reject the expectations of others. Expect to be mocked and ridiculed for displaying the audacity of attempting to follow your dream, and be prepared for the humiliation of failing and failing again...and again...and again. If you do ever miraculously reach a point where you can sustain yourself with your artistic endeavors alone, prepare to be hated—weak and jealous people will always try to mask the pain of their own unfulfilled dreams by pissing all over yours. Now more than ever, the world is full of critics, always ready to point out where and how you have failed, how something you are trying will never work, how someone else has already done it and done it ten times better, but to hell with those people. Never ever ever EVER give a single solitary fuck about what people who are not successful at what you are trying to do think about your work. If I wanted to be a mechanic, would I pay attention to a stand-up comedian with no automotive experience beyond driving their car to the grocery store telling me how to rebuild a carburetor? *Fuck no.* No one else's opinion matters, not well-meaning friends', not concerned family's, and especially not random anonymous internet commenters'. Note that I am *not* saying "Don't listen to *anyone*. You do you, baby!" Sometimes we all need a little adult supervision to help guide us in life, and an incredibly valuable skill to develop, one you should start working on immediately, is learning how to shut up and listen to people who actually know what they are talking about if and when they are generous enough to share their time and knowledge with you.

How do you know whether someone is an artist worth listening to? Their work speaks for them.

In the end, the work and the process are all that matters. The artist at work is like an antique-hunting auctioneer walking into a pitch-black warehouse full of an untold variety of things. You leave the noisy outside world behind and step into the dark and bang around in the blackness for a while, cursing and bruising your shins as you blindly bump into things until you remember you have an old book of matches in your wallet. You strike a couple and they immediately go out, but in those brief flashes of light you spot a dusty candle stub sitting on a crate. You fumble over to it, and after a few nerve-wracking tries with the last of your matches, you manage to get the candle lit. You hold the flickering flame up, and even though it gives only a tiny bit of light, it's just enough to make out the vague outlines of what looks to possibly be beautiful objects all around you.

But you still can't see much, and your candle is burning fast, so you stumble around some more, looking for additional sources of light. Eventually, you find a few old oil lamps, and you light them and place them around the room until you have a clear picture of your surroundings. And the warehouse is indeed full of beautiful things—now you have to decide which you want to carry out to auction. You examine these objects. Right in front of you is a lovely old velvet jewelry box, but you've seen way too many just like it on the auction block lately, so it's not going to fetch much. Over there is a nice piece of furniture, a trendy midcentury chair you know for sure will be a hot-ticket item, but when you pick it up it disintegrates in your hands, destroyed by an infestation of termites.

Finally, you spy a large rectangular item standing in a corner, covered in dust. You walk over to it, carefully turn it around, and it turns out to be a massive nineteenth-century French Baroque style beveled mirror in an elaborate hand-carved gilt frame—it looks to be solid, relatively intact, and you're fairly certain it will be worth quite a lot. *Bingo*. But to inspect it, you need more light, so you feel along the warehouse walls until you find a switch. You flip the switch, the warehouse fills with brightness, and sure enough, it holds many other things that look pretty valuable. But you are by yourself, and you can carry out only one item at a time, so you make a mental note to come back later, and you return to the mirror.

The frame appears to be mostly intact, but a lot of elbow grease will be needed to clean it up, maybe to apply a careful dab of paint here and there where it has chipped. With your handkerchief, you carefully wipe away the thick coat of dust that covers the mirror's glass, sneezing from time to time as it flies into your nose and makes your eyes water. When you have gotten the glass mostly clean, you step back and take a look.

There you are, and there is everything around you, perfectly reflected in this magnificent old object, this carefully handcrafted work of art. *This will work,* you think, *now I just have to get this thing out of here.*

If you are willing to look through the eyes of an artist, life can be a warehouse full of beautiful ideas—you just have to be brave enough to search the dark until you find one worth working on, putting your back into it, and whipping it into shape, then bringing it into the light. Maybe no one will care about your ideas, maybe they will even think your ideas are stupid or ugly. Or perhaps people will eventually see the truth, beauty, and value of those ideas, but not until long after you're dead. It doesn't matter, though, because it is through this search, the artistic process, that we learn how to see and come to know ourselves.

To be an artist of sober mind and body—that is how I have learned to see, to navigate this world, to make life happen *for me*, not *to me*.

Art saves lives. I know it saved mine. Who knows? It might save yours.

Chapter Ten

THE FRIEND CATCHER

I n April 2021 I was stuck at home, and things were starting to get a little weird in my head.

Lamb of god had released our self-titled album almost a year previously, but because venues remained closed with the ongoing coronavirus pandemic, we hadn't been able to tour to support it. In fact, it had been almost two years since I had stepped foot on a stage to perform for a live audience, the longest time I had ever gone without doing so in my entire adult life, and I was beginning to feel like I wasn't even a musician anymore. Write album, record album, tour to support album, rinse and repeat—that had been my routine for over two decades, and although the touring musician's

251

life is not nearly as structured as a nine-to-five office worker's, to have that admittedly rough outline of a regular life plan removed totally destroyed the little sense of normalcy I might have had.

We did book a tour to start in just four months, and after it had been rescheduled several times, it looked like it might actually happen this time. But after a solid year of watching everyone's lives and plans be repeatedly turned upside down by the pandemic, I wasn't holding my breath.

Yes, during our unintended touring break, my band had already started writing and demoing out a new album—what else were we supposed to do? However, unlike some musicians, I am not a fan of the recording process. I view it as a necessary evil, a headache-inducing pain-in-the-ass step I must periodically take so that I can continue to feel the biggest rush that being a musician provides: getting out in front of a large mass of people and interacting with them through the intensity of a live show. I want to feel connected to *human beings* through my music, not a computer in a recording studio—this requires a living, breathing audience.

I had spent most of my life throwing my voice into a sea of people, then hearing their voices come roaring back in answer, crashing over me like a mighty wave. I missed that push and pull of energy, the earth-shaking back-and-forth that lets you physically see when your music is actually *moving* people. For a performer, there is nothing like that communicative experience, and I was starting to get a little frayed around the ol' edges in its absence.

On days when I caught myself stuck in the house, growing restless and going way too far up in my head over things I could not control, I would get out and take a walk across the Mayo Bridge that spans the James River in downtown Richmond—if I couldn't move my body in front of a crowd, at least I could march it over to Southside and back. I was returning from one of those walks on April 10, 2021, when I stopped to ask an older gentleman fishing from the bridge if he was having any luck (always the polite thing to do). "Some," he replied. "Got couple of little flatheads, but I don't know what in the hell this thing is—do you?" The fisherman reached into his blue five-gallon bucket and pulled out a hideous eel-looking fish—*Agh! A snakehead!*

Snakeheads are an invasive species, an aquatic apex predator native to China, Korea, and Russia. Some moron released these fish into American waters years ago, and they have been spreading ever since, first appearing in Virginia in 2004. Snakeheads can breathe air, live out of water for up to four days, and can even *crawl across land* on their slimy little bellies in search of different bodies of water to hunt in, like some sort of awful nightmare commando fish from hell. I know they are a part of nature and all that hippie-dippie tree-hugging crap, but they should be doing their creepy crawling around the Yangtze River basin in China, not Shockoe Bottom in Richmond, so I was very unhappy to see one. I've been told they *are* pretty delicious to eat—never tasted one myself—so I told the fisherman to be sure to kill the damned thing and cook it up later. Then

I snapped a picture to send to the Virginia Department of Wildlife Resources.

I was stomping away angrily muttering to myself, *It's bad enough we can't go on tour because of COVID and now I can't even take a walk across the goddamned river without fuckin' snakeheads swimming all over the goddamned place around here trying to eat up all our goddamned small mouth bass and fuck that thing because I don't know where the goddamned snakehead hotline number is and I want to kill all these motherfuckers, grrrrrr...* when I noticed that lamb of god's publicist Maria had forwarded me an email. The subject line read "Lamb of God Be The Match."

Hey there—

I was just hoping you could pass a message along to lamb of god. Their EP, "The Duke," inspired me to get involved with the Be The Match organization back in 2016. Fast-forward to today and I got the email that I'm a match for a 67-year-old leukemia patient... and it's all because of them.

Anyway, I just wanted them to know that they made a difference.

Thanks,

Todd Seaman

And just like that, my whole attitude changed.

Holy shit, I thought. *We did it! Wayne, we actually fucking did it, bro!* I looked out over the river that runs through my city, and I thought about the song I wrote for Wayne Ford, a fan of my band dead from leukemia for over six years, and I started to cry. It felt good, though, because I had just been reminded of what I was—a musician—and I was now remembering just how powerful music could be. Beyond being a creative outlet and beyond being just a job, this was all I ever wanted from my music: for it to help people, to give them courage, and to make things better, just as other people's music had helped me get through so many tough times.

I stood there on the bridge for a moment rereading the email, then I wiped away my tears, walked home, and immediately emailed Todd Seaman. I thanked him for letting us know, told him how much this meant to me and how his message had just reminded me that what we do matters, and I asked him to please keep me updated on the situation. Todd hit me back within an hour.

"Finding out I'm gonna get to help save somebody's life is possibly the coolest feeling I've ever experienced in my life," he wrote, "and I've been fortunate enough to do a lot of cool things, ha-ha." With that one sentence, I knew immediately that he and I were going to be friends. He promised to keep me updated and let me know that he and his father would be coming to our August 8 show in Arkansas, their home state. We made plans to meet up near the venue before the gig and then I messaged my bandmates with the good news.

It's strange to look back now and remember how vastly different things were just a few short years ago at the height of the coronavirus pandemic. I watched a movie recently that was set in late 2020, and it brought back so many things I realized I had practically forgotten—all the uncertainty and complete upheaval of normal day-to-day existence. The dark and shuttered businesses. The children stuck at home, unable to go to school to learn and properly socialize with other kids. The uncomfortable, intentional physical distancing from my older family members. The odd feeling of walking away from a street-corner conversation with a masked stranger and realizing you had no idea of what their face looked like. The anger and the fear and the deaths, all those lonely deaths that so many elderly people had died, isolated from their loved ones in an apartment, nursing home, or hospital bed. Once before, I had been physically disconnected from my family, friends, countrymen, and native soil by the walls of a foreign prison, but this was something entirely different—a discomforting sense of disconnection from humanity itself.

It was a bizarre time to be alive, but it did make me appreciate the good occurrences in my life with a much greater intensity. Receiving Todd's email would have made me ecstatic during the best of times, but reading it in those dark days was a positively transcendent experience. I actually felt *high* and floated around on a cloud of gratitude for days.

Two and a half months later, Todd emailed to let me know that the patient's oncologist had determined he was the best donor candidate and that Be The Match would be flying him to Washington, DC, so that he could donate his stem cells at a medical facility in nearby Annandale, Virginia. I got very excited when I saw he would be coming to my beloved Old Dominion.

"Bro!" I replied. "When is the procedure? Annandale is about an hour and a half away from me—I would love to drive up and buy you dinner!" Todd wrote back that the procedure was supposed to happen on August 17…the day I was supposed to fly to Austin, Texas, to start tour. Dammit! It didn't look like we would be able to meet up in Virginia after all, but I would hopefully still get to meet him at our gig in Arkansas in September. I say "hopefully" because at that point I still wasn't convinced the tour would happen: The show in Rogers, Arkansas, was originally scheduled for July 14, 2020. Then it was moved to August 8, 2021. Then one of the opening acts, our friends in the band In Flames from Sweden, had to drop off the tour because they couldn't get visas to get into the States. Our friends in Hatebreed jumped on as replacements, but they were having an extremely hard time finding a bus to carry them and their road crew. Then the show got moved *again*, this time to September 22, 2021. As well, the few tours that *had* managed to get up and running were constantly postponing or canceling shows as band and crew members fell sick from COVID.

The pandemic was still constantly pushing and shifting everything around in the touring world, and tours are monumentally complex undertakings even when the world is running normally. Booking and preparing for a big tour is not like making tentative plans to meet a friend for lunch on some undecided day next week. ("Call me Monday and we'll figure it out!") There are hundreds of moving pieces, and everything has to be nailed down months in advance if there is to be any hope of getting a bunch of lunatic musicians out their front doors and on the road. This whole thing was frustrating for everyone involved, including the fans, but I was very grateful that I was merely the singer guy, not a manager or booking agent. Trying to plan a tour back then must have been like waking up every day and throwing a handful of darts at thirty different constantly moving targets.

Eventually, we got lucky, and lamb of god finally got out on the road. I flew to Austin on August 17 as planned, and after all the chaos, the tour did extremely well. But our schedule was not the only one being moved around. Shortly before we hit the road, Todd emailed me to let me know that his donation procedure had been moved to a week later in August for some unknown reason. Then it got pushed until the end of September because the patient had to undergo some other medical procedure. Then it got pushed back another eight weeks because the patient had gotten very sick and needed to get healthier before he would be able to receive a transplant—the doctors were now shooting for late November for Todd to donate.

Every time it got close to his scheduled donation date, Todd would have to go to a local oncologist in Arkansas, undergo a battery of tests and get checked to make sure he hadn't suddenly developed cancer himself. He would get cleared, begin preparing to donate, then a message would come that the patient wasn't healthy enough to receive Todd's bone marrow. Remembering how quickly leukemia took out our merch girl Evie, a healthy young woman, not a senior citizen, I worried that the patient would die before he ever got the chance to receive Todd's donation. But all we could do was keep our fingers crossed and wait.

One bright spot amid all this was meeting Todd and his father, Scott, when we played Arkansas. We got along famously, just as I knew we would. Sometimes you just get a good feeling about a person, and my instincts were right. We met up for lunch on the patio of a restaurant near the venue (fittingly named "Tacos 4 Life") and had a great chat over our meal about the amazing thing Todd had been given the opportunity to do, what life was like in that part of Arkansas, and (of course) music. Todd and Scott were both accomplished musicians, both had done some touring, and both were in bands that, just like mine, hadn't played a gig in quite some time because of COVID. These were two good men, and I could tell Scott was very proud of his son and Todd's selfless nature.

That evening's show was the first one Todd attended since February 2020 (599 days, to be exact—he did the math!), and it was a great one—the Arkansas crowd was tremendous, our band was on fire, and I made sure to give Todd a shout-out from the stage. Then I loaded them up with merch after the show (by the way, this is how you get free band swag outta me: do something *awesome* for other people out of the kindness of your heart) and told them I hoped to see them in Virginia soon.

Months of back-and-forth between the patient's doctor and the Be The Match people went by, and finally on November 18, 2021, Todd texted me to let me know all systems were go—it was *on*. He and Scott would be flying into DC on December 21, and the donation would happen the next day on the twenty-second, just in time for Christmas. *Oh, hell yes!* I was done touring for the year, so I got the oil changed in my truck, reserved a room at the Hilton in McLean, where Todd and Scott would be staying, and started counting the days.

On the morning of the twenty-first in December, Todd and Scott caught an early flight to DC. I rolled out of bed, tossed back a few cups of coffee, got in my truck, headed north on I-95, and arrived at the hotel in the early afternoon.

It was good to see those two Arkansas boys again, and we were all definitely in extremely high spirits, with high-fives and hugs all around. Todd had gotten his final injections of filgrastim at a nearby clinic that morning—for the whole week leading up to this, a nurse had come to Todd's house twice a day to give him injections of the drug. As Todd explained, filgrastim basically puts your system into overdrive, greatly increasing the release of blood-forming cells from bone marrow and into the bloodstream. In nonscientific terms, it gives you leaky bones.

The next day, Todd would be hooked up to an apheresis machine, his blood would be drawn into the machine, which would spin it around at a super high speed in a centrifuge to separate and collect the healthy stem cells that had leaked from his bones into his blood, and then pump it back into his body. The procedure was supposed to be relatively painless, he would be awake for it, and it would last just a few hours. The only other things I had heard before about bone marrow donation was that it involved large needles poking into your actual bones to directly collect marrow and a long and painful recovery period. Bone marrow donation is still done this way sometimes, when a donor cannot produce enough cells to use the comparatively pain-free apheresis method; luckily Todd was not one of those people. But had that been the only option, I know he would have manned up and done it without a second's hesitation—that is the kind of man he is, and I am so very proud to call him my friend.

The first afternoon, we were all a bit hungry after our travels, so we went to a nearby ramen restaurant and got a quick bite to eat. Then I asked Todd if he felt like going into DC for an hour or two to see a little of the town. Tomorrow was a big day for him, and the Seamans had already put in a long day's journey from Arkansas, so I didn't know if he just wanted to rest up, but they were both game for a little sightseeing. The Tyson's Corner DC Metro station was under a mile away, so we walked to it, hopped on the subway, and rolled through the underground out of my home state and into our nation's capital. When we got out at the Capitol South station at the eastern end of the National Mall, the sky was overcast, and there was a chill in the air as the sun began to set, but it was a fine, brisk evening to walk and talk—and walk and talk we did.

Like many Virginians, I have been going to Washington, DC, since I was a child on school field trips or on vacation with my family to see the wonderful Smithsonian museums. In the eighties and nineties, I often made the hour-and-a-half trip from Richmond to see shows at the venerable old 9:30 Club only to finally wind up playing gigs myself at the new 9:30 Club and have photo exhibitions at galleries in the District. I've been to DC so many times that I tend to forget that for most people in our country, Washington is a faraway place, seen mostly in movies or on television on the nightly news during discussions of our nation's contentious halls of power. Famous landmarks like the Washington Monument, at one time the world's tallest structure (and still the world's tallest obelisk), have become a commonplace sight to me over the years, just another part of the landscape I often pass by on I-95 heading up the eastern seaboard on tour.

But Todd had only ever been to DC on tour himself and had never had time to see the sights; Scott had never been in the city before, period. Washington, DC, is a fine walking town, and I always enjoy feeling the weight of history as I look at its beautiful old buildings and stroll through the imposing grandeur of its stately monuments, so it was a pleasure to play tour guide and show the two men from Arkansas around. We started out walking around the Capitol, pausing to take photos by a giant Christmas tree that stood on the Capitol's west lawn. Many families out enjoying the evening were also taking photos by the tree; a really good feeling of Christmas joy and cheer filled the air. I did have a brief, strangely unsettling moment standing among all those happy people by the Christmas tree: I looked up at the staircases climbing to the still-blocked-off western entrance to the Capitol and suddenly remembered what had happened there earlier that year on January 6. History is a strange thing, and I was reminded that sometimes its weight is not pleasant. But there was no angry mob storming the Capitol that evening, only smiling couples, laughing children, and three Southern musicians out for a peaceful evening walk. It felt good to see everyone walking among each other in peace at a place so recently and famously marred by violent division, and my unease disappeared as quickly as it had arisen.

We left the Capitol and made our way across the National Mall to stop and crane our necks skyward beneath the Washington Monument. Then we walked down the gently sloping hill to the National World War II Memorial, with its fifty-six columns representing the men and women of each state and US territory who served during that terrible war for the soul of our world. We found the columns for Arkansas and Virginia and then ambled along the almost half-mile length of the iconic Lincoln Memorial Reflecting Pool, ending up at the steps of the Lincoln Memorial. Looking out over the Reflecting Pool toward the Washington Monument, we stood at the very same spot where Martin Luther King Jr. gave his magnificent "I Have a Dream" speech. We walked up the steps and into the Lincoln Memorial and stood there in the hushed silence staring up at the massive 175-ton statue of Lincoln, powerfully seated with a look of deep contemplation furrowing his famously craggy brow.

The Lincoln Memorial is as fine a piece of neoclassical architecture as you will find anywhere in the world, and my favorite time to visit it is at night during the colder months, when the ever-present throngs of tourists that crowd DC in the spring and summer are absent. It was a perfect night to visit Honest Abe, chilly and empty, and we spent a good amount of time there. Then we took the short walk over to the low black granite walls of the Vietnam Veterans Memorial, an intensely solemn place where people often leave notes, candles, flowers, and various other objects beneath the engraved name of a loved one taken by that senseless war. More than fifty-eight thousand names of men and women killed or missing in action are carved into those dark mirror-like walls. Being there never fails to move me.

The entire time we walked, I periodically asked Todd if he was tired or wanted to head back to the hotel to crash. I didn't want to wear him out, but he kept saying he was fine. We were having such a good time that I said, "You can't come to DC and not see the White House!" so off to the White House we went. As we walked around the White House, I told Todd one of my all-time favorite DC history stories.

One December day in 1970, Elvis Presley got into a huge argument with his wife and father over him spending too much money on Christmas presents (reportedly $100,000 on thirty-two handguns and ten Mercedes-Benzes). Presley had had about enough of his family's nagging and lack of Christmas cheer, so he decided to get out of town. He flew to Los Angeles by himself, grabbed a couple of his buddies, and then immediately caught a red eye back east to Washington, DC. Once he and his boys landed, they hopped in a limousine and took it straight to the White House, arriving at the crack of dawn. Elvis, wearing a black velvet suit and cape, got out of the limo and handed a note to the astonished officers guarding the front gate stating that he wanted to meet with President Richard M. Nixon. The King of Rock and Roll desperately wanted to discuss his plan to help save his country by going undercover to fight "the drug culture" and "hippie elements." He was sure he could do this if only President Nixon would do him the small favor of making him a "Federal Agent at Large" (whatever that means).

In the note, Elvis went on to assure Nixon that he would remain in DC for however long it took to obtain the credentials of a federal agent because he had "done an in-depth study of drug abuse and Communist brainwashing techniques" and was certain that his elevated status as an entertainer would enable him to gain the trust of the enemies of our country who lived in our midst—oh, and also that he had brought Nixon a personal gift he wished to give him. The King included his hotel room number and alias he was staying under, hopped back in the limo, and went to his hotel to await Nixon's call.

Incredibly, Tricky Dicky's people set up a meeting, so a few short hours later, Elvis Presley strolled into the White

House, looking like some sort of bouffanted hillbilly Dracula in his black cape and sunglasses. In his hands he carried Nixon's gift: a small display case containing a World War II commemorative Colt .45 pistol and seven silver bullets. Understandably, the Secret Service were slightly alarmed by this and would not allow Elvis to bring the pistol into the Oval Office, but they did accept it on Nixon's behalf. (According to Presley, they missed the two-shot derringer he had in his boot; I've seen that very gun at Graceland.)

After this tiny security concern was addressed, Elvis was led in to meet Nixon, and despite initially alarming the president by giving him a big ol' Tennessee hug—Nixon wasn't really the cuddly sort—the meeting was by all accounts a success. Presley wound up getting some sort of honorary badge and nonsense federal ID from the president (which was all he really wanted in the first place—Elvis collected those sorts of things), and Nixon got publicity photos his team hoped would help spiff up his stuffy image with younger voters—the black-and-white photo taken by the White House photographer of Elvis and Nixon shaking hands in the Oval Office remains to this day the most requested photo in the National Archives.

We had a good laugh over Elvis's adventure as we stood in front of the White House in Lafayette Square. It was only when I started writing this that I realized that I had told Todd the story of Elvis and Nixon *exactly* fifty-one years to the date after it actually happened, December 21, 1970. Incredible.

By this time, it was fully dark, and we were getting cold and hungry. We walked down F Street in search of food, passed by Ford's Theatre where John Wilkes Booth assassinated Abraham Lincoln 156 years ago, eventually wound up at a fancy Mediterranean restaurant called Fig & Olive, and I got to do what I had come to DC to do in the first place: buy these guys dinner. The three of us felt a bit underdressed among the suit-and-tie-wearing businessmen and politicians in the dinner crowd, but I am used to feeling like that pretty much anytime someone takes me somewhere "respectable" to eat on the road. I'm a singer in a heavy metal band, not a stockbroker or congressman, so I don't usually bother to pack a dinner jacket and dress shoes along with my grubby show clothes. However out of place we may have looked, my money was as green as anyone else's, and obviously that's all that really matters in DC. Plus, the staff was cool, the food was absolutely delicious, and it was nice to be in the warmth for a bit. We finished eating and all of us could have fallen asleep right there at the dinner table, but we hopped on a Metro train back to McLean and were in our hotel rooms by ten o'clock. We had walked more than eleven glorious miles that evening, and every inch of them had been a treat.

At 6:00 a.m. my alarm went off, I did my old man stretches, met Todd and Scott in the hotel lobby, and we were out the door and on the road in my truck by seven. Todd was scheduled to be at the clinic at 7:30 a.m., and it being a short eight-minute drive to Annandale, we arrived in plenty of time. Somehow Todd had finagled it so that I could be present during the donation, and I had brought my camera to document the process. We walked into the clinic, met Cathy and Brendan, the two nurses who would perform the procedure, and then Scott and I sat down while they prepped Todd. They checked his temperature and blood pressure, injected him with some drug that raised his body temperature, put an IV into each of his arms, hooked ol' Leaky Bones up to the apheresis machine, and started pumping his blood into the machine so it could extract the good stuff.

It was absolutely freezing in the clinic, and with good reason—it was almost Christmas, but the air conditioning was set to an inhumanly low temperature. This helped preserve the vital platelets being extracted from Todd's blood until the procedure was over and they could be put into cold storage. I shivered under a blanket, but Todd was totally fine, sitting in the arctic air and looking as unbothered as a polar bear in his Steve Vai T-shirt and socks printed with the same pattern as the infamous rug in the movie *The Big Lebowski*. Every now and then, one of the nurses would place microwaved bags of saline on Todd's neck and hands to keep him toasty. Cathy and Brendan were awesome people and didn't seem to be annoyed by my endless stream of questions. I shot a bunch of photos, we talked about music, joked around with each other, and generally had about as much fun as one can have while hanging out in a refrigerator. It was honestly a good time. Todd had to sit perfectly still, or the machine would start beeping like crazy—that seemed to be the worst part of the procedure for him. I texted a picture of Todd attached to the machine to my friend Nergal, the singer of Poland's Behemoth who had beaten leukemia himself with the help of a bone marrow donor.

Nergal sent back a video thanking him: "Todd, thank you so much for being brave as fuck—you are a giver of life," Nergal said into his cell phone camera. "You are a *light bringer*. Sending love from Poland."

And it's true, Todd was those things. At one point, Scott and I walked to a nearby café to grab some sandwiches. When we returned, we met a man in a Star Wars T-shirt in the lobby. He was in the Air Force and had flown in from Ohio that morning for a physical examination to get cleared to donate stem cells. He had been matched with a cancer patient himself. He was scheduled to return to Annandale to donate next week, and we stood around talking for a bit about how cool Be The Match was and how we had found out about it. Then he said, "Oh, you're in lamb of god? I knew you looked familiar. I used to listen to your band!" It's always *hilarious* to me when I meet people who say things like that ("Wait, you're Randy from lamb of god? I used to be a big fan!"), and I wanted so badly to ask him why he stopped listening to us, but he was a really cool guy, so we wished him luck and went back upstairs to hang out with Todd. After four hours of sitting (mostly) perfectly still, the apheresis machine began loudly beeping in Morse code: SOS.

Todd was finished. He had done his bit to save an unknown stranger's ship, so the nurses unhooked him from the apheresis machine, and he hopped up and ran to the bathroom in his Big Lebowski socks to take a much-needed leak. I yelled, "Dude! Don't pee on the rug!" Todd returned looking much relieved, changed into a T-shirt that said I AM A BE THE MATCH DONOR, and we took more photos together in celebration, Todd holding up the one bag of stem cells and one bag of plasma the apheresis machine had just extracted from his blood. Brendan took the bags of stem cells and plasma, the "magic sauce," as we had begun to call it, threw them in a medical cooler, sealed it up, and a courier quickly came and took it away. We thanked Cathy and Brendan, who had both been really funny people and a real pleasure to hang around. "I love my job," Cathy said. "I get to help people save lives all day!" She also ordered my first book online right then and there, so hopefully she'll read these words about herself one day, too.

We said our goodbyes and drove to a pizza place to have lunch, then I dropped Todd and Scott off at their hotel, gave them both a big hug, and headed south for Richmond. Driving home, I became very emotional, and more than once I had to wipe tears from my eyes to see the road clearly. The greatest Christmas ever had come a few days early. The last two days had been hands down two of the best days of my entire life. I felt so good because I had played a small part in doing something important, something that mattered, something *real*.

When I got home, Todd sent me a text message: "Go enjoy Christmas with your family. Take the day in and be thankful for all of it. What you do really does make a difference. Dude...lamb of god saved a man's life today. That's amazing."

"No," I replied, "YOU saved a man's life today—lamb of god just helped you a little."

I had just watched it happen with my own two eyes.

———————

Later that evening, somewhere in the United States, a man in his late sixties lay in a hospital bed slowly dying, his body battered by leukemia and his immune system purposefully weakened by radiation and chemotherapy.

But at an airport on the outskirts of this man's city, a cooler was carefully taken off a plane just arriving from Washington, DC, and rushed to the hospital where he lay.

Nurses took a bag of stem cells and a bag of plasma from the cooler, attached them to an IV that ran into the man's arm, and he watched as life—*pure life*—freely given by a stranger from the state of Arkansas began flowing into his body to wage holy war on the disease that was killing him.

———————

On August 23, 2023, I paced back and forth outside my tour bus in the parking lot of the Ball Arena in Denver, Colorado. I was full of nervous energy because I was about to meet a seventy-year-old man who had fought death to a standstill... with a little help from a song.

One week before Todd and I had met up in DC for his donation nearly two years ago, Todd had texted to let me know he was writing a letter to his recipient, a letter that would be delivered the same day as Todd's stem cells. Because of HIPAA privacy laws, Todd would not be told the recipient's name, and the recipient would not be told Todd's, but after a year, the recipient would be given the option to find out who his donor was if he so desired. Todd was a little nervous about the letter and was having problems finding the right words, so I told him to go from the heart and say what felt right to him. If he did, I was sure it would be good. I offered to look it over for him if he wished. The next day Todd sent me the letter, and it was absolutely magnificent—honest, open, empathetic, and encouraging. Todd let his recipient know how honored he was to be given this opportunity to help, that he and many other people were putting a lot of love into the bag of magic sauce the recipient would be receiving, and that he knew in his heart that they were "gonna beat this together." I cried my eyes out as I read the last few sentences:

> You've got work left to do here, man. You're not going anywhere anytime soon. With all the love a stranger could have for somebody,
>   Your donor

What a *champion*.

Throughout 2022, the year after our trip to DC, Todd and I stayed in touch fairly regularly and even visited again when he and his family made a road trip to see lamb of god play a gig in Oklahoma. During this time, Todd let me know that the Be The Match people had informed him that his recipient had survived, which was great news. But I often wondered who that man was, where he was, and what his life was like today. I was hoping the recipient would contact Todd, and I knew Todd was, too, but there was no guarantee that would ever happen—some recipients never did. I did not understand why someone *wouldn't* contact a person who had saved their life, but it was not my place to judge—if I had learned one thing from talking to Todd about his experience, it was that it was a deeply personal and profoundly emotional thing to go through, creating a sense of connection with a complete stranger that is something only other donors can understand. And sadly for some donors, their recipients do not make it, which can lead to a sense of failure, a weird sort of survivor's guilt. Of course, it is *not* the donor's fault the procedure didn't work. They did their best and literally gave of themselves in such a selfless manner to try to save a stranger, but I can definitely see why it would hurt so badly if that stranger died.

If even a successful donor could be affected so profoundly by the process (as I knew Todd was), I couldn't imagine what it must have been like for the recipient. Every now and then I would ask Todd whether he had gotten any updates, but there was no news, so I would just think to myself, *Well, bro, I hope you're doing well, whoever and wherever you are.*

But on January 17, 2023, a little over a year after we'd met in DC, Todd texted a message that simply said, "DUDE." Beneath it was a screenshot of an email from Be The Match saying that all forms had been signed, all legal hoops jumped through, and the recipient had agreed to exchange direct contact information. *Yes!* A couple hours later, Todd sent me another message—he had just spent an hour on the phone with his recipient.

The mysterious figure we had both wondered about so often was a sixty-nine-year-old man from Denver named Michael. After receiving Todd's donation, within a year his cancer had disappeared, he was healthy and active, was out and about enjoying life again, spending time with his lady and family. Todd and I had joked around about the unknown recipient's character a few times before ("Bro, what if he's like just a *total jerk*? What if you are saving the Grand Wizard of the KKK or some bullshit like that? What a waste of the magic sauce, hahaha!"), but as it turned out, Michael was just a *cool dude* in general. During their conversation, he and Todd had laughed and cried, and Todd said later it was like catching up with an old friend. He also found out that Michael was smart, well-spoken, loved the arts, and was a photographer (and a talented one, as I discovered when Todd sent me some of his work).

"Dude, he's *so awesome*," Todd wrote, "and we're making plans to meet up soon!"

"Rad," I replied. "You're going to have to tell him the story of 'The Duke' when you meet him!"

"I already did!" Todd replied. "Bro, he's a drummer and used to play a little rock and roll with a few guys when he was younger—he says he wants to meet you when you come through Denver on tour!"

Reading all this, my head started spinning. *WHAT?!? Wait…how?* I thought *He's cool* and *he's a photographer* and *he's a freakin' musician? Holy cow—this dude is one of us!* Todd's bag of magic sauce had definitely gone to the right person—it was almost too good to be true, an absolutely perfect match.

On August 4, 2023, I was sitting on my bus after a gig in New Jersey when Todd sent me a photo of him hugging a gray-haired man on that man's front lawn. Michael was turning seventy, and after planning it out secretly with Michael's girlfriend, Todd and his lady had driven from Arkansas to Colorado to surprise him. "I bawled like a baby," Todd wrote me. They arrived in time for Michael's surprise seventieth birthday party, a festive occasion attended by family and friends who came from all over the country. They ate a bunch of good food, went hiking, and visited the top of Colorado's highest drivable peak, Mount Evans. Michael even took Todd to see one of my favorite venues to play, the world-famous Red Rocks Amphitheatre. In the Red Rocks Visitor Center they spotted my band's name among the long list of legendary acts that have played there, one of the most stunning venues in the entire world.

Aside from the birthday festivities and seeing the sights of that very beautiful part of our country, Michael and Todd were simply enjoying the unique nature of each other's company for the first time—and "unique" is a bit of an understatement. When a bone marrow recipient receives a transplant, they are not just getting a plastic sack of healthy cells that will go to work kicking cancer's ass. The long-term effects of the magic sauce are not that simple. The recipient also gets their donor's DNA, which takes hold within their very bones and then proceeds to replicate itself in its new habitat, adding a second set of DNA to, and in some instances even *replacing*, the recipient's original DNA. A recipient inherits aspects of a donor's physiological blueprint, and those aspects become their own, including such things as allergies and immune responses. Michael was a seventy-year-old man, but now had the immune system of a thirty-five-year-old. It's amazing to think about, but in a very real and scientific way, on a cellular level, Todd and Michael had to a certain extent become the *same person*. Totally *wild*.

Eleven days later after meeting Michael, Todd was back home and lamb of god was playing Arkansas, so we had a nice visit again. He gave me Michael's phone number, and as my band traveled across the country toward Colorado, Michael and I exchanged messages and made plans to meet in Denver in a couple of weeks. Show by show, I felt my excitement growing over actually meeting this man I had thought so much about before even knowing his name, increasing a bit more each night as we pulled away from the gig and continued onward to the next town. A touring musician marks his passage through time with a geographic calendar divided into cities and states, not months and days, and I was counting the gigs until Denver like a child counts the days until Christmas. The tour headed west, and finally one sunny day we arrived in the Mile High City.

A huge smile broke out across my face when I saw Michael get out of his car, wave, and head my way. As I watched him walk across the parking lot, I noticed that despite his recent debilitating illness (not to mention the inevitable wear and tear that comes along with spending seventy years on earth), he was still a tall and leanly muscled man, his long legs carrying him forward in large, confident strides. Tall men like Michael and me are built to *cover ground*, born to move and range the earth, and I was very happy to see him so obviously strong and mobile. We gave each other a big hug, then he stepped back, shot me a grin, and said, "Boy, I'll bet you're glad to see me!"

Truer words had never been spoken.

Michael and I spent a great afternoon in downtown Denver that day, walking and talking about life, mortality, our families, his battle with leukemia and our friend Todd, politics, music, travel, and photography. The conversation flowed easily as we walked the streets of Denver and eventually stopped for lunch and a coffee in the beautifully restored Denver Union Station. As we ate, Michael recalled memories of catching trains from that station as a child. I quickly seized this opening to indulge in one of my favorite activities—asking members of older generations about their experiences growing up in times gone by, eras that I never knew. These men and women are living history books, and their perspectives on the past are invaluable to me, keys that help me grasp the good and bad built into the time frame of my own existence.

We discussed his coming of age during the turbulent sixties, seeing the Beatles the only time they ever played at Red Rocks, his memories of America during the Vietnam War era, and his various jobs, including a stint driving a truck. After years of working in IT, at some point in the nineties Michael decided he was sick of sitting in one place, so he got his CDL and set out to see the country from behind the wheel of a truck. It was then that he really fell in love with photography, and as a professional rambling man myself, I understood both the need to travel and what great photographic opportunities the road provides. And of course, we also did what we photographers always do when we get together, shot a bunch of photos. After a while another photographer friend of mine from Denver, the great and powerful Mike Thurk, joined us, and he got some shots of me and Michael that I truly cherish—thanks, Thurk!

After a few hours, we returned to Michael's car and drove back to the venue. I still had a show to play, and he had a bit of a drive to his home on the outskirts of Denver. Michael wouldn't be attending the show that evening because if he didn't get to bed by eight o'clock, he "turned into a raging maniac" (his words, not mine), and there would already be more than enough of those in the building that night. Plus, lamb of god is not for everyone, and that's perfectly okay.

Michael had already given me a truly great day on tour, and I hadn't even sung a note yet. At the venue, I gave Michael the backstage tour and introduced him to my bandmates and then we hugged it out and he got in his car and left. I watched him pull away, then went inside and got ready to do my job. I took the stage with an extra full heart that evening, because I had just spent the day walking and talking with living proof that what we do in this crazy, improbable, infuriating, exhausting, and highly fulfilling thing that is our band, lamb of god, well, it *matters.*

Earlier that day, Michael and I had run into a couple of fans on the street who were going to the show that evening. We stopped briefly to say hi, and I did the usual thing and took a few quick photos with them. "Man, you just really made their day—they were so happy to see you," Michael said as we walked away, and I laughed and said, "Yeah, I guess I did." As strange as it often is to me, I try not to forget the humbling truth of this, that people I don't even know are actually happy to see me—because things definitely weren't always this way. I well remember a time in my life when people—*especially* the people who knew and loved me dearly—would watch me weave my drunken way toward them, and all they saw was trouble and heartache. I am very grateful that I do not live that way anymore and that I haven't for many years now. I also know that I never have to return to that nightmare again . . . as long as I don't forget what I am and where I come from. My old life of misery and insanity is very much still there, alive and kicking, just waiting for me inside a single bottle of beer. All I have to do is pop the cap and take just one drink, but today I have zero desire to do so. No, I don't think I'll be doing that today, thank you very much. Tomorrow I may feel differently, but I can't worry about that because tomorrow may never come. Tomorrow is going to have to take care of itself because I am too busy taking care of right now.

Right now isn't perfect by any means, but it's pretty damn good. Plus, it's all I have—why throw it away?

We'd almost reached Michael's car when he pointed out one of his old haunts, El Chapultepec, Denver's longest-running jazz club. Entire generations of jazz legends had walked through those doors to play, the greatest of the greats, names like Miles Davis, Ella Fitzgerald, John Coltrane, Chet Baker, Tony Bennett, Count Basie, Etta James, Frank Sinatra, all three Marsalis brothers, Harry Connick Jr., and Chick Corea. Sadly in 2020, after eighty-seven years of hosting music, "The Pec" permanently shuttered its doors, lost like so many other businesses during that brutal year. I was a bit saddened looking at the building from the outside, as I invariably am when I see a silenced music venue, and I stood there in front of it, imagining all the incredible sessions that must have gone down inside. But I also knew that all the songs played there over the years lived on, for music is boundless and eternal, incapable of being held prisoner by the constraints of a particular time or place or even a specific genre. Born in the nineteenth century in Congo

Square in New Orleans, jazz has traveled through time and space, snaking its way through the electric blues of the 1930s and 1940s, picking up its pace and stomping its feet in the early rock and roll of the 1950s, becoming louder and more distorted as it flowed into the blues rock of the 1960s, violently accelerating into the punk rock and heavy metal of the 1970s, and smashing at warp speed through the thrash and hardcore of the 1980s to finally crash into our twenty-first-century songs today. No one would ever refer to lamb of god as jazz, but jazz is buried deep in the heartbeat of the music we make today. Who knows where it will go from here? Not me. I only know that it lives on within us. I can feel it and all the other music that came before ours, running wild and free and immortal in my blood, because music cannot be silenced as long as we musicians continue to play.

And of that one thing I am certain: the music we make will continue to travel on into eternity, so I want to put things of importance into it, to give it my heart and add the very best of what I am to that endless and beautiful legacy. I must give this music all my joy and pain precisely because I can never know where it will go, who it will touch, or what it might inspire. And long after I am dead, I myself will travel through time and space within that music, just as Wayne Ford traveled from beyond the grave on the back of a song to help save a stranger he had never met. After he was set free from his pain, Wayne's spirit spoke to me in the language of the heart and told me to put him in a song. I listened, then sent the song out into the world, and it went into Todd, grew and became part of his own heart. The song left Todd, flew to Colorado inside a magic bag of life that gave Michael a little more time—and Michael still walks the earth today, carrying the music within him wherever he goes.

Don't you see? As long as we continue to listen for the song, that eternal song called love that resides in all our hearts... well, we will *never die*.

A few months ago I got a message from Todd. The Be The Match people had just contacted him to let him know that he matched *again*, this time with a sixty-four-year-old woman suffering from chronic leukemia. *Incredible*. "What are you, some kind of superhuman, bro?" I asked. Todd contacted Wayne's father, too, to let him know his son was staying busy. "Wayne's still got work to do," he told that proud Arizona father, and he spoke nothing but the truth.

So, lady, wherever you are, whoever you are—keep on fighting. Hang in there just a little while longer, okay? Because help is on the way. You just have to stay here long enough to get it. And although you don't know it, there are a lot of people behind you, and we are trying everything we can to give you just a little more time. I hope we meet one day, because I have a song I want to sing for you.

Now, once again, we wait for the word. When it comes, my friend from Arkansas will board a plane, and if I am not onstage in some far corner of the world, I will go to meet him, wherever he is. We will sit in a freezing-cold room beneath fluorescent lights, laughing and joking and talking music. It will be a good opportunity to relax and catch up on each other's lives because Todd will be trying his best to sit very still...while magic flows from his veins.

It's going to be a great day, one of the greatest of my life. I'm so looking forward to it.

Epilogue
SINKING

S itting in the window of my study directly in front of my desk as I write this are two photos of me—but I am not alone in these pictures.

In one I'm standing on an Arizona street corner on a fall night back in 2012, my left arm around a bald young man wearing a lamb of god T-shirt and a big grin. My right hand points to this fan beside me, a man named Wayne Ford, already two years into a brutal five-year fight with the leukemia that would eventually take his life. Directly to the right of that picture, in another photo, this time I'm standing beneath the fluorescent lights of a medical clinic once again pointing with my right hand to a fan standing beside me, a bearded man from Arkansas named Todd Seaman. Todd is wearing a Be The Match T-shirt and holding in one of his hands a bag of healthy stem cells, in the other a bag of plasma, both just taken from his body—he is holding life itself. In between these two photos on the windowsill is a small wooden frame my friend Greta made. In that frame is a typewritten invocation to the muse from the introduction to Homer's *Odyssey*—it is an artist's prayer, one I learned about from a book called *The War of Art* by Steven Pressfield.

The two photos each depict a short chapter in the life stories of two extraordinary men, chapters that I was privileged enough to play a tiny role in, for I am just a bit character in their much grander tale. And although these men never met each other in this life, their stories are as inextricably connected as the words of this sentence, and I know they will meet as brothers in the next. I keep their pictures in front of me as a map and a reminder of the lesson I'm still trying to learn each day as I write the tale of my own life: how to live and die a good man.

As for the prayer to the muse, it's part of the lesson, too, and I read it aloud every time I sit down to work on this book. That prayer fits squarely in the middle of those two photos as a reminder of my duty: to quiet my own voice and listen for the muse's so that I may fulfill my function. Every day, I must push my own petty self out of the way, open my eyes, ears, and heart, and let the universe use me as it will. Hopefully, it will run through me, use me and my ever-disappearing artist's life as a dab of glue to bind the bits of light that cross my path and make the world just a little brighter until my own light goes dark and disappears.

I am so very lucky to have been given this life.

I must not waste it.

ACKNOWLEDGMENTS

Thanks to:

You, for reading this book.

All y'all who read my last book.

Anyone who has relapsed into active alcoholism or drug addiction, somehow survived, jumped back into the sobriety lifeboat, and spoken to me about it. Not a single one of you has told me a pretty story, so I thank you from the bottom of my heart for going out there and taking that ass-whoopin' for me. You are living reminders that I don't need to do any more "research"— now do yourself a favor and stay here with us, among the living.

Anyone trying to get clean and sober. I see you. Hang in there—trust me, you don't need that poison, and life gets unimaginably better without it. Just keep on trying.

Marc Gerald, for once again bugging me to write a book. Ben Schafer, for once again editing said book and being my friend. Sean Moreau, Thomas Mis, and everyone else at Grand Central/Hachette for giving me a literary home.

My bandmates in lamb of god. For thirty years we've been doing this together, and somehow we get along better now than we ever did before—we must be finally growing up or some such bullshit. Martin Atkins and Pigface—we need to tour again. Chuck Doom and Saudade. All the other bands I've recorded guest vocals for or filled in for on tour—when duty calls, I will answer. The lamb of god road crew who works way harder than us musicians for none of the glory—we ain't shit without you, and y'all are our family. The fans, for enjoying what we do while simultaneously paying our rent. Brad Fuhrman, Cory Brennan, Bob Johnsen, and everyone else at 5B Artist Management, for wrangling me and the other cavemen so that we don't have to go back to restaurant gigs and sweating on a roof. Tim Borror and Paul Ryan, for throwing darts at a map and sending us off to work. Josh Wilbur and family. All the bands we tour with. Monica Seide-Evenson at Speakeasy PR. Maria Ferrero at Adrenaline PR, for the years of tireless service. Kirsten Sprinks at Cosa Nostra PR in the UK. Rest in peace, Michelle Kerr— you were a total badass, Roger Brilliant loves you, and he shall come visit you in Highgate soon.

Willie Adler, Brandy Adler, and Berkley McDaniel, for granting me a temporary Mechanicsville visa when the chips were down—I love y'all.

East Coast surf crew—Patty Platinum, Andrew "Big Rig," and Mat "Nukie" Clemmons—stop burning the old man, okay? David and Norma Edralin—aloha, Mister Hand! Kane Barrie at Nightmare Shapes—release the kook! Don Sharp at Planet Don—yes, I will go surf that slop for one hour with you, you maniac. Ryan McPherson. Brian Gerney. Jason at Rodanthe Surf Shop. Reflections Surf Co. Robert Siliato, for always holding me down up in Jersey. Commander Vander and Connie—them boys just don't get it, y'all.

West Coast—the homie Dez Fafara/Suncult—let's get waves soon, brah. Joe Lambert at San Onofre Surf Co. for being rad and rescuing me when the diabolical cliff kooks stole my wallet and locked me outta my car at Sano. Brian Bent, for making people smile. Cory Brennan, for sessions at Manhattan Beach and letting me store a board—you use way too much wax, dude.

Ecuador—*a mi hermano Carlos Ojeda y su hermosa familia—los quiero muchísimo.* Fred and Graciela, for amazing fiestas and food. Gallo, for party waves and porch hammocks. João and Ivan at Casa Banana. Eduardo Fernandez, for the laughs. Sol Funk, for tower internet and Leica talks. Mercer— stay safe in the jungle. Sergio, for maintaining Secrets.

Anyone else I've caught waves with in North America, Central America, South America, Asia, and Australia—I'll go left, okay?

The Outer Banks and Cape Fear regions of North Carolina.

The fine citizens of Richmond, Virginia—way too many of you to list, so just insert your name here. I'll see y'all at Kroger sooner or later.

Ed Calderon, for answering my endless Spanish questions, Sneakreaping, and interesting life discussions. All the makers out there who ponder the riddle of steel. Pat McNamara— basic dude stuff is the truth.

Bad Brains and all the other bands that have kept me alive since I was a kid.

ACKNOWLEDGMENTS

My entire family—somehow y'all still haven't disowned me, and for that I am so very grateful. See, I told y'all I'd write a happier book than the last one! Y'all are my heart.

Lisa Marie Bartelli—thanks for reminding me what it is to be a man. I love you. PS—I don't know yet, okay, Questions? Let's just watch and find out.

The Ford family and Courtney for sharing about Wayne with me. I've tried to honor him again here the best I could. Todd Seaman and family—love you, don't die.

Catherine Baab-Muguira, for writing the utterly hilarious *Poe for Your Problems* and being the first to get back to me with a blurb. Mark Manson, for the blurb and such thoughtful emails about marketing and subtitles. Anyone else who blurbed this book—I am honored y'all took the time to read my ramblings—I would list you individually, but these acknowledgments are due by end of business today. Steven Pressfield, for writing *The War of Art*—you are a genius. Jay Kristoff for using lamb of god lyrics as dialogue in the fantastic *Empire of the Vampire* series—please turn me into a vampire in the next book. Rest in peace, Pat Conroy—thank you for reading *Dark Days*, for sending the personalized copy of *The Prince of Tides*, and for writing so beautifully about life and the Low Country. All the authors I love to read so much—books rule.

Kiran Karnani, for always chasing light—you are a beautiful soul, my friend. Leica Camera USA, for providing me with the best tools. Kevin Wilson, for friendship and giving me my first gallery show. Alan Evans, for Resurrection Man and photo stuff. All the photographers who have taught me so much.

All you future writers, musicians, photographers, dancers, actors, filmmakers . . . all you *artists to be* who will express yourselves so beautifully. You are the lifeblood of our culture, the moral conscience of civilization. A world without art is a world not worth living in, so bend yourself to your art, and *never* let the bastards grind you down.

Marcus Aurelius, Seneca, Epictetus.

Bill and Bob.

The H.P.

Memento mori.

SOUNDTRACK

INTRODUCTION

"Knowledge"
   by Operation Ivy

CHAPTER ONE

"The Duke"
   by lamb of god

CHAPTER TWO

"Doomsday"
   by Discharge

CHAPTER THREE

"My War"
   by Black Flag

CHAPTER FOUR

"Heaven Knows I'm
Miserable Now"
   by The Smiths

CHAPTER FIVE

"I'll Fly Away"
   by Albert E. Brumley

CHAPTER SIX

"Soul Craft"
   by Bad Brains

CHAPTER SEVEN

"Money Is Not Our God
(Babylon Dub)"
   by Killing Joke

CHAPTER EIGHT

"You're Never Alone"
   by Hatebreed

CHAPTER NINE

"Bonzo Goes To Bitburg"
   by Ramones

CHAPTER TEN

"The Friend Catcher"
   by The Birthday Party

EPILOGUE

"Sinking"
   by The Cure